History of the Śākta Religion

The present work deals comprehensively with the genesis and development of Śāktism as an organised but flexible and receptive religion, its primitive, ancient, medieval and modern forms, its involvement with other religious systems and finally its functional role, in every turning point of Indian history. The social forces determining the process of historical development of Śāktism from crude primitive fertility beliefs to more refined ideas and broader sentiments have been reviewed in this book in the general background of the corresponding historical development of other forms of Indian religious system as well.

The author has succeeded in making a comparative analysis of their contents in chronological sequences and form a carefully worked out sociological approach. This has made the work indeed valuable for the basic understanding of the religious history of India as a whole. This is a revised and enlarged edition and some of the views and conclusions of the earlier edition have been changed besides new chapters have also been added.

Narendra Nath Bhattacharyya does not require any special introduction in the field of Indological studies. Though religious history is his forte he works at ease in diverse branches of ancient Indian history and civilization.

His important publications in English include *Indian Puberty Rites; Indian Mother Goddess; History of Indian Cosmogonical Ideas; Ancient Indian Rituals and Their Social Contents; History of Indian Erotic Literature; Jain Philosophy: Historical Outline; History of Researches on Indian Buddhism; History of Tantric Religion; A Glossary of Indian Religious Terms and Concepts; Geographical Dictionary of Ancient and Early Medieval India; Ancient Indian History and Civilization: Trends and Perspective; Buddhism in the History of Indian Ideas;* and *Indian Religious Historiography,* vol. I.

He has edited R.P. Chanda's *Indo-Aryan Races* and N.C. Bandyopadhyay's *Development of Hindu Polity and Political Theories;* besides these, he also edited *Medieval Bhakti Movements in India,* a collection of papers by eminent scholars, on the occasion of Sri Caitanya's Quincentenary celebration and *Prakrit and Jain Studies,* essays in honour of Prof. J.C. Jain.

Prof. Bhattacharyya was teaching in Department of Ancient History and Culture, University of Calcutta and passed away in 2001.

History of the Śākta Religion

Narendra Nath Bhattacharyya

MUNSHIRAM MANOHARLAL

Munshiram Manoharlal
Publishers Pvt. Ltd.

ISBN 978-81-215-0713-4
Reprinted 2015
Second revised edition 1996
First published in 1974

Printed in India
Published by Vikram Jain *for*
Munshiram Manoharlal Publishers Pvt. Ltd.
PO Box 5715, 54 Rani Jhansi Road, New Delhi 110 055, INDIA

www.mrmlbooks.com

Contents

Preface to the Second Edition

The first edition of the *History of the Śākta Religion* appeared in 1974. Despite shortcomings it was able to evoke scholarly interest. For a long time it was out of print. It was owing to the insistence and pressure of Shri Devendra Jain of Messrs Munshiram Manoharlal Publishers that I set myself in preparing a second edition. This revised and enlarged edition is substantially in agreement with the first, though some of the views and conclusions expressed therein have been changed with the passing of time. Apart from the alterations and additions in the chapters that have been retained, a few major changes have also been made. A new chapter on Śākta philosophy has been added. The reviews and criticisms of the book in the first edition have been taken into account. The Bibliography has been updated to include important publications on the subject. In preparing this new edition I have received help from my daughter Dr. Parṇaśabarī Bhattacharyya and my pupils Sri Amartya Ghosh, Smt. Saṅgītā Chaudhuri and Sri Ardhendu Roy. I extend my sincere thanks to them.

N.N. Bhattacharyya

Dept. of Ancient Indian
History and Culture,
Calcutta University
Calcutta
1 January 1996

Preface to the First Edition

There are numerous works on different aspects of the cult of the Female Principle, but virtually nothing has as yet been written comprehensively on the history and historical role of the Śākta religion. The present work is therefore meant for filling up this lacuna in the study of the religious history of India.

Greater emphasis has been laid in this work upon the functional role of the Śākta religion in Indian society and life throughout the ages, because the study of any cult or religion in itself is of little significance unless it is used as a means to understand the vast and enormously complicated problems of social history. Here it has been shown how the role of Śāktism changed from time to time in accordance with the changing social demands, from the guiding principle of hunting rituals and agricultural magics to that of the movement of national awakening, from the esoteric cults and practices arising out of the former to a liberal universal religion which had left a deep impress upon the latter. In between the two there were many turning points in each of which Śāktism was a driving force standing for something new, owing to its flexible nature which made it subject to various interpretations in different ages and by persons and sects belonging to a variety of ideas and beliefs. It will be significant to observe that throughout the ages the Female Principle stood for the oppressed peoples, symbolizing all the liberating potentialities in the class-divided, patriarchal and authoritarian social set up of India, and this alone explains why attempts were made from different corners to blacken Śākta-Tantric ideals.

The origin of Śāktism was spontaneous which evolved out of the pre-historic Mother Goddess cult symbolizing the facts of primitive life. But its development was manifold—not through any particular channel—like a lot of streams, some big some small, issuing from a single source. Each of these streams and also their combined courses have been dealt with on the basis of the material mode of life providing the rationale for the type of religious beliefs and practices developing among peoples belonging to different cultural grades and on that of the diverse historical conditions under which the

Female Principle made its way into other forms of Indian religious systems. The evidences which we derive from the temples and sculptural specimens and also from coins and other objects have been collated with those furnished by literary works and epigraphs to find out the process through which the tribal cults of the female deities were cleverly woven in the texture of the intellectual and rational scheme of the doctrine upheld by the higher religions.

Since the precise nature of the material culture and social institution of the early Indians is a question which the internal evidence is in itself too fragmentary to solve, it has been studied in the light of what is known of the surviving institutions and ideas, races and languages, beliefs and rituals and also from that of what we have been able to derive from the archaeological explorations and excavations. Important results have been obtained by applying this method to the understanding of the nature of evidence furnished by the Vedic literature. It has also been possible to form a clear idea of the post-Mauryan streams of the ancient Mother Goddess cult giving rise to Śāktism as a specialised religion by arranging the available materials systematically in a chronological set up. It has not been very difficult to deal with the history of the later and developed phases of the Śākta religion because there are numerous literary works supplying sufficient materials.

Now it is for my readers to judge how far I have been successful in this attempt. I crave the indulgence of my sympathetic readers for the mistakes and blemishes that must have crept into this book. In formulating some of my views I have been immensely helped by the works of V. Gordon Childe, E.O. James, O.R. Ehrenfles, R. Briffault, G. Thomson, D.P. Chattopadhyaya, and others. I am also grateful to Prof. D.C. Sircar, Prof. Niharranjan Ray, Dr. Amita Ray, Dr. Dilip K. Chakrabarti and Dr. Dipakranjan Das who have helped me in many ways. To my wife Manjula I am indebted for patient co-operation and very much else besides.

N.N. BHATTACHARYYA

Dept. of Ancient Indian
History and Culture,
Calcutta University
Calcutta
15 August 1974

Abbreviations

AA	*American Anthropologist*
AB	*Aitareya Brāhmaṇa*, Eng. trans. by A.B. Keith, HOS, XXV, Cambridge Mass., 1920
ABORI	*Annals of the Bhandarkar Oriental Research Institute*
AI	*Ancient India*
AMSJV	*Ashutosh Mukherjee Silver Jubilee Volume*
AN	*Aṅguttara Nikāya*, PTS, ed. by R. Morris and E. Hardy, 6 vols., 1885-1900; Eng. trans. by F.L. Woodward and E.M. Hare, London, 1935-36
ARSIE	*Annual Report of South Indian Epigraphy*
ASIAR	*Archaeological Survey of India: Annual Report*
AS(I)R	Cunningham's *Report of the Archaeological Survey of India*
AV	*Atharvaveda*, Eng. trans. in part by M. Bloomfield in *SBE*, XLII, Oxford, 1897; by W.D. Whitney, Cambridge Mass., 1905
BCLV	*B.C. Law Volume*, ed. D.R. Bhandarkar, Calcutta, 1945
BRKMIC	*Bulletin of the Ramakrishna Mission Institute of Culture*
Bṛ U	*Bṛhadāraṇyaka Upaniṣad*, Eng. trans. by R.E. Hume in *Thirteen Principal Upaniṣads*, Oxford, 1921
Camb. HI	*Cambridge History of India*
CHI	*Cultural Heritage of India*
CII	*Corpus Inscriptionum Indicarum*
Ch U	*Chāndogya Upaniṣad*, Eng. trans. by R.E. Hume in *Thirteen Principal Upaniṣads*, Oxford, 1921
CV	*Culavaṃsa*, ed. W. Geiger, PTS, London, 1925
CWV	*Complete Works of Swami Vivekananda*, Advaita Asrama, Calcutta
DKCV	*Das Kapital Centenary Volume*, ed. Mohit Sen and M.B. Rao, New Delhi, 1968
Dh. A	*Dhammapada Aṭṭhakathā*, ed. by H.C. Norman, 4 vols., PTS, London, 1906-14
DN	*Dīgha Nikāya*, ed. T.W. Rhys Davids and J.E. Carpenter, PTS, 1890, 1903, 1911; Eng. trans., *Dialogues of the Buddha* by T.W. Rhys Davids, London, 1899, 1910, 1921
DRBV	*D.R. Bhandarkar Volume*

EA	*Eastern Art*
EI	*Epigraphia Indica*
ERE	*Encyclopaedia of Religion and Ethics,* ed. J. Hastings, Edinburgh, 1902 ff
FL	*Folklore*
GS	*Gṛhyasūtra*
HB	*History of Bengal,* Dacca University, Calcutta, 1943
HPEW	*History of Philosophy: Eastern and Western,* ed. S. Radhakrishnan, 2 vols., London, 1953
IA	*Indian Antiquary*
IC	*Indian Culture*
IHC	*Indian Historical Quarterly*
ISPP	*Indian Studies Past and Present*
JAOS	*Journal of the American Oriental Society*
JAS	*Journal of the Asiatic Society*
JASB	*Journal of the Asiatic Society of Bengal*
Jāt	*Jātakas,* Eng. trans. by E.B. Cowell, 7 vols., Cambridge, 1895-1913
JBBRAS	*Journal of the Bombay Branch of the Royal Asiatic Society*
JBORS	*Journal of Bihar and Orissa Research Society*
JBRS	*Journal of Bihar Research Society*
JEA	*Journal of Egyptian Archaeology*
JGNJRI	*Journal of Ganganath Jha Research Institute*
JKHRS	*Journal of the Kalinga Historical Research Society*
JMU	*Journal of Madras University*
JRAS	*Journal of the Royal Asiatic Society*
JUB	*Journal of the University of Bombay*
JUB	*Jaiminīya Upaniṣad Brāhmaṇa*
KS	*Kāṭhaka Saṃhitā,* ed. by A.B. Keith in *JRAS,* 1910, 517 ff; 1912, 1095 ff
KS	*Kāmarūpaśāsanāvalī* by Padmanath Bhattacharya, Rangpur
MASI	*Memoirs of the Archaeological Survey of India*
Mbh	*Mahābhārata,* critical ed., Poona, 1927 ff; Eng. trans. by K.M. Ganguly, pub. by P.C. Roy, Calcutta, 1884-96; rep., Calcutta, 1926
MI	*Man in India*
MN	*Majjhima Nikāya,* ed. V. Trenckner and R. Chalmars, 3 vols., PTS, 1888-99; Eng. trans. by I.B. Horner, *Middle Length Sayings,* PTS, 1954-59
MR	*The Modern Review*
MS	*Maitrāyaṇī Saṃhitā,* ed. Von Schroeder, Leipzig, 1881-86

NINQ	*North Indian Notes and Queries*
OHRJ	*Orissa Historical Research Journal*
Pan	*Pāṇini*
PNQ	*Punjab Notes and Queries*
Rām	*Rāmāyaṇa*, Eng. trans. by M.N. Dutt, Calcutta, 1893-94; by R.T.H. Griffith, Benaras, 1915
RV	*Ṛgveda*, Eng. trans. by F. Max Müller in *SBE*, XXXII and H. Oldenberg in *SBE*, XLVI; by R.T.H. Griffith, Benaras, 1896-97
S	*Science*
San G.S.	*Sāṅkhyāyana Gṛhyasūtra*
SB	*Śatapatha Brāhmaṇa*, Eng. trans. by J. Eggeling in *SBE*, XII, XXVI, XLI, XLIII, XLIV, Oxford, 1882-1900
SBE	*Sacred Books of the East*, ed. F. Max Müller
SCT	*Śakti Cult and Tārā*, ed. D.C. Sircar, Calcutta University, 1967
SHB	*Studies in the History of Buddhism*, ed. A.K. Narain, Delhi, 1980
SII	*South Indian Inscriptions*
SKACV	*S.K. Aiyangar Commemoration Volume*
SPB	*Sāṅkhya Pravacana Bhāṣya*, ed. by R. Garbe, HOS, Cambridge Mass., 1895
SN	*Saṃyutta Nikāya*, ed. L. Feer, 5 vols., PTS, 1884-91; Eng. trans., *Book of the Kindred Sayings* by C.A.F. Rhys Davids and F.L. Woodward, London, 1917-30
SPD	*St. Petersburg Dictionary*
SPP	*Sāhitya Pariṣad Patrikā*
TA	*Taittirīya Āraṇyaka*, ed. R.L. Mitra, Bib. Ind., Calcutta, 1872
TB	*Taittirīya Brāhmaṇa*, ed. R.L. Mitra, Bib. Ind., Calcutta, 1890
TS	*Taittirīya Saṃhitā*, ed. E.B. Cowell, Bib. Ind., Calcutta, 1899; Eng. trans. by A.B. Keith, Cambridge, 1914
UE	*Ur Excavations*, London, 1927
VA	*The Vedic Age*, ed. R.C. Majumdar, Bombay, 1951; rep., 1965
VA	*Vita Agricolae* of Tacitus
VS	*Vājasaneyī Saṃhitā*, ed. with Mahīdhara's com. by A. Weber, London, 1852
YV	*Yajurveda*
ZDMG	*Zeitschrift der Deutschen Morgenlandischen Gesellschaft*

1

Introduction: The Pre-Vedic Elements

Śāktism is a very important religion among the Hindus of the present day all over India. Those who worship the supreme deity exclusively as a Female Principle are called Śākta. Śakti is worshipped in various forms and numerous shrines are dedicated to her images in different parts of the country. The Śāktas conceive their Great Goddess as the personification of primordial energy and the source of all divine and cosmic evolution. She is identified with the Supreme Being, conceived as the source and spring as well as the controller of all the forces and potentialities of nature.

Nowhere in the religious history of the world do we come across such a completely female-oriented system. This obviously requires an historical explanation. Some scholars hold that, though in its present form Śāktism is essentially a medieval religion, it is a direct descendant of the primitive Mother Goddess cult which was so important a feature of the religion of the agricultural peoples who based their social system on the principle of mother-right. The origin of the anomalous position of the Male Principle of creation in the Śākta religion can presumably be traced to the anomalous position of the males in a matriarchal society.

In fact there was a general tendency among the earlier historians to associate the concept of the Female Principle of creation with the ancient matriarchal societies.[1] The superiority of the goddesses over the gods and the priestesses over the priests may possibly be explained in terms of a social system in which maternity counts more than paternity, descent being traced and property handed down through women rather than through men. That the cult of the Indian Mother Goddess might have some bearing on the principles of mother-right was held by a number of scholars,[2] but it was R.P. Chanda who asserted categorically in 1916 that Śāktism arose in India under the same social conditions as those under which Astarte or Ashtart was conceived in Syria, Cybele in Phrygia and Isis in Egypt.[3]

Modern anthropologists, however, do not subscribe to the theory of a universal existence of mother-right or matriarchy as an inevitable stage of social evolution.[4] But they are not disinclined to treat specific institutions like matriliny, matrilocal marriage and residence and so forth from the viewpoint of the structure of society with the totality of social usages stressing on the comparative analysis of the social structures, or from that of explaining them in terms of their function, by the part which they play within the integral system of the culture and by the manner in which they are related to each other within the system. Claiming social anthropology to be the natural science of society, to which the conjectural reconstruction of history resorted to by the older anthropologists of the evolutionist school is irrelevant, they seek to establish general tendencies or laws underlying the diversities of human social life. Speculations about the early origins of human institutions which formerly provided the main drive of the anthropological studies have been abandoned by them as unprofitable.

But a historian's perspective is somewhat different. His methodology in some cases, especially when he deals with the facts of remote antiquity, should be similar to that of the earlier anthropologists of the evolutionist school. As regards the customs and social institutions of the surviving tribes, reviewed by the modern anthropologists, the historian's viewpoint is that the evidences which are frequently cited are largely of the nature of the extant cases from one stage to another. For example, when he comes across the *alia-santāna* system of inheritance (from mother's brother to sister's son, mentioned in the *Mahābhārata* and followed till recently by the kings of Travancore and various tribes and castes of Southern India), he can not treat it as an isolated phenomenon, a thing-in-itself. He correlates it with other forms of matrilineal inheritance and shows how the original form of succession from mother to daughter was later converted into that from man to man, but in the female line, from mother's brother to sister's son, or from father-in-law to son-in-law before the establishment of the purely patriarchal form of inheritance. While dealing with the process of social evolution, the historian is also aware of the fact that the growth of many primitive communities is retarded by economic difficulties of their habitat and that the more backward peoples are continually subjected to the cultural influence of the more advanced.

The earlier concept of an elaborate and all-pervading absolute matriarchy is not encouraged by the historians, but they find no reason to reject the vast mass of literary evidence in favour of the existence of the matriarchal social norms, institutions and cultures which suggest that in the prehistory and early history of the civilized peoples matriarchal elements persisted to a much higher degree than the ethnographical data might lead us to expect. Matriarchal institutions have been traced by Herodotus[5] among the Elamites, Persians, Lykians, Karians, Lydians and Mysians. Arrian[6] refers to the matriarchal system found among the Karians, while Strabo[7] describes the same as was prevalent among the Kantaberians. Polybius[8] and Justin[9] refer to the matriarchal institutions among the Greeks. Aristotle[10] makes mention of matrilineal inheritance among the Spartans. The Greek gods and heroes are specifically referred to by the names of their mothers, such as, 'Apollo, the son of Leto', 'Dionysos, the son of Semele', 'Heracles, the son of Alkmena', 'Achillis, the son of Thetis', and so forth. The *Old Testament, Iliad* and *Odyssey* are full of matriarchal elements. The Greek literary traditions associated with matriarchal institutions and cultural elements have been collected and analysed by Gilbert Myrray,[11] Ridgeway[12] and Bulter,[13] the Egyptian by Hall,[14] Petric,[15] Erman,[16] Mespero[17] and Breasted,[18] the Semitic by Robertson Smith[19] and the Teutonic and Celtic by Chadwick,[20] Freeman,[21] MacCulloch,[22] Nutt,[23] and others.[24]

Ancient Indian literary tradition refers to Strīrājya or 'Women's Kingdoms'. The *Jaiminibhārata*[25] account of the kingdom of Pramīlā, queen of the land of the Amazons, may be mythical, but the existence of Strīrājyas in ancient India was not merely a flight of fancy, as it seems to be supported by works such as the *Si-yu-ki* of the seventh century Chinese pilgrim Hiuen Tsang in which it is stated that, to the north of Brahmapura in the present Kumaon-Garhwal region lay the Suvarṇagotra country (Su-fa-la-na-kin-ta-lo) which was the 'Eastern Women's Country' where, according to the Chinese pilgrim "for ages woman has been the ruler, and so it is called the kingdom of women."[26] Hiuen Tsang also mentions another Strīrājya called by him 'Western Women's Country' near Lāṅgala in the present Baluchistan region.[27] Long before Hiuen Tsang, Megasthenes heard of queen-rulers in the Pāṇḍya country. Arrian says that Pandaia was the daughter of Heracles who entrusted her with the sovereignty of the land in which she was born. According to Polyaenus her empire comprised 365 villages and it was the rule that one village should each day bring to the treasury the royal-tribute so that the queen might always have the assistance of those men whose turn it was to pay the tribute in coercing those who for the time being were defaulters in their payments. According to Solinus the Pandeon nation was always governed by queens.[28] The *Mārkaṇḍeya,*[29] *Garuḍa*[30] and *Skanda*[31] Purāṇas mention Strīrājyas or women's kingdoms which is also attested by the *Bṛhatsaṃhitā,*[32] *Mahābhārata*[33] and *Rāmāyaṇa.*[34] Strīrājya is also mentioned in the *Rājataraṅgiṇī*[35] which H.C. Chakladar considers to have been lying in the extreme northwest, being same as described in the *Bṛhatsaṃhitā.*[36] The Survarṇagotra country with its typical social system described by the Chinese pilgrim is also mentioned in the *Vikramāṅkadevacarita.*[37]

In India, particularly in her eastern and southern zones, there are various peoples who have retained to this day a primitive social organisation of matriarchal character. Indeed, a predominantly agricultural country like India with her stunted economic development accounting for the strong survival of tribal elements is only likely to be full of matriarchal relics, and this explains the cause of the popularity and survival of the concept of the Female Principle. Baron Omar Rolf Ehrenfels to whom goes the credit of collecting all the matriarchal data and organising them in a theoretical set up, observed that mother-right elements in India were stronger, both in extent and in degree, than those in any part of the world and that the Indian mother-right, based on a primitive form of agricultural economy, appeared to have created the ancient matriarchal civilizations in the Mediterranean Basin. Oriental Africa, the Near East and especially South Arabia. His hypothesis of India being the original home of mother-right may not be correct, but the extensive survivals of mother-right in India of which copious examples have been furnished by him are of great importance to any historian or sociologist. According to him, notwithstanding ruthless efforts to establish male superiority through hypergamy, child-marriage and *satī* (burning of widows), mother-right elements could not be stamped out from the lives of the masses. Such extravagant means was called for, parallels of which are, according to Ehrenfels, scarcely to be found elsewhere in human history.[38]

How far the observations of Ehrenfels on the violent overthrow of the ancient mother-right in India are valid from a purely historical point of view is, however, a different question. But Ehrenfels himself has admitted that the matriarchal cultural elements could not be stamped out from the life of the masses. What then could have been the reason for the extensive survival of the mother-right elements in India? Debiprasad Chattopadhyaya, one of the exponents of Marxist historiography, has dealt with this question from an economic point of view and argued that, if the undeveloped agricultural economy had a natural tendency to create matriarchal society and if by far the largest proportion of the Indian masses remained predominantly agricultural, it was but logical that the most extravagant methods would have been necessary to force upon them the supremacy of the male. He holds that, because agriculture was the discovery of women, the initial stages of agricultural economy created the natural conditions for the supremacy of the female. Thus mother-right in India was historically connected with the early agricultural economy, and the peculiar tenacity with which its elements have survived is due to the fact that the majority of the people still remains the tiller of the soil. By contrast the economic life of the early Vedic people was predominantly pastoral. This accounts for their highly organised patriarchal society with a characteristically male-dominated world-outlook. It is here that we have the real clue to the basic difference between the two main currents of the subsequent religio-philosophical thought in India, the Vedic and the non-Vedic.[39]

We have thus dealt with the principal arguments of those who want to view the emergence of Śāktism in terms of the principles of mother-right. We have already had the occasion to refer to the observation of R.P. Chanda who in 1916, six years before the dramatic discovery of Mohenjodaro, wrote:

> For the conception of a godhead analogous to that of the Śākta conception of the Devī we should travel beyond the countries dominated by the Vedic Aryans and the Avestic Iranians to Asia Minor, Syria, Egypt and other countries bordering on the Mediterranean. There is a strong resemblance between the Indian Śākta conception of Śakti and the Śākta ritual of the followers of Vāmācāra and Kulācāra, who practised ceremonial promiscuity on the one hand, and the Semitic conception of Ashtart, the Egyptian conception of Isis and the Phrygian conception of Cybele, on the other.[40]

In the Śākta scheme of cosmogonical process, the unmanifested *prakṛti* alone existed before creation. She wished to create, and having assumed the form of the Great Mother, the created Brahmā, Viṣṇu and Śiva out of her own body. Referring to the Mother Goddess cult of Mohenjodaro, Marshall[41] observes that, in the later Śākta phase of the primitive Mother Goddess cult, the Devī is transformed into the eternally existing all-powerful Female Principle, the *prakṛti* or *śakti,* and having associated with the Male Principle, the *puruṣa,* she becomes Jagadambā or Jaganmātā, the mother of the universe, the creator of the gods. In her highest form she is Mahādevī, the consort of Śiva but, in spite of her being the consort of the latter, she is his creator. In Asia Minor and round the shores of the Mediterranean are found many examples of the Mother Goddess with a young subordinate god by her side.

> In Punic Africa, she is Tanit with her son; in Egypt, Isis with Horus; in Phoenicia, Astaroth with Tammuj (Adonis); in Asia Minor, Cybele with Attis; in Greece (and especially in Greek Crete itself), Rhea with young Zeus. Everywhere she is unwed, but made the mother first of her companion by immaculate conception, and then of the gods and of all life by the embrace of her own son. In memory of these original facts her cult (especially the most erotic mysteries of it) are marked by various practices and observances symbolic to the negation of true marriage and obliteration of sex.[42]

Such stories of Virgin Goddesses are relics of an age when the father had no significance at all and of a society in which man's contribution to the matter of procreation was hardly recognised. From the written records of ancient civilizations it appears that the earlier peoples were worshippers of the Earth Mother, the Creatrix, the goddess whose moods were reflected by natural phenomena, whose lovers were the spirits of season, and whose qualities were specialised by the later goddesses. The story of the annual death and resurrection of the lover of the goddess, found in the agricultural mythologies, is suggestive of the death and revival of plant life in the annual cycle of seasons.

II

In primitive society the clan centred in the women on whose responsibility rested the essentially important function of rearing the young and for imparting to them whatever could be characterised as the human heritage at the economic stage of hunting and gathering. All cultural traits including habits, norms of behaviour, inherited traditions, etc., were formed by and transmitted through the females. The woman was not only the symbol of generation, but the actual producer of life. Her organs and attributes were thought to be endowed with generative power, and so they had been the life-giving symbols. In the earlier phases of social evolution, it was this maternity that held the field, the life-producing mother being the central figure of religion. This may be suggested on the basis of the plentiful discovery of palaeolithic female figurines in bone, ivory and stone with the maternal organs grossly exaggerated.

At a subsequent stage increased knowledge about the function of the male in the process of generation introduced a male element into the cult of the Mother Goddess. The male partner was at first supplementary because his precise function in relation to conception and birth was less obvious and less clearly understood. With the concentration of creative energy in the Male Principle as the begetter, the male element was introduced at first as the insignificant lover of the goddess, but at length he became co-equal and eventually the predominant partner. The process was quickened in those places where the hunting and gathering stage was directly replaced by the pastoral means of subsistence. Cattle-rearing being basically a masculine affair, the pastoral societies were necessarily patriarchal. In pastoral societies the cult of the Mother Goddess or the concept of the Female Principle did not go out of vogue, but greater importance was attached to the characterisation and exploits of the male deities. But where the transition from hunting and food-gathering to higher forms of production was marked by an extensive development of agriculture, the influence of the life-producing mother as the central figure of religion was naturally extended to the realm of vegetation and fertility. Mother Earth thus became the womb in which crops were sown.

The material mode of life of a people ordinarily provides for the type of the deity and the manner of worship prevalent in a given society. This accounts for the extensive development of the cult of Mother Earth among agricultural peoples. Rituals based upon fertility magic must have played a very significant part in the agricultural societies.

> So long as they have pasture, cattle feed and breed of themselves, but by comparison with cattle raising the work of tilling, sowing and reaping is slow, arduous and uncertain. It requires patience, foresight, faith. Accordingly, agricultural society is characterised by extensive development of magic.[43]

The magical rites designed to secure the fertility of the fields seemed to belong to the special competence of women who were the first cultivators of the soil and whose power of child-bearing had, in primitive thought, a sympathetic effect on the vegetative forces of the earth.[44]

> The fertility of the soil retained its immemorial association with the women who had been the tillers of the earth and were regarded as the depositories of agricultural magic.[45]

Peoples of the past instinctively projected their own experiences into the objects around them and thus associated various ideas in order to constitute a practical philosophy of life, making unconscious use of the only principle available to them, viz. the principle of analogy. Thus they came to the conclusion that natural productivity should be viewed in terms of human productivity, earth-mother in terms of human mother. "The identification of earth with woman," writes Briffault, "pervades the thought of all stages of culture, and pages could be filled with illustrations of the universal equation."[46] The same preconditions which fertilises women are also thought to fertilise Mother Earth. This explains why in different parts of the world Mother Earth is believed to menstruate and why there are so many rites and customs in which all fluxes of blood are treated alike as manifestation of the life-giving power inherent in the female sex.[47] The conception of Mother Earth is as varied as the degree of culture, or rather cultures, attained by separate communities of mankind, and this can be shown with reference to the various types of the Mother Goddess cult prevailing in different regions of the ancient world.

> So intimate appeared to be the relation between the process of birth and generation and those of fertility in general that the two aspects of the same 'mystery' found very similar modes of ritual expressions under prehistoric conditions.[48]

Of such 'ritual expressions' the erotic rites were really significant for they were employed as expedients to increase the generative powers of nature represented by the Earth or Mother Goddess. Certain Tantric ideas and practices of later times are evidently rooted in these primitive sex rites. The *dehavāda* or the theory and practices of the body and the cosmogony of Tantrism, so elaborately revealed in the Śākta religion, are but ramifications of the corollaries of a most primitive belief. Also the Śāṅkhya philosophy was originally a development of the primitive proto-materialism which formed the substratum of Tantrism itself. The primitive empirical and analogical belief in the equation of earth and woman, of natural and human fertility, forming the infrastructure of numerous agricultural rites, revealing the mode of securing the material means of subsistence, invariably connects the mystery of nature with that of the human body, from which it transpires that the birth of the universe is the result of the same or similar process as the birth of the human beings.

The Tantric sex rites might have something to do with the Phrygian mysteries associated with the cult of Kubele or Cybele, the Eleusinian mysteries observed in Greece and in the Hellenistic colonies, and those associated with the rituals of Isis and Osiris. Ideas similar to the primitive Tantric cosmogony may also be traced to the myths of the vegetative cycles current in Western Asia and the Mediterranean and Aegean region which were clustered around a great goddess and her young subordinate male partner—the Devī and her Bhairava of the Tantric tradition. The psycho-physical personality of the goddess was perhaps attributed to the woman of flesh and blood whose energy was though of, as it were, to be transmitted into the psychic centres or planes of consciousness of the aspirant impersonating her male partner, thus calling forth a new orientation to the earlier concept of Indian Yoga.

III

Archaeological explorations and excavations have revealed that in India the transition from food-gathering to food-production and that from rural settlement to urbanism did not follow a uniform and orderly sequence of events. With the end of the threefold Stone Age the course of change varied widely. In some cases there was reasonable advancement in accordance with the changing productive conditions while in others the development was arrested. The Early and Middle Stone Ages correspond roughly to the Lower and Middle Palaeolithic respectively of the archaeological tradition as found in Europe and Western Asia, but in the case of the Late Stone Age, comparable to the transitional Mesolithic stage of European prehistory and characterised by microlithic tools of various shapes, there is some difficulty, because in India there is no major phase corresponding to the Upper Palaeolithic blade and burin industries of other countries. Although in certain parts of India, there are traces of a blade and burin culture flourishing towards the end of the late-pleistocene period, these sporadic occurrences have been regarded as a peculiar growth of the existing flake industries and not as an essential part of the three-fold sequence of the Stone Age.

Economically the Palaeolithic or Stone Age societies relied for a livelihood on hunting, fishing and collecting, but their methods and equipments did not remain static. In a hunting society a special relationship had developed between man and animal which led its members to perform certain rites, religious or magical, to ensure the prey in the hunting expedition. The Palaeolithic female figurines as those of the 'Venuses' with emphasised sexual characters, though having no face, carved out of stone or mammoth ivory were probably used in some sort of fertility ritual to ensure the multiplication of game. Very probably peoples like the Gravettians who made such figurines grasped the generative function of women, and sought magically to extend it to the animals or plants that nourished them. In the Indian context no such figurine has been found. The sites of Panchmarhi in Madhya Pradesh, Lekhahia and Baghai Kor in Uttar Pradesh, Bagor in Rajasthan, Langhnaj in Gujarat and Sarai Nahar Rai in the Ganga-Yamuna Doab have yielded burials. The crouching posture in which a number of skeletons have been found leaves no doubt that they were deliberately buried with some tender beliefs regarding the fate of the departed ones. It is, however, difficult to say whether these Stone Age interments nascently imply the later concept of the Mother Goddess as the guardian of the dead.

In the Indian context, Neolithic conditions are rather complex and are interrelated with the problems of uneven development. This is due to regional peculiarities caused by local environments and external influences. The number of pure or full-fledged Neolithic sites, characterised by gray wares, polished stone-axes and bone-tools, is not large. Polished stone-tools, occasionally associated with hand made pottery and bones of domesticated animals have often been found below the levels of the first metal using cultures. But in many cases metals have been found along with polished stones. We came across the use of black-painted red wares, long stone blades and copper-bronze implements which are characteristics of Chalcolithic conditions. Thus the presence of the Chalcolithic elements in the Neolithic and vice versa has made it very difficult to make a sharp distinction between the cultural stages or to say when the Late Stone Age cultures developed into the Neolithic and the latter into the Chalcolithic. Because of this overlapping the term Neolithic-

Chalcolithic is sometimes used jointly to explain the Indian situation.

The religious beliefs and practices of the hunters and food-gatherers were modified according to the new social ideals introduced by the Neolithic-Chalcolithic conditions. Magic must have been still practised in order to ensure the fruitfulness of the earth despite the enlarged real control over nature, thus introducing agricultural rituals in addition to those connected with hunting. Most Neolithic societies buried their dead with more pomp and social effort than had the Palaeolithic hunters. That the dead so reverently deposited to the earth was supposed somehow to affect the crops that sprang from the earth and was probably brought in relation to the existing Mother Goddess cult, the Earth Mother thus becoming the guardian of the dead, connected alike with the corpse and the seed-corn beneath the earth.[49] The Neolithic goddess was not simply the life-producing mother. The earth from whose bosom the grains sprout was imagined as a goddess who might be influenced like a woman by entreaties and gifts as well as controlled by imitative rites and incantations. Female figurines were moulded in clay or carved in stone or bone by Neolithic societies in Egypt, Syria, Iran, all around the Mediterranean and in South-Eastern Europe. These figurines were undoubtedly the direct ancestress of the images of admitted goddesses made by historical societies in Mesopotamia, Syria, Greece and other countries.

Among the few settlements of the unmixed Neolithic type in which metal is absent, reference may be made to those of Baluchistan, especially the Quetta region, and the valleys of the Loralai and the Zhob which are evidently pre-Harappan belonging to the middle of the fourth millennium BC. In Kashmir, the earliest period of Burzahom and at sporadic sites of Assam and Meghalaya, pure Neolithic features are also found. In the earlier periods of the settlements of Baluchistan we have evidence of houses made of mud-brick or hard-packed clay while in the subsequent periods greater sophistication and more compactness are found. In a few cases the transformation of the settlement into a town with massive defensive walls and square bastions of sun-dried bricks is observed. The second aspect of the cultural evolution is indicated by the transition from hand-made to wheel-made, often painted, pottery. The third and fourth features are indicated by the transition from blades made of coarse flakes to those made of better lithic elements showing remarkable advance in execution, shape, smoothness and sharpness and by the transition from stone to metallic implements. Terracotta bulls and Mother Goddess figurines testify religious belief. The latter has been found not only in the Zhob Valley but also in Kulli and Mehi as well as in Gumla and Hathala. The Kulli figurines finish at the waist in a splayed pedestal, arms bent with hands on the hips, breasts usually shown, eyes fashioned from small stones, hair elaborately dressed, ornamented by oval pendants resembling cowrie shells, and bangles on arms and wrists. In the Zhob valley sites the same type of female figures recurs with necklaces, large and beak-like noses, hooded heads, exaggerated breasts, circular eye-holes and slit mouths. That they had a fertility significance is shown by the cowrie shells and by that of a phallus carved in stone at the mound of Moghul Ghundai on the left bank of the Zhob river and at the neighbouring mound of Periano Ghundai on the right bank of the river where a *yoni* is depicted with great prominence.[50]

The Neolithic village farming and pastoral communities of Baluchistan and the Indus valley had a quick transition into the Chalcolithic stage and eventually culminated in the Harappan urban civilization. Remains of Harappa civilization are scattered over an area no less than about half a million square miles and containing more than seventy centres. This area extends up to Sutkagendor to the west on the Makran coast near the border of Iran, Lothal on the gulf of Cambay and Bhagatrav on the Narmada to the south, the Himalayan foothills as far as Manda in Jammu to the north and Ganga-Yamuna region beyond Delhi to the east. Much has been written on the town-planning of Mohenjodaro and Harappa, the earliest excavated sites situated respectively in the Larkana district of Sind and in the Montogomary district of Punjab, which was characterised by well executed roads and lanes, an elaborate drainage system, brick-built buildings of various sizes and shapes and different arrangements for civic amenities, the two most prominent being the Grath Bath at Mohenjodaro and the Great Granary at Harappa. Subsequent excavations at Harappa have revealed evidence of fortification. Kalibangan, where traces have been discovered of the remains of massive brick walls around both the citadel and the lower town and where the transition from pre-Harappan to Harappan can be successfully detected, has much in common with Mohenjodaro. At Lothal the town is divided into six blocks, each on a raised platform and separated by roads, the principal one running from north to south. The situation of the famous dockyard with artificial channels for entrance and exit is on the eastern side. The rectangular town also has a massive protective wall.

The following features of the Harappa civilization are to be noted. (i) The population was heterogeneous and comprised different racial types, the principal ones being Mediterranean, Proto-Australoid and Alpinoid. (ii) Harappan society was a class-divided society. Within the urban population itself architectural remains reveal that there was a difference of wealth. The rows of mud-brick tenements contrast visibly with the spacious two-storeyed houses comprising courtyards, bathrooms, private wells, etc., which accommodated what may be termed as the Harappan bourgeoisie. (iii) There was a rapid growth of professionalism. Major sections of the mixed population came from the adjacent villages to seek fortune as craftsmen, artisans and manual labourers. The discovery of a variety of objects for day-to-day use proves that apart from the priests, rulers, traders and agriculturists, there was a network of specialised professions. (iv) The uniformity of weights and measures all over the area, the similarity of the seals, the evidence of extensive trade, the common patterns of town-planning and also of art and religion, suggest political, economic and cultural unity of the Harappa civilization and the existence of a functioning state system. (v) The total time-span of Harappa civilization has been fixed between 2300 and 1750 BC. This dating also holds god in regard to the Harappan phases of Kot Diji, Lothal and Kalibangan.

The Harappans were not conversant with the metallurgy of iron. The principal metals for manufacturing tools and other objects were copper and bronze. Gold contained a substantial proportion of silver and was very light in colour. Lead objects were known and lead occurred often as an alloy in copper tools. Objects made of ivory, steatite, etched carnelian beads, lapis lazuli, shells, etc. have been recorded. Spinning of cotton and wool is indicated by the discovery of spindles and spindle whorls, Dyers' vats indicate that dyeing was practised. Pottery consisted mostly of wheel-made wares, found in many shapes and sizes for daily practical use. Most of the pottery is of pinkish colour with a bright red slip. The majority of terracotta human figurines are those of females. Animal figures have also been found. The steatite bust from Mohenjodaro with well-arranged hair and beard and half-shut eyes, and the statue of the dancing girl in bronze reveal a striking anatomical faithfulness. Copper vessels were raised from sheet-metal while those of bronze were cast by *cire perdue* method. The seals and sealings are of three classes—large intaglio seals of steatite and terracotta, miniature seals or amulets of steatite, and seals of terracotta or faience made from moulds with devices and inscriptions in relief. The script found on the seals has not yet been deciphered.

The cultural uniformity of the Harappa civilization is reflected not only in its town-planning but also in other aspects on social, economic and religious life. Harappan urbanism rested on the capability of producing food on a large scale and the use of rivers which were sufficiently dependable to facilitate transport, irrigation and trade. Apart from the existence of an extensive inland trade, there was also intimate cultural and economic interaction between the Harappa civilization and the West. The Harappan posts of Sokta-koh and Sutkagendor on the Makran coast and the dockyard of Lothal point to the maritime trade with Iran, Mesopotamia and Western Asia. Circular button-seals and bun-shaped copper ingots have been found both at Lothal and in the Persian Gulf region. Seals of Harappan type discovered from Ur, Kish, Susa, Lagash and Tell Asmar are also indicative of trade contacts.

Gordon Childe went as far as to suggest that the Harappan manufactures were imported to Sumer and Akkad and that the Indian cults were actually celebrated there.[51] Marshall also stressed upon a common cultural bond between the Harappa civilization and the West. What was the exact nature of this cultural bond is not very clearly known to us, but it may be inferred that religiously these civilizations had something in common. Marshall wrote:

> Now it is well known that female statuettes akin to those from the Indus valley and Baluchistan have been found in large numbers and over a wide range of countries between Persia and the Aegean, notably in Elam, Mesopotamia, Transcaspia, Asia Minor, Syria and Palestine, Cyprus, Crete, the Cyclades, the Balkans and Egypt....
>
> The generally accepted view concerning them is that they represent the Great Mother of Nature Goddess, whose cult is believed to have originated in Anatolia (probably in Phrygia and spread thence throughout most of Western Asia. The correspondence, however, between these figurines and those found on the bank of the Indus is such that it is difficult to resist the conclusion that the latter also represented Mother or Nature Goddess and served the same purpose as their counterparts in the West, viz.

either as votive offerings or, less probably, as cult images for household shrines; and this conclusion is strengthened by the fact that the range of these figurines now extends practically without a break from the Indus to the Nile, over tracts that are not only geographically continuous but which in the Chalcolithic Age were united by common bonds of culture.[52]

The Sumerian Mother Goddess, whose qualities were later absorbed by Nana of Urk, Nina of Ninevah, Inanna of Erech, Bau of Lagash, Ninlil of Nippur, Annuit of Akkad, Zarpaint of Babylon, etc., belonged to the same category of the Harappan Magna Mater whose attributes were also specialised by various goddesses of the historic age. Some of the aforesaid deities had evidently an eastward migration in subsequent ages. The goddess Inanna, also known as Nana, Nanai, etc. who was supposed to by the mother of Attis and identified with Ishtar, Astarte. Artemis, Anaites and Aphrodite, was able to extend her cult into India through the Śakas and Kuṣāṇas in later times. Examples are the Nainā Devī of the Kulu valley, Sirmur and Bilaspur, Bībī Nānī of Baluchistan, Nainā Devī or Nainī Devī of Nainital etc. Goddesses of the Ishtar group (Ishtar, Astarte, Astaroth, Atargatis, etc.) might also have contributed something to the later Tantric conception of Tārā, as is indicated by the similarity of their names.

Many of the Mother Goddess figurines from Mohenjodaro are painted with red slip or wash[53] as in ancient Egypt, Mesopotamia and Malta[54] but those from Harappa retain no trace of paint.[55] The goddess wears a distinctive head-dress which rises from the back of the head, in some cases directly from the head, while in others it forms part of the coiffure. The goddess is significantly nude save for a very short skirt round the waist secured by a girdle. The figurines, as a rule, are burdened with jewellery consisting of elaborate neck collars, long chains, armlets, bangles, anklets, ear-rings, etc. The figurines from Harappa do not represent mere busts, as the Kulli and Zhob figurines do, but are modelled with legs and hands, showing a variety of positions. They suggest a greater freedom of movement indicating a stylistic advance on the figurines of the preceding peasant cultures of Baluchistan, though the religious association of both are the same.

A seal, unearthed at Harappa shows, on the obverse, a nude female figure, head downwards and legs stretched out upwards, with a plant issuing out of her womb.[56] This may be regarded as the prototype of the Earth Mother Śākambharī of the Purāṇas from whose body grow the life-sustaining vegetables. On the reverse, we find a female figure with dishevelled hair and arms raised in alarm, and a male figure standing in front of her in a threatening attitude with a shield-like object in one hand and a sickle-like object in the other. Marshall suggests that the seal is intended to portray a human sacrifice connected with the Earth Goddess depicted on the other side. The association of the Earth Goddess with the vegetative forces of nature is not confined to the Śākambharī-seal alone. There are many others in which trees and plants are associated with the goddess. In one such seal the goddess stands between the bifurcated branches of a *pīpal* tree in front of which appears a half kneeling worshipper behind whom stands a goat with a human face, and in the lower section there are seven persons dressed in short kilt and wearing long pigtails.[57]

Many of the living features of later Hindu religion and philosophy may be traced directly to this pre-Vedic source, and in this connection we may refer to the principles of Tantrism, the philosophical Sāṅkhya, the practice of yoga and the present day Śāktism. They came into view only slightly in the *Ṛgveda,* but more elaborately in the later Vedas and in the still later Brāhmaṇas, Upaniṣads, Epics and Purāṇas, when the pastroal Vedic people had long since amalgamated with other races and absorbed some measure of their culture. Evolving out of a mother-oriented world view, the aforesaid features of Hindu life stand in reciprocal relation, the one being intimately associated with the other. The deep-rooted influence of this world-view, in terms of an all-pervading Female Principle of creation, persisted in the field of religion and rituals through the ages.

IV

The Mother Goddess figurines, scenes on seals and ritual objects, notably large stone *liṅgas* and *yonis,* give glimpses of Tantric survivals, of magic fertility rites that formed the basis of a primitive Tantrism, and of personal deities arising out of them. In popular Hinduism *liṅga* and *yoni* (male and female organs) stand respectively for Śiva and Devī, and the prototype of the former is found in seals unearthed at Harappa and Mohenjodaro. Provided with horns on the head, and in one instance surrounded by animals, the three-faced male-god, who is seated in the posture of a yogin on several seals, may rightly be regarded as the prototype of the Indian god Śiva, the consort of the Devī.

The existence of a Male Principle, as is thus found in the Harappan religion, is not inconsistent with a female-dominated religious system. In the later Śākta theology we find that the Male Principle has some part to play, although he is described as connotative of static existence and, dissociated with Śakti or the Female Principle, he is no better than a corpse. Also in the Sāṅkhya, *prakṛti* is all in all, *puruṣa* or the Male Principle being nothing but a passive spectator. The Vedic metaphysical speculation ultimately culminated in the monistic conception of the immaterial Brahman as the ultimate reality. The dualistic Sāṅkhya conception of *puruṣa* and *prakṛti* is basically different from the Vedic conception of an absolutistic and monistic Brahman which was developed in the Upaniṣads and further elaborated in the Vedāntic speculations.

Referring to the anomalous position of the Male Principle in the Sāṅkhya, Śaṅkara asked: *kathañcodāsīnaḥ puruṣarpradhānam pravartayet?* If creation is possible by the union of *puruṣa* and *prakṛti*, how is it that the role of *puruṣa* is so insignificant? Or, if the *puruṣa* is so insignificant and indifferent, how is it that he takes so important a part in the affair of creation? This contradiction cannot be explained except by postulating a matriarchal origin for the system. In a matriarchal society the father has no kinship with his children who belong to their mother's clan. The early philosophers must have thought, in accordance with their social system, that just as a child is born as result of union of the male and the female, so also the universe is a result of union of the *puruṣa* and *prakṛti*. Just as a child in a matriarchal society has no real kinship with the father, so also the universe has no real relationship with the *puruṣa*. But in a matriarchal system, the father has a significant role in the matter of procreation, though in his family he is insignificant and a passive spectator, exactly like the *puruṣa* of the Sāṅkhya.[58]

The root of the Sāṅkhya philosophy may therefore be sought in the pre-Vedic matriarchal tradition in India in which the conception of a material *prakṛti* evolved from that of a material Earth Mother supposed to represent the forces that stimulate the generative powers of nature. Magical fertility rites, originally performed by women to ensure the process of nature were inavariably associated with such a conception of a material Earth Mother. These rites, surviving through the ages in popular beliefs and customs, were conserved and crystallized in the later Tantras while some of their theoretical aspects centering round the conception of a material Earth Mother (*prakṛti*) developed subsequently into a distinct metaphysical form which came to be known as the Sāṅkhya system.

What was the exact influence of this matriarchal tradition upon the material culture and social institutions of the Harappans is impossible to determine at the present state of our knowledge. Ehrenfels who believed that India was the original home of mother-right insisted that the Harappa civilization was matriarchal.[59] Marshall also emphasised on the matriarchal character of this civilization.[60] But only on the basis of some Mother Goddess figurines and sex symbols such type of generalisation is untenable and unwarranted. Though the aim of prehistoric archaeology is to define the social traditions expressed in the material cultures, the archaeological finds do not tell by themselves facts about the social organisation of a people or the main aspects of their world-view. It is also to be observed that prehistory survived late in some parts of India when other areas within the same country were already developing higher cultures. While the Harappa civilization was at its zenith, other parts of this subcontinent were occupied by peoples even belonging to Late Stone Age culture. To reconstruct the religious history pertaining to the remotest period of a country characterised by uneven socio-economic and cultural development, facts obtained from archaeological sources should therefore be substantiated by other evidence coming from literary sources as well as from anthropological and linguistic researches. A study of the surviving tribal religions and of the tribal elements as found in the literary records of the comparatively advanced peoples, evidently belonging to different periods of history is likely to throw some light on this subject.

V

The main racial types with their various ramifications that have gone to make the people of India are included within one or the other of the four distinct speech-families, viz. the Austric, the Tibeto-Burman, the Dravidian and the Indo-European (Aryan). The Austro-Asiatic dialects belonging to the Austric family of languages survive in the Kol or Munda, the Nicobarese and the Mon-Khmer speeches of India, but once their speakers were spread over the greater part of northern India. The Austric speakers were mainly food-gatherers, but some of their groups became accustomed with the elementary forms of agriculture. They used a a common word (*lakuṭa, laguḍa, liṅga*), later adopted in the Indo-Aryan vocabulary, for denoting their digging stick and also their cult object, the *liṅga* or phallus.[61] They also worshipped a Mother Goddess called Mātṛkā (Polynesian *mātariki*), sometimes identified with the Pleiades, and the word had been, in subsequent religious history of India, the common term for the Divine Mothers. The Moon was also regarded as a goddess and she is still worshipped by the surviving Austric speakers under the name Ninda Cāndo whose lover was the Sun-god Siñ Bongā. Rākā and Kuhū, old Austric names for full-moon and new-moon, survive as goddesses in the Vedic literature.[62] Another Vedic goddess Sinīvālī, supposed to be of Austric origin, was also connected with the new-moon. These goddesses are specifically associated in the Vedic literature with vegetation and fertility.[63] In the *Bṛhaddevatā*[64] as well as in the *Vājasaneyī Saṃhitā*,[65] Rākā and Sinīvālī are identified respectively with Śrī and Vāk, the prototypes of Lakṣmī and Sarasvatī of the later period. In many agricultural communities of India, especially in Bengal, the Austric goddesses of the full-moon and the new-moon are worshipped as the goddesses of abundance in the full-moon night of *kojāgarī pūrṇimā* (Oct-Nov during Durgā-pūjā fortnight) and the following new-moon night of Dīpāvalī. The goddess is represented by a heap of rice kept in a basket made of cane and by cowrie-shells, symbolising female generative organ, fixed around the basket. It is held by some scholars that the cult of the Female Principle was first developed in India by the Austric speakers.[66] Very probably the Austric speakers with their dark skin and snub nose were known to the Vedic peoples as Niṣādas, and they gradually became Aryan-speaking roughly between *c.* 1500 and 600 BC. Racially the majority of the Austric speakers belonged to the proto-Australoid stock, but the Khasis of Meghalaya, who still have a female-dominated society, were of Mongoloid category. Their tribal mother Ka-me-kha was probably Sanskritised or Hinduised as Kāmākhyā whose shrine at Guwahati in Assam in one of the most important centres of Hindu pilgrimage where the goddess is worshipped in the form of a *yoni* or female organ of generation.[67]

The Tibeto-Burman speakers, probably the Kirātas of Indian literature[68] settled in the northern, north-eastern and eastern borders of India. These people of the Mongoloid stock inhabited the Himalayan region by the middle of the first millennium BC. There were apparently wave after wave of migrations of the Tibeto-Burman speakers to North-Eastern India even down to the early medieval period. These peoples, because of their late arrival, could not penetrate far into the interior plains and were not in a position to leaven the whole of it, so to say, in the way the Austrics, the Dravidians and the Aryans did. In the *Manusmṛti*[69] they are described as dwellers of the Himalayan region, especially of the Eastern Himalayas, having golden or yellowish complexion, who were rich in gold and silver and gems and experts in making cloths of various kinds. In the Kirātaparvādhyāya of the *Mahābhārata*, the episode of Śiva meeting Arjuna as a Kirāta, accompanied by Umā, also in the guise of a Kirāta woman is narrated. In the *Varāha Purāṇa*[70] the goddess is addressed as a Kirātinī or Kirāta woman. Matriarchal survivals among the Himalayan tribes[71] and also countless Mother Goddess shrines in the lower Himalayan region, stretching from west to east give us some idea about their female-oriented religion and it is likely that these Kirāta peoples contributed something to the esoteric side of the Tantric rituals which is indicated by the story of Vasiṣṭha's initiation into the secrets of the Tārā cult.[72]

Among the three groups of the Tibeto-Burmans, the Naga and Kuki speakers were driven to the hills and the Bodo became the dominant language which included all the surviving non-Aryan languages of the plains, the Garo Hills and the North Cachar Hills. The Kachaṛi, Mech, Garo, Dimasa, Tipra, Lalung, Rabha, Chutiya, etc., are derivations of the Bodo. Even before the Mongoloid hordes were entering this region from the east and the north, the protagonists of the Sanskritic culture took up their trek into the North-East along the Brahmaputra in consequence of which a fusion took place of the Sanskritic and Mongoloid cultures. The example of Assam proper shows how a dominant culture can absorb and impose itself on weaker cultures, how a people, by and large Mongoloid, adopted Assamese which is a Sanskritic language. Even the powerful Ahoms had not only adopted the Hindu way of life but also the Assamese, forgetting their own Ahom language. In this process of Sanskritisation or Hinduisation the original tribal divinities of these peoples became identified with the Vedic and Purāṇic gods and goddesses. Thus, the Nuting or Muring or Nuring of the Garos—also known as Dingipa-Ba-Pra—was identified with Śākti and came to be regarded as the source and spring of all the myriad phenomena of nature, the great transformer, the source of light and wisdom, the moulder of the firmament.[73] Mainao of the Bodo-Kacharis was equated with Lakṣmī and also with Pārvatī, Durgā and Kālī under the name Balkungri.[74] Other tribal goddesses such as Khan-Khampapha and Ja-ching-pha of the Ahoms, Heremdi, also known as Lairidi and Gomadi, of the Dimasa-Kacharis, Bāyakho of the Rabhas, Mailu-ma, Khulu-ma and Tui-ma as well as the seven Buḍirak sisters of the Tipras and so forth were identified with popular Hindu goddesses.[75] The celebrated Kāmākhyā of Assam, who might have originally been a Khasi goddess, and Kechāi-khāti (goddess who eats raw) of the Chutiyas, upgraded as Tāmreśvarī or Dikkaravāsinī, had also votaries among various tribes of the North-East. Among the Meitheis of Manipur seven Lairemas or goddesses are regarded as the ancestresses of the seven *shalais* or clans which are again identified with seven Brahmanical *gotras* with the expansion of Hinduisation.[76]

The Dravidian speakers now from solid bloc in the Deccan and South India, and there is reason to believe that in other parts of India Dravidian was at one time fairly widespread. In Baluchistan we have still the Dravidian Brahui speech which is just a surviving fragment of a very widespread Dravidian tract extending from Baluchistan and Sind through Rajasthan and Malwa into Maharashtra, Mysore, Andhra, Tamiḷnadu and Kerala. Like other linguistic communities the Dravidians also belonged to a variety of races. The Dravidian problem is also basically similar to that of the Aryan. It is believed by a section of scholars that the original homeland of the Dravidian speakers was situated in the islands of the Aegean and the tracts of mainland along the Aegean sea. Later they came to the Eastern Mediterranean tracts and from this region migrated in different directions. This, however, is a wishful thinking unsupported by genuine evidence. The assumption that the Harappans spoke a primitive Dravidian speech is favoured by many a historian, but there is no definite evidence to support the Dravidian authorship of the Harappa civilization.

From the evidence of the words in use among the early Tamils, we can derive the following of the material culture and social institutions of the pre-Vedic Dravidians. They were agricultural peoples (*ér,* plough, *velānmai,* agriculture) living in villages (*paḷḷī*) and towns (*ūr, peṭṭai*) which formed parts of districts (*nāṭu*) of a country ruled by kings (*ko, véntaṇ, mannaṇ*) who lived in palaces (*koṭṭai, araṇ*) and maintained the laws and customs (*kaṭṭalai, pazakkam*). The soldiers were armed with bows (*vil*), arrows (*ampu*), spears (*vel*) and swords (*vāḷ*) which testify the use of metals. Canoes, boats and even ships (*toṇī, otam, vallam, kappal, patava*) were known to them. They also knew the art of writing on palmyra leaves (*olai*) and bundles of such leaves were known as books (*eṭu*). The title *ko* denoting the king was also attributed to god to whose honour they used to dedicate temples (*koil, koyil, kovil*). Spinning (*nūl*), weaving (*ney*) and dying (*niram*), and also all the necessary arts of life, were known to them.[77] The Dravidians contributed a great many elements of paramount importance to the evolution of Indian civilization and that in certain matters the Dravidian and other pre-Vedic contributions were deeper and more extensive than that of the Vedic peoples. Temple worship along with the conception of the divine in a more concrete form, the religious and philosophical ideas centering round the conception of the divinity as Śiva and Devī, worship of *liṅga* and *yoni*, pilgrimage to holy places, the practice of Yoga, the ideas of *karma* and transmigration, the ritual of *pūjā* as opposed to the Vedic ritual of *homa,* fertility cult and image worship, etc. are evidently pre-Vedic contributions in which the Dravidian speaking peoples had a great share.[78]

But more important in this connection is the worship of the Female Principle. S.K. Chatterji pointed out that the name Umā, evidently of non-Sanskritic origin, recalls Mā, the Great Mother of the Asian and East Mediterranean peoples, and that Durgā corresponds with Trqqas, a deity mentioned in the Lycian inscriptions of Asia Minor. From this he came to the conclusion that Śiva or Umā were in all likehood of Dravidian origin, and as such, they were the Indian modification of the Great Mother Goddess and her consort of the Mediterranean peoples.[79] Further researches exhibit the ancient cults which inspired those of Mā or Kubélé (Cybele) and Attis, or Hepit and Tashup, the former having as her vehicle the lion, and the latter bull, formed undoubtedly one of the bases on which the Śiva-Umā cult of Hindu India grew up.[80] According to Chatterji:

> The patriarchal social organisation of the Aryans presented a contrast to the matriarchal one of the Dravidians. The Great Mother Goddess of a matriarchal society, who was brought into India by the Dravidians from Asia Minor and the Eastern Mediterranean islands, was also conceived as an all-powerful force which was identical with Nature itself. In front of this puissant and eternally active Śakti or power that was the Great Mother of the Universe, her male counterpart was virtually an ineffective being. This idea also developed in India; and in the Tantras one of the basic concepts is that of the Śakti or the wife or the Female

counterpart of a god. The god was a mere male and all his power lay in his female form who was looked upon as his wife, repository or mainspring of his Śakti or power.[81]

Certain features of the village goddesses worshipped by the Dravidian-speaking peoples of the South in modern times may be observed. Most of them bear the epithet *amman* or *amma*, meaning 'mother'. They symbolize the village life and are related, not to great world-forces, but to such simple matters as cholera, small-pox, cattle-disease, etc. They are connected with agriculture because the idea of fertility pertains exclusively to the females. They are almost universally worshipped with animal sacrifices. The priests are not Brāhmaṇas, but are drawn from all other castes. The names of the goddesses are legion, some of them having an obvious meaning and many quite unintelligible even to the people themselves. They differ almost in every district and often the deities worshipped in one village are quite unknown in other villages five or six miles off. The characters of the goddesses vary considerably. The villagers do not regard them as evil spirits, but neither do they regard them as unmixed benefactors. The functions of the different goddesses are not at all clearly marked. Some of their shrines, especially in the Tamil country, are fairly large buildings, but the majority of them are mean little brick buildings of various shapes and sizes. In many villages, the shrine is simply a rough stone platform under a tree, and in many of the Telugu villages there is no permanent shrine at all. In some villages there is no permanent image or symbol; a clay figure of the goddess is made for each festival. In other villages the deity is represented simply by a stone pillar. Very often the goddess is represented in processions by a brass pot filled with water. There is no act of uniformity and no ecclisiastical calendar regulating the festivals or forms of worship of the village deities. In many places there is a fixed annual festival which generally takes place after the harvest. In some places, however, there is no regular annual festival. Again, there is no uniformity as to the duration of a festival.[82]

The aforesaid features must have also characterised the religious life of the south Indian villagers even in the remotest antiquity. The reason is simple. There has been no significant change in the pattern of village life since time immemorial. Some of the village goddesses, however, received an elevated position in the course of time under various conditions. The process of this transformation has been outlined by S.K. Chatterji as follows with reference to the religious life of Bengal.

The original or national cults of the pre-Aryan peoples are found in the worship of many caste or tribal deities, of village gods, who have no place in the official Hindu pantheon of pan-Indian acceptance; at times they have just succeeded in finding place in some Sanskrit Purāṇa, but in other cases they have advanced only as far as the threshold or the ante-chamber of the hall of official Hinduism by having their legends rendered in the vernacular only. Thus there are village godlings of the type of Gabhur Dalan and Mochra Singh worshipped in the South Bengal Delta, who are unknown to any Purāṇa, and unsung even in the vernacular; there are Dakṣin Rāy and Kālu Gāzi godlings who control the tigers in the Sundarbans of the forest lands of the southern Delta whose exploits are narrated in Bengali, and whose fame has not yet travelled beyond Bengal; and finally, there are deities of the type of Śītalā, the goddess of small-pox, and Manasā, the goddess of serpents, who have received admission into the pantheon of Purāṇic gods and goddesses, honoured, although they were newcomers, beside Śiva and Devī, Viṣṇu and Lakṣmī. The nature of pre-Aryan religion and ritual, in its mythology and its idea and practices, among the various pre-Aryan groups of peoples, it has not been possible to establish as yet: most of it now survives in the rites and cults obtaining to remote villages, which are now always under the aegis of official Brahmanical Hinduism.[83]

According to a similar process, Mariamma, the South Indian pox-goddess, was identified with the Purāṇic Reṇukā, the mother of Paraśurāma. It is said that when Paraśurāma cut off the head of Reṇukā at his father's command a Pariah woman who embraced Reṇukā out of sympathy also lost her head. Both of them, however, were later restored to life, but in his eagerness to do it Paraśurāma put Reṇukā's head on the body of the Pariah woman and vice versa. The woman with the Brāhmaṇa head and Pariah body was afterwards worshipped as Mariamma, and the woman with Pariah head as the goddess Yellamma. Referring to this story Whitehead observes:

> The story... probably describes the fusion of the Aryan and Dravidian cults in the days when the Aryans first found their way into South India. A Pariah body with a Brāhmaṇa head is an apt description of the cult of Śiva; while a Pariah head with a Brāhmaṇa body might well describe some of the cults of the ancient Dravidian

deities, modified by Brāhmaṇa ideas and influences.[84]

Some of the ancient Dravidian goddesses were later identified with powerful Purāṇic goddesses. Thus Kanaka-Durgā-Amman was originally a protectress of animals worshipped during cattle epidemic. She had no temple or image. The Durgā-Amman of Bellary was originally worshipped in an ant-hill. Later owing to her elevation she came to be worshipped in temples and images. Caṇḍeśvarī of Kurnool was originally the tribal goddess of the Togatas who was later inducted in the Brahmanical pantheon with a Sanskritic name. Likewise the Cokkalingam and Mīnākṣī of Madura were identified with Śiva and Devī.[85] Kāli or Kālī-Amman is worshipped in many villages as a protectress deity. In the villages of Trichinopally Kālī is known as Mādurai-Kālī-Amman. In the Mahakalikudi village of the same district Kālī is worshipped as Ujinihamkālī who has four female attendants—Elli-Amman, Pullathal-Amman, Visalakṣmī-Amman and Angal-Amman. The priests of this goddess were originally non-Brāhmaṇas. In her Sanskritised form this goddess is known as Vīramahākālī and Ugramahākālī.[86] In Kerala Kālī was worshipped in Kabu or open place and the goddess was a shapeless stone. Various forms of Kālī included Kandam, Kurim, Kurumba and so forth. In Malayalam the world 'Kali' means 'terrible': The Chutal-Bhadrakālī lives in the cremation ground and dances with her companions at midnight. Originally the cult of Kālī in Kerala was the exclusive affair of the people belonging to the lower ranks of social hierarchy. Later it was taken up by the Nayars and subsequently by the Brāhmaṇas.[87] Her festival is known as *puram* which lasts for many days. The place of worship is decorated by red cloth and painted with geometrical designs. The drama dealing with the slaying of the Asura Daruka is enacted. Women fill plates with rice, put lamps on them and circumambulate the Kabus. The Malayalam literature contains songs on Kālī.

Cult of the Female Principle was a major aspect of the Dravidian religion.[87] The concept of Śakti was an integral part of their religion, and their female deities eventually came to be identified with the Purāṇic Pārvatī, Durgā or Kālī.[88] Among the ancient Tamils Koṭṭavai or Korravai was the principal goddess. Koṭṭavai means victorious.[89] In various parts of South India seven goddesses or seven sisters are worshipped conjointly. In Mysore they are called Mārīs. In Kannada, 'Mari' means 'Śakti' or energy. They are village goddesses, regarded as the wives of Śiva, and worshipped as protectresses. In Tanjore district these seven Śaktis are regarded as consorts of Śiva.[90] Not only in Mysore and Tanjore, but in other parts of South India these seven sisters are worshipped. They have a brother who is everywhere regarded as Patu Raju. But the names of the sisters vary from place to place. In the Nellore district these seven sisters are known as Paleramma, Ankamma, Muthyalamma, Dillipolasi, Bangaramma, Mathamma and Reṇukā. One should not fail to recall in this connection that in various parts of northern India seven goddesses as sisters are worshipped. This might have been due to Dravidian influence. Skanda-Kārttikeya, who appears to have been a very popular god in the South, was also nourished by seven goddesses Kāki, Halimā, Mālinī, Vṛnhilā, Āryā, Palālā and Vaimitrā. The cult of Sapta Matṛkā or Seven Divine Mothers which is an integral part of the Śākta religion may thus be of Dravidian inspiration.

VI

The precise nature of the social and religious institutions of the pre-Vedic Indians is a question which the internal evidence in itself is too fragmentary to solve. Apart from some Mother Goddess figurines and fertility symbols found from pre-Harappan Baluchistan, the Harappan sites and the post-Harappan site of Inamgaon we have little archaeological evidence on the basis of which the religious history of pre-Vedic India can be reconstructed. The internal evidence, such as the stray archaeological findings, must therefore be studied in the light of what is known of the surviving institutions and ideas, races and languages, beliefs and rituals, because the past is always contained in the present. Scholars have worked and are still working on these diverse fields, and we have referred to their views pertaining to the cult of the Female Principle, especially from their study of the tribal survivals on which they insisted for ascertaining the original cultural features of the ancient races and linguistic families such as the Austric or the Tibeto-Burman or the Dravidian. But there is one difficulty. The conclusions drawn from some fragmentary surviving evidence are liable to the fallacy of over-speculation, in some respects the formulations themselves even going far beyond its normal suggestivity. For example, it is quite logical to hold that the cult of a Female Principle as the Supreme Being of religion is a natural outcome of a matriarchal social system. It is equally logical to hold that at a remote antiquity when there was uncertainty regarding paternity, when the precise function of the male in relation to procreation was less clearly understood, in other words, when absolutely no connection was known to exist between pregnancy and sexual intercourse, it was the females whose maternal functions gave them the real authority in social life and it was through them that all the cultural traits including the habits, norms of behaviour, inherited traditions, etc., were formed and transmitted. But, as we have seen above, despite the existence of matriarchal features and cultural elements, the theory that there were full-fledged matriarchal societies or that such societies preceded everywhere the patriarchal ones can not be proved historically. Though the concept of the Female Principle of creation can be associated with the relics of matriarchal cultural elements, no universal concomitance can be established between the two.

Scholars of the earlier generations sought to trace the worship of the Female Principle in the literal interpretation of some of the hymns of the Vedas and in the philosophical interpretation of the Sāṅkhya system. They argued that the Sāṅkhya principle of *prakṛti* served as the basis of the conception of an all-pervading Female Principle and in order to find out the origin of the former they depended on the Vedic literature. Their line of approach was as follows: At first the sky was personified as the heavenly father, and the earth as the mother of all creatures. Then evolved the idea of *prakṛti* in the place of the earth. This *prakṛti* began to be conceived as the germinal productive principle—the eternal mother capable of evolving all created things out of herself, but never so creating unless united with the eternal spiritual principle, the *puruṣa*. But archaeological excavations and linguistic studies have revealed the fact that some fundamental ideas of Hinduism as well as many ancient beliefs and observances, including the conception of a Female Principle of creation, may be traced to a pre-Vedic period. There was once a time when it was believed that the Dravidian and other pre-Vedic contributions to the subsequent Hindu religion were negligible and barbaric, comprising only the worse features. But now the idea is completely changed and it is admitted that the Dravidians contributed a great many elements of paramount importance to the evolution of Indian civilization and that in certain matters the Dravidian and other pre-Vedic contributions were deeper and more extensive than that of the Vedic peoples. Many traits of later Hinduism, especially those like the cult of the Mother Goddess are legacies of the Harappa civilization. The predominance of the Mother Goddess cult in the earliest levels of culture in which they occur in the ancient Near East from the Eastern Mediterranean to the Indus Valley shows that attention was first concentrated of the feminine aspects of the process of generation, leading to a female-dominated world-view which was subsequently crystallised in the form of what is known as the Śākta religion.

References

1. "Female deities have often enjoyed the highest place among the gods. This depends upon the nature of the social organisation and the respect in which women are held. Clan life in which the mother is the head of the group is likely to lift the Mother Goddess into a supreme position." (Starbuck in *ERE*, V, 828.) "There is a large body of evidence to show that the Semites before their separation passed through a matriarchal form of society. All those traits which are the oldest and most permanent in the character of Ashtart-Ishtar are those which for other reasons we must predicate of the ancient Semitic tribal mother." (*ERE*, II, 15.) "In old Arabian religion gods and goddesses occur in pairs, the goddess being the greater, so that the god cannot be her Baal, that the goddess in often a mother without being a wife, and the god her son, and the progress of things was towards changing goddesses into gods or lowering them beneath the male deity. (Robertson Smith, *KMEA*, 306.) "When we reflect that this practice of mother-kin as opposed to father-kin survived down to the latest times of antiquity, not in an obscure or barbarous tribe, but in a nation whose immemorial civilization was its glory and the wonder of the world, we may, without being extravagant, suppose that a similar practice formerly prevailed in Syria and Phrygia, and that it accounts for the superiority of the goddess over the god in the divine partnerships of Adonis and Astarte, of Attis and Cybele." (Frazer, *AAO*, 398.)
2. Cf. Hopkins, *RI*, 541.
3. *IAR*, 148 ff.
4. From the time when the concept of mother-right was formulated it was assumed that the treatment of the subject lay in organizing all available materials pertaining to descent, kinship, inheritance, succession, authority, marriage, etc., within one vast theoretical set-up, usually of an evolutionary nature (cf. Rivers in *ERE*, VIII, 151 ff). The matriarchal theory was introduced by Bachofen (1861), McLenan (1865) and Morgan (1869) who held that marriage was evolved from promiscuity through a series of progressive stages to monogamy and that descent through the maternal line had preceded that through paternal, the former passing to the latter when property relations were established and paternity was no longer doubtful. Subsequently, Bloch (*SLOT*, 189), Maine (*DELC*, 202), Hartland (*PP*, II, 3), Thomas (*KGMA*, 15) and others held that the less important fatherhood was in a society, the more that society would be driven to base its right upon the mother and that mother-right had everywhere

preceded father-right. The matriarchal theory did not, however, find much favour with Westermarck (*HHM*, I, chs. 3-9), Goldenwiser (*AA*, NS, XIII. 603 ff.), Horatio Hale (*S*, XIX. 30), Van Gennep (*MLA*, intro. XXXII) and some other anthropologists. It was reasserted by Robert Briffault in 1927. One of the strongest supporters of Morgan, Briffault marshalled on his side a mass of data, far more copious and concrete in favour of the matriarchal theory than had ever been adduced against it. He suggested that the differentiation of men as the warrior was not due to any constitutional indisposition or incapacity in primitive woman, but to economic necessities. While women were frequently known to share in the active pursuits of men, the constructive occupations which had given rise to the development of material culture belonged almost exclusively to the sphere of women's work. All industries were first home industries and developed in the hands of women. But with the decline of the evolutionist mode of approach in anthropological studies, the classical concept of mother-right came to be treated will diminishing importance. For details see my *IMG*, 253-77.

5. I.73, 93, 171; III.31, 68, 88; VI.192-99; VII.3-4, 74-99; VIII.17-88, 93, 103; passim.
6. I.23.
7. III.165.
8. XIII.6.
9. II.6, 7.
10. *Politika*, II.6, 11.
11. *RGE*, 98 ff.
12. *OT*, 198 ff.
13. *AO*, 107 ff.
14. *ERE*, V.733.
15. *SLAE*, 109, 119.
16. *LAE*, 92 ff.
17. *IAEA*, 22 ff.
18. *HE*, I.96 ff.
19. *KMEA*, 74 ff.
20. *HA*, 312; *OREN*, 331 ff.
21. *HNC*, I.410 ff.
22. *RAC*, 222 ff.
23. *SLHG*, 232.
24. Cf. Tacitus *VA*, XV.
25. XXII.
26. Watters, *YCTI*, I.330.
27. Ibid., II.257, cf. Beal, *BRWW*, II.277 ff.
28. Majumdar, *CAI*, 222-23, 456-58.
29. LVIII.39.
30. Ch. LV.
31. M/K, XXXIX.27 ff.
32. XIV.22.
33. XII.4, 7.
34. IV.43, 20.
35. IV.173, 185, 587, 666.
36. *ABORI*, VII.144 ff.
37. XVIII.57.
38. *MRI*, 18 ff., 121-29, 201-04.
39. *L*, 232 ff.

40. *IAR,* 148-49.
41. *MIC,* I.48 ff.
42. Hogarth in *ERE,* I.147.
43. Thomson, *AA,* 21-22.
44. Frazer, *GB* (ab), 11-82, 399-423.
45. Briffault, *M,* III.117. In ancient Greece agricultural magic was the monopoly of women (Farnell, *CGS,* V.180 ff.). The term 'thesmophoria' appears to have been loosely used for all the agricultural rites of Greece. All other Attic festivals of agriculture and fertility such as 'aretophoria', 'sthenia', 'haloa', 'skira', etc. were likewise celebrated by women (Harrison, *PSGR,* 131, 134, 146). The rites of Dionysos, Demeter and Kore (Persephone) were confined exclusively among women at Pyreai, Briseai, Pelline and Halicarnassus (Cf. Herodotus, VII.178; Pausanias, III. 20; VI. 20; VII. 27; VIII. 48; IX.12, 20). In Babylonia and Assyria women were inspired prophetesses of the gods. None but a woman was allowed to enter the secret cave of Bel-Marduk (Sayce, *RAEB,* 446, 455). In ancient Egypt, the queen was the high priestess of Ra, and at the time of the New Empire, there was scarcely a woman from the highest to the lowest who was not connected with the service of the temples (Erman, *LAE,* 295).
46. *M,* III.56.
47. See my *IPR,* 8-19. In India it is believed that in the time of *ambuvācī* (from seventh to eleventh day of the third month of Hindu calendar) Mother Earth menstruates during which period there is an entire cessation of all ploughing, sowing and other farm work. In many parts of India great importance is attached to the menstruation of the goddess Pārvatī (*IA,* XVIII, 155 ff.). The same holds good in the case of the goddess Kāmākhyā of Assam, (B.K. Kakati, *MGK*). In Punjab Mother Earth sleeps for a week in each month (*NINQ,* II.172; *PNQ,* II.205). In the Deccan, after the *navarātra,* her temple is closed from the tenth to the full moon day while she rests and refreshes herself (Underhill, *HRY,* 34). A similar rite of purification is made in the case of the goddess Bhagavatī at her temple in Kerala (Nagam Aiya, *TSM,* II.89 ff.). In Malabar region Mother Earth rests during the hot weather until she gets the first shown of rain (Iyer, *CTC,* II.78).
48. James, *PR,* 172.
49. Cf. Piggott, *PI,* 127.
50. Stein, *ATWNB,* 38 ff; *ATG,* 37 ff.
51. *WHH,* 129.
52. *MIC,* I.50.
53. Mackay, *FEM,* I.349; Marshall, *MIC,* I.341.
54. Cf. Brunton and Canton-Thompson, *BC,* 29.
55. Vats, *EH,* 292.
56. Marshall, *MIC,* I.52.
57. Ibid., 63 ff.; Mackay, *FEM,* I.337-38.
58. Chattopadhyaya, *L,* 359 ff.; Bhattacharyya *IMG,* 92-94.
59. *MRI,* 1.
60. *MIC,* I.58.
61. Bagchi, *PPI,* 4, 10.
62. Chatterji, *IAH,* 36 ff.
63. *RV,* II.32.6; X.184.2; *AV,* XIX.31.10; *Nir,* XI.31.
64. II.77.
65. XI.55.
66. *SPP,* 1345 BS, 247.

67. Kakati, *MGK*, 6-7, 35-36.
68. Cf. *AV*, X.4.14; *VS*, XXX.16; *TB*, III.4.12.1; passim.
69. X.44.
70. XXVIII.34.
71. Bhattacharyya, *IMG*, 81-89.
72. *Infra*.
73. Playfair, *G*, 80 ff.; Dawan Singh, *FG*, 369; Bardoloi, *D*, 293.
74. Basumatari, *BKSKA*, 16 ff.; Narzi, *BKSS*, 245 ff.
75. Sen, *RM*, 131-32; Chatterji, *KJK*, 57.
76. Shakespeare in *FL*, XXIV.409.
77. Caldwell, *CGDL*, 113.
78. Kunhan Raja in *HPEW*, I, 39.
79. *MR*, 1924, 679.
80. Raychaudhuri, *SIA*, 200-204.
81. *JAS*, I, 1959, 107-08.
82. Whitehead, *VGSI*, 23 ff.
83. *BCLV*, 76.
84. *VGSI*, 117.
85. Elmore, *DGMH*, II, 41, 57, 74-75, 84-85, 110-19.
86. Whitehead, *VGSI*, 32, 80, 92, 104-08.
87. *ERE*, V.6.
88. Elmore, *DGMH*, 40.
89. Eliot, *HB*, II.213.
90. Whitehead, *VGSI*, 29, 32, 124.

2

The Vedic Age

The Vedic literature reveals the existence a composite but structurally uniform civilization constituted by a variety of standardized cultural streams which flourished especially in northern India between *c.* 1500 and 600 BC. The Vedic language which later came to be known as Sanskrit after its subsequent refinement was supposed to belong to the Indo-European or Aryan family of languages. But the concept 'Aryan' was never confined to the exclusive domain of philology. It developed racial, psychological and also political connotations and came to be used to serve a variety of purposes.

Notwithstanding Max Müller's warning that the implication of the term 'Aryan' should not go beyond its purely linguistic suggestivity, many scholars insisted on a racial interpretation, arguing that the original language must have evolved within a particular race, the migration of which into different countries led to the propagation of the language far and wide. Psychological considerations were also there. Since a good number of the languages belonging to the Aryan family belonged to Europe and since the nineteenth century Europe was materially superior in many respects to the other parts of the world, the concept 'Aryan' acquired a connotation of superiority. From this viewpoint the Western scholars held that in remote antiquity the Aryans spread in different directions, especially in the Oriental world inhabited by the 'aboriginals' with a civilizing mission. This idea obviously contributed to the cause of imperialism and colonialism: 'white man's burden', in the language of Kipling, or 'thousand years' Aryan rule', in the words of Hitler.

Starting from North Pole and Greenland, almost every region of Asia and Europe, including India as well, has been claimed, at different times and on different grounds, by scholars belonging to different disciplines, to be the original homeland of the undefined Aryans. For the last two hundred years theories after theories, based on imaginary and far-fetched evidence regarding the so-called Aryan migration, were formulated. But, apart from the fact that a vast region of Asia and Europe was inhabited by peoples speaking in various languages, attributed by the philologists to the Aryan family, all the overgrowths of Aryanism are nothing but figments of scholarly fancy.[1]

The *Ṛgveda,* the earliest literary record of India, the *terminus ad quem* of the composition of which is 1200-1000 BC, reveals a socio-economic and religio-philosophical process in transition. Its older portions indicate that the stage of a highly developed agriculture was reached only after passing through a purely pastoral phase of long duration. In fact, out of 10,462 verses of the *Ṛgveda,* only 25 refer to agriculture.[2] Side by side the importance attached to the possession of cattle is shown in numerous passages. The word *go* denoting the cow is used as one of the synonyms of *pṛthivī,* the earth. According to the *Nighaṇṭu,*[3] nine other terms were also used to denote the cow. Even in the *Ṛgveda* the gods are invoked as offsprings of the cows[4] and the poets did not hesitate to compare their songs with the lowing of the cow[5] or to designate the starry heaven after the term *gāvaḥ.*[6]

> Again and again in the songs and invocations to the gods the prayer for cattle and horses occurs. Also the strife amongst hostile aboriginal inhabitants turns on the possession of cattle. Therefore, too, the old word for 'war' or 'battle' is originally desire for cattle (*gaviṣṭi*). In most extravagant expressions, cows and bullocks are praised as most precious possessions.[7]

The accumulation of wealth came in primitive societies in two ways: by the development of agriculture and by the domestication of cattles. Where agriculture developed considerably without any intervening pastoral stage, women, due to their traditional association with agriculture, could naturally exert greater hold on social life and affairs. But where agriculture developed in its most productive form in the societies which were originally pastoral, we have the opposite result. Instead of raising the economic power and importance of earth-cultivating women, it gave rise to the most pronounced type of patriarchal societies.[8]

The most ancient forms of the Ṛgvedic religion were therefore patriarchal, a reflection of the society of the pastoral warriors. The pastoral tribes require greater courage and hardihood than the agicultural, and also an efficient leadership to protect the cattle. So the cult of heroes and ancestors attains its highest degree of development among the pastorals. The herder in his nomadic life has to live under the scorching heat of the sun, the dreadful thunders, the devastating storms. So his religion is mainly connected with the sky, in which astral and nature myths, often personified as secondary gods and godlings, make their appearance. The Supreme Being of a pastoral religion is generally identified with the sky-god who rules over other deities like the headman of a patriarchal joint family.

II

But this does not mean that goddesses should have always a subordinate position in pastoral-patriarchal societies or that the conception of a Female Principle of creation should have no room in the patriarchal world-view. Apart from being the Earth and Corn Mothers of the agricultural societies, the primitive Mother Goddesses had many features in connection with procreation, generation and regeneration, sustenance, protection, healing and other facts of day-to-day life which the pastoral people, with male-dominance on social life, could hardly ignore, especially when the existing cult of the Mother Goddess of various peoples was visibly present before them. To quote Farnell:

> The Aryan Hellenes were able to plant their Zeus and Poseidon on the high hill of Athens, but not to overthrow the supremacy of Athena in the central shrine and in the aboriginal soul of the Athenian people.[9]

The same held good in the case of the pastoral-patriarchal tribes of the *Ṛgveda*. Guided by the belief that female deities have very little to do in a patriarchal society, Macdonell wrote:

> Goddesses occupy a very subordinate position in Vedic belief and worship. They play hardly any part as rulers of the world. The only one of any importance is Uṣas, who judged by the statistical standard ranks as a deity of the third class.... Goddesses as wives of the great gods similarly play an insignificant part in the Veda. They are altogether without independent character, simply representing the spouses whom such gods as Indra must have had. Hardly anything about them is mentioned but their names, which are simply formed from those of the gods with the feminine suffix *-ānī*. Thus Indrāṇī is simply 'wife of Indra'. Varuṇānī and Agnāyi also occur in the *Ṛgveda*, but rarely. Rudrāṇī is not found till the Sūtras, but she plays a decidedly a more important part in the cult than any of the other goddesses in *-ānī*. The wife of the Aśvins is once in the *Ṛgveda*, called Aśvinī. The 'wives of the god' (*devanāṃ*

patnīḥ) occasionally mentioned in the *Ṛgveda* have in the Brāhmaṇas an established place assigned to them in the cult apart from the gods.[10]

In order to determine the relative position of the Vedic deities scholars depended on statistical standard. According to this standard since Indra is mentioned in 250 hymns and Rātri in only one hymn, the former must be the highest deity and the latter a minor one. There is of course some justification in following this standard, but this does not explain the whole situation. Although the Vedic poets describe in glowing terms the heroism of Indra in overcoming the enemies or the greatness of Varuṇa as the guardian of moral order, there is some sort of democracy among the early Vedic gods. Individual gods, whether invoked in a good number of hymns or in one hymn, are always described as the highest deity which has given rise to the much discussed theory of Max Müller—Henotheism or Kathenotheism—according to which the Vedic poets attributed to the god, they happened to be addressing, all the highest traits of divinity, treating him or her for the moment as an absolutely independent and supreme deity.[11] No one is superior to any one, Varuṇa and Sūrya are subordinate to Indra;[12] Varuṇa and Aśvins submit their power to Viṣṇu;[13] and Indra, Mitra-Varuṇa, Aryaman and Rudra can not resist the ordinances of Savitṛ.[14] It should not be forgotten in this connection that the composers of the hymns of the *Ṛgveda* were basically poets, and hence in their conceptions of deities poetic norms and imageries were maintained so that the personification of natural phenomena suited well with their anthropomorphic forms, whether male or female.

Aditi, the Vedic Mother of the Gods is mentioned about eighty times in the *Ṛgveda,* though she is not subject to any separate hymn. The derivative meaning of Aditi is 'unbinding', 'bondlessness', etc., and hence as a goddess she is naturally invoked to release her worshippers from fetters. According to Max Müller, Aditi is the earliest name invented to express the infinite as visible to the human eye, the endless expanse beyond the earth and the clouds.[15] Roth has explained Aditi as a personification of the boundlessness of heaven as opposed to the finite earth.[16] The concept of Aditi's motherhood is found in such expressions as *dyaur aditih,* 'the boundless sky,' the mother who supplies the gods with milk.[17] The expression *aditeḥ putrāḥ,* sons of Aditi, several times applied to the Ādityas in the *Ṛgveda,* is also to be noted in this connection.[18] Her epithet *pastyā* or housewife may possibly also allude to her motherhood.[19] She is the mother of Indra, Varuṇa, Mitra, Aryaman, Bhaga, Dakṣa, Rudra and others.[20] She is described as *anarvā* or unimpaired, expanded, mistress of wide stalls, bright and luminous and a supporter of creatures, frequently invoked along with Agni, Savitṛ, Mitra, Varuṇa and Aryaman to release from guilt or sin.[21] This has brought her in close relation with Varuṇa whose fetters bind the sinners.[22] She is spoken of several times as protecting from distress and she is said to grant complete welfare or safety.[23] As the mother of the luminous Ādityas, Aditi in often connected with light, implored to protect or bless her worshippers, their children and cattle and also to bestow wealth.[24] Terrestrial Soma is compared to the milk of Aditi.[25] Priests with their ten fingers are said to purify Soma on the lap of Aditi. Sometimes she has been regarded as the personification of universal nature: 'Aditi is the sky; Aditi is the air; Aditi is all-gods and the five tribes; Aditi is the mother, and father, and son; Aditi is whatever shall be born.'[26]

The *Nighaṇṭu* gives Aditi as a synonym of *pṛthivī* (earth); *vāc* (speech), *go* (cow) and *dyāvā-pṛthivī* (heaven and earth).[27] In some passages of the *Ṛgveda* and in the *Vājasaneyi Saṃhitā* Aditi is spoken of as a cow.[28] In the *Atharvaveda* Aditi is described as 'mother of heroic sons', 'mother of eight sons', 'mother and sister of the Ādityas, Rudras and Vasus', 'the great mother of the devout', 'the mistress of Ṛta', 'strong in might', undecaying, protecting and skilfully guiding and also identified with the earth.[29] In a cosmogonic myth of the *Ṛgveda* it is stated that the earth sprang from Uttānapad; from the earth sprang the regions; Dakṣa sprang from Aditi and Aditi from Dakṣa.[30] Yāska who considers Aditi as the 'mighty mother of gods' and locates her in the atmospheric region, explains the Aditi-Dakṣa myth saying that Aditi and Dakṣa might have originated from the same source or derived their substance from each other.[31] This myth of reciprocal generation can be explained if we take into account the idea that the patriarchal world-view of the Vedic Indians was in search of a Male Principle of creation, the incipient form of which was represented by Dakṣa who was later identified with Prajāpati in the Brāhmaṇa literature. Even in the later portions of the *Ṛgveda,* as the myth suggests, Aditi remained the Female Principle of creation and Dakṣa was conceived of as the male creative agent or force standing in inseparable relation with the former which accounts for their reciprocal generation. In later mythology, the goddess Satī was the daughter of Dakṣa who was reborn as Umā or Pārvatī.

According to Macdonell, a review of the evidence indicates that Aditi has two prominent characteristics. The first is her motherhood. She is the mother of a group of gods whose name represents a matronymic formation from hers. Her second main characteristic, in conformity with the etymological meaning of the name, is her power of releasing the bonds of physical suffering and moral guilt. The Ādityas are frequently described as *aditeḥ putrāḥ* which might have meant in the pre-Vedic age 'sons of freedom or bondlessness' like *sahasaḥ putrāḥ* or 'sons of strength'. Hence Macdonell wonders: "How are we to account for so early a personification of such an abstract idea, and in particular for Aditi becoming the mother of the Ādityas?"[32] V.M. Apte gives the following explanation.

> Aditi is unmistakably connected with light in the *Ṛgveda*. Varuṇa—the Āditya—is connected prominently and almost exclusively with Ṛta; so is Aditi. This Ṛta has for the physical basis the belt of the zodiac. Now the Devas, the lights of heaven, seemed to the ancients to recover their freedom from the clutches of darkness and to restart on their bright career from a fixed point in the east, lying on the belt of the zodiac or the Ṛta. This point in all probability was Aditi. No wonder, the luminaries suddenly emerging thus into freedom and light (emerging in other words into life itself) from this fixed point (Aditi) received epithet 'sons of Aditi'.[33]

In view of what has been stated above it may be said that Aditi was the most ancient mother of the gods whose original features became obscure even in the Vedic age. Ṛgvedic references of Aditi associate her with the celestial region and heavenly bodies. Diti, whose name as a goddess seems to be merely an antithesis to that of Aditi,[34] is mentioned only three times in the *Ṛgveda*. In the first place, Mitra and Varuṇa are said to behold from their car Aditi and Diti.[35] In the second place, Agni is besought to grant wealth to Diti for the preservation of Aditi.[36] In the third place Diti is mentioned along with Agni, Savitṛ and Bhaga for the bestowal of what is desirable or divisible (*vārya*, meaning the divisible wealth).[37] According to Roth, while Aditi stands for the eternal, Diti stands for the mundane and perishable.[38] Muir regards Diti as the 'entire aggregate of visible nature'.[39] According to Apte, Diti is the exactly opposite point of the zodiac in the west where the light goes out. Diti is named along with

Aditi as a goddess also in the later Saṃhitās.[40] Her sons are mentioned in the *Atharvaveda* who in the post-Vedic mythology are the enemies of the gods.[41]

III

While Aditi represented the most rudimentary forms of the principles of infinity and liberation and Diti those of finiteness and bondage which, in their developed and perfected forms, characterised the later religious and philosophical conceptualizations of India, two other goddesses, Uṣas and Rātri, representing two complementary principles in the functioning of natural process, occupy a very important position in the *Ṛgveda.* Uṣas, the goddess of dawn, is celebrated in about 20 hymns and mentioned more than 300 times.[42] In the case of Uṣas the personification is slight, the poet never losing sight of the beautiful physical phenomena behind the deity. Gaily attired like a dancer with a garment of light she displays her bosom; like a maiden decked by her mother, she shows her form, appearing in the east and unvailing her charms. Ever youthful, being born again and again, though ancient, never aging, immortal, rising resplendent as from a bath, Uṣas drives away darkness, awakes before all the world, revolves like a wheel, awakens creatures and every living being to motion, reveals the paths of men of all the five tribes, manifests all beings and bestow new life, drives away evil dreams to Trita Āptya, wards off evil spirits, makes the birds fly, discloses the treausres concealed by darkness and distributes them bountifully, illumines the ends of the sky, opens the gates of heaven and the doors of darkness, protects the cattle, goes straight along the path of order and renders good service to the gods by causing all worshippers to awake and the sacrificial fire to be kindled. She is borne on a shining, will-adorned, massive and spontaneously-yoked car drawn by ruddy powerful bulls or steeds. She is also said to arrive on a hundred chariots.

Uṣas is urged to arouse only the devout and liberal worshipper leaving the ungodly niggard to sleep on; asked not to delay so that the sun may not scorch her as a thief or an enemy; besought to bring the gods to drink Soma; and implored to bring to the worshipper wealth and children, to bestow protection and long life and to confer renown and glory. She is born in the sky and is constantly called the daughter and the beloved of heaven. Various gods are associated with her origin. Indra is said to have generated or lighted up Uṣas; Soma made her bright at birth; Bṛhaspati discovered her; and ancient Fathers generated her by efficacious hymns. Uṣas is the sister of Bhaga and a kinswoman of Varuṇa. She is associated with the moon which being born ever anew goes before her and with the Aśvins, the twin-gods of the early morning who accompany her as friends. She is invoked to arouse the Aśvins and she appears when their car is yoked. As the sacrificial fire, Uṣas is associated with Agni who is sometimes called her lover, often meeting her for fair riches. But the closest connection of Uṣas is with the Sun as she opens the path for Surya to travel. She shines with the light of the Sun who is her lover and follows her just as a young man follows a maiden. She is also described as the wife or mistress of the Sun and is occasionally thought of to be his mother. Savitṛ who shines after the path of Uṣas is also said to have been generated by her.

The Uṣas-hymns are among the most poetic of the *Ṛgveda*. One cannot help feeling that the lyric beauty and love of nature reflected in these hymns were inspired from the direct experience of the poets. Thus the goddess is resplendent, shining, bright, white, ruddy, golden-hued, divine, immortal and characteristically bountiful. In her anthropomorphic form she is conceived as a beautiful damsel with a soothing personality. But there are certain aspects which are also to be noted in this connection. Unlike other gods, she receives no share in the Soma offering. The real attitude of the Vedic peoples towards this goddess was certainly not of reverence but of flattery. In *Ṛgveda,* IV.30.8-11, the poet does not besitate to admire the heroism of Indra in overcoming Uṣas.

> This Indra, was a deed of might and manliness which thou didst achieve that thou didst smite the daughter of the sky (Uṣas), a woman who was bent on evil. Thou Indra, the great (god) didst crush Uṣas, though daughter of the sky, who was exalting herself. Uṣas fled away in terror from her shattered car, when the vigorous (Indra) had crushed it. This chariot of hers lies broken and dissolved while she herself has fled afar off.[43]

What may be the cause of Indra's hostile attitude towards Uṣas? Was it a typical patriarchal attitude in which a woman, though appreciated for her beauty, grace and manners, was treated as a sheer object of enjoyment? Or did she belong to a pre-Vedic period, enjoying greater popularity among the non-Aryan-speaking tribes?

What is strikingly significant is that the same hymn which describes Indra's rape of Uṣas also describes his success in plundering the cities of Susṇa, defeating the Dāsa Kaulitara, slaying five thousand followers of the Dāsa Varcin, making a gift of hundred stone-built cities to Divodās and slaying thirty thousand Dāsas for the sake of Dabhīti.[44] Circumstantial evidence thus connects Indra's rape of Uṣas with his destruction of the hostile tribes. Are we then to conclude that Uṣas was the Great Mother Goddess of a different cultural tradition and that the Vedic peoples inducted her to their pantheon by clipping many of her original attributes though retaining her features pertaining to the physical phenomenon of dawn? The *Ṛgveda* in one place refers to Uṣas as *māta devānāṃ aditer anīkam,* 'Mother of the gods and rival of Aditi, as Sāyaṇa interprets it.[45] The word *anīka* also means 'face' and 'manifestation'. Aditi, as we have seen, was the most ancient Mother of the gods whose features had become hazy even in the age of the *Ṛgveda.* Uṣas, who was either a rival or a manifestation of Aditi, must have therefore been a very ancient goddess whose diverse attributes have only been touched in the *Ṛgveda* but not given the fullest expression.

Uṣas is described as the sister or elder sister of Rātri, the goddess of Night.[46] The names of Dawn and Night are often conjoined as a dual compound, Uṣāsānaktā or Naktoṣāsā, Rātri is invoked only in one hymn in the *Ṛgveda.*[47] Like her sister Uṣas, she is called the daughter of heaven. Rātri probably became a goddess by way of antithesis to Uṣas with whom she is invoked in several verses as a dual divinity. Rātri is not conceived as absolutely dark, but as the bright starlit night. She shines manifoldly with her eyes. Decked with all spelndour, she fills the valleys and heights, driving away the darkness with light. At her approach men return home like birds to their nests. She is invoked to keep away the wolf and the thief, guiding her worshippers to safety. She is all-pervading. She covers the atmospheric and the terrestrial regions with darkness. Owing to her grace the villagers, the birds and beasts sleep peacefully. She is as benevolent as the cow. She repays all the debts of her worshippers and infuses energy in them to vanquish their enemies.

Though Rātri is invoked in a single hymn in the *Ṛgveda,* in the subsequent religious history of India, she was able to exert more influence than her glamorous sister Uṣas. In the *Bṛhaddevatā*[48] Rātri has been identified with Sarasvatī, Durgā and Aditi. She has thus some role in the process of the development of the later concept of

Śakti. In the Purāṇas it is stated that at the request of Brahmā, Rātri entered the womb of Menakā and blackened the complexion of Umā who was in her womb.[49] Rātri is thus the precursor of the later mythological conceptions of Pārvatī, Kauṣikī, Kālī and similar goddesses.

IV

To a third group belong Dyaus and Pṛthivī (Heaven and Earth) who are regarded as the parents not only of the gods, but of the men also. The conception of a Sky Father fertilising the Earth Mother is met within a number of mythologies. A Greek parallel of the Ṛgvedic Dyaus and Pṛthivī is found in Uranus, the Sky Father and Gaea, the Earth Mother. In a Greek magic formula the sky is invoked to rain and the earth to conceive and yield which, as Farnell points out, "savours of a very primitive liturgy that closely resembles the famous Dodenaean invocation to Zeus, the Sky God and Mother Earth; and it belongs to that part of the Eleusinian ritual *quod ad frumentum attinett*".[50] Aeschylus wrote:

The pure Sky yearns with love to wound the Earth,
The loving Earth yearns likewise to be wed,
And from the heavenly bridegroom showers descend
Upon the bride, who brings forth for mankind
The grazing cattle and Demeter's corn
With precious moisture riping the fruits
To autumn fulness. (*Danaides*)

In various passages of the *Ṛgveda,* Dyaus and Pṛthivī are said to have made and to sustain all creatures.[51] It is said that they have augmented Bṛhaspati by their power[52] and they are described as having in conjunction with the waters begotten Agni.[53] They are characterised by a profusion of epithets not only by such as are suggested by their various physical characteristics[54] but also by such as are of moral or spiritual character.[55] In many passages of the *Ṛgveda* Dyaus and Pṛthivī are described as universal parents.[56] The two together are styled *pitarā*[57] or *mātarā*[58] or *janitrī.*[59] In other passages Heaven is separately styled father and the Earth mother.[60] The same is found also in the *Atharvaveda*[61] and the *Vājasaneyi Saṃhitā.*[62] But it appears that, even in the age of the *Ṛgveda* their cosmogonical importance was not fully recognised. The sky is visible, and so the earth. The idea therefore soon developed that heaven and earth were, after all, produced by some greater being. In many passages we come across various speculations about their origin. In a verse of the first *maṇḍala* we find that the poet wants to know how the Heaven and the Earth have been produced.[63] In another passage the poet asks: 'what was the forest, what was the tree, from which they fashioned the Heaven and the Earth?' This question is repeated in another passage in which their creation is ascribed to the sole agency of Viśvakarman.[64] Again, Indra is described as their creator, as having beautifully fashioned them by his power and skill and as sustaining and upholding them.[65] The creation of Heaven and Earth is also ascribed to other deities like Soma, Puṣan, Dhātṛ, Hiraṇyagarbha and others.[66] They are declared to have received their shape and variety of forms from Tvaṣṭṛ to have sprung respectively from the head and the feet of Puruṣa and to have sustained or supported by Mitra, Savitṛ, Varuṇa, Indra, Soma and Hiraṇyagarbha.[67]

Dyaus is coupled with Earth in the dual compound *dyāvā-pṛthivī.* No single hymn of the *Ṛgveda* is addressed to Dyaus alone. According to Macdonell, as a father he is most usually thought of in combination with Earth as a mother which is indicated by the fact that his name forms a dual compound with that of Pṛthivī oftener than it is used alone in the singular, that in a large proportion of its occurrences in the singular it is accompanied by the name of Pṛthivī and when regarded separately, he is not sufficiently individualised to have a hymn dedicated to his praise, though in conjunction with Pṛthivī he is celebrated in six. In about 20 passages the word *dyaus* is in feminine, even when personified.[68] Pṛthivī, when mentioned with Dyaus frequently receives the epithet of 'mother'. She is spoken of a 'kindly Mother Earth' to whom the dead man is exhorted to go.[69] The *Ṛgveda* refers to Pṛthivī as 'the broad one' which is in accordance with its etymological meaning. Indra is said to have upheld the earth and spread it out.[70] The *Taittirīya Saṃhitā*[71] and the *Taittirīya Brāhmaṇa*[72] while describing the origin of the earth, expressly derive the name of Pṛthivī from the root *prath,* to extend, because she is extended. Pṛthivī is lauded in only one short hymn in the *Ṛgveda*[73] and in a long and beautiful one in the *Atharvaveda.*[74] In her case, anthropomorphism is less, both in extent and in degree, the attributes of the goddess being chiefly those of the physical earth. She abounds in height bears the burdens of the mountains, and supports the trees of the forest. She fertilises the soil through the rains. The showers of heaven are shed from the lightning of her cloud. She is great (*mahī*), firm (*dṛḍha*) and shining (*arjunī*). The *Atharvaveda* hymn consists of 63 stanzas in which it is said that Mother Earth is sustained by supreme truth, consecration and penance, holiness and sacrifice; that she is the mistress of everything visible in the extensive space; that she bears the mountains and rivers, the ocean, the herbs of various virtues and food and cattle for peoples; that in the beginning she was in water; that she bears peoples of various speeches and of varying customs; that she is the bestower of plenty who grants wealth in a thousand streams; and so forth.

V

Vāc, personified speech, is celebrated in one hymn of the *Ṛgveda*[75] which is popularly known as Devīsūkta. Though this hymn belongs to the later portion of the *Ṛgveda*, its importance can not be underestimated because it contains the nucleus of all aspects of later Śāktism. In this hymn the goddess describes herself. She accompanies the Rudras and the Vasus, stays with the Ādityas and all the gods and supports Mitra-Varuṇa, Indra-Agni and the Aśvins, as also Soma, Tvaṣṭṛ, Puṣan and Bhaga and bestows wealth on the person who pleases the deities with clarified butter and prepares Soma. She is the controller of the universe, bestower of wealth, greatest among the objects of sacrifice, principle of consciousness, established variously within the constituents, of the universe and among all beings. He who partakes of food, sees, breaths or hears does so because of her energy. She is at the root of power, greatness and intelligence. She fights for the welfare of mankind. She encompasses the celestial and terrestiral region. She has produced *dyāvā-pṛthivī*, the sky and the earth. Her generative function starts from the waters of the ocean whence it manifests in the world and reaches the celestial region. In the *Nighaṇṭu*[76] Vāc is enumerated among the deities of atmosphere. The *Nirukta*[77] refers to *madhyamikā-vāc* or the voice of the middle region which presupposes the later concept of *śabda-brahman* according to which the real form of Vāc lies far beyond the range of ordinary perception and it has four stages, namely, *parā, paśyantī, madhyamā* and *vaikharī*.

A legend in the *Śatapatha Brāhmaṇa* says that Vāc brought Soma for the gods from the Gandharvas.[78] According to the *Aitareya Brāhmaṇa* version of the story, Soma was purchased from the Gandharvas at the price of Vāc who presented her naked form (*mahānagnā bhūtayā*) to them for the sake of the gods.[79] In Devarāja's commentary on the *Nighaṇṭu*[80] the goddess is also called naked. This nakedness of Vāc may be considered as a remote source of the conception of the nakedness of Kālī. According to a legend found in the *Śatapatha Brāhmaṇa*[81] Vāc or Sarasvatī being angry, assumed the form of a lion which reminds us of the later conception of the lion-mount of Durgā. The identification of Vāc with Sarasvatī took place in the age of the later Saṃhitās and Brāhmaṇas.

In the *Ṛgveda*, Sarasvatī is a river goddess lauded in three hymns and in numerous detached verses. She is mentioned along with other rivers and described as flowing with fertile flood surpassing all other rivers in greatness, on whose banks princes and people offer sacrifice.[82] She is the best of mothers, of rivers and of goddesses. She fills the terrestrial regions and the wide atmospheric space and occupies three abodes. She is invoked to descend from the sky, from the great mountain to the sacrifice.[83] She bestows vitality and offspring and is associated with deities who assist procreation.[84] Besides Puṣan and Indra, Sarasvatī is particularly associated with the Maruts and connected with the Aśvins.[85] The *Vājasaneyi Saṃhitā* speaks of Sarasvatī as the wife of the Aśvins.[86] It also states that when the gods celebrated healing sacrifice, the Aśvins and physicians and Sarasvatī through speech (*vāc*) communicated vigour to Indra.[87] In the *āprī* hymns she is associated with Ilā and Bhāratī, with whom she forms a triad, and sometimes also with Mahī and Hotrā.

Although in the *Ṛgveda* Sarasvatī is no more than a river goddess, whose personification never obscures her original character, we find her identified with Vāc in the Brāhmaṇas,[88] and in post-Vedic mythology she has become the goddess of eloquence and wisdom and regarded as the wife of Brahmā. In the *Bṛhaddevatā*,[89] Sinivālī, Rākā, Anumati, Kuhū are mentioned as various forms of Vāc or Sarasvatī. In the *Atharvaveda* Vāc or Sarasvatī is invoked to bestow progeny (*prajāṃ devi rarāsva naḥ*).[90] In the *Śatapatha Brāhmaṇa* Vāc or Sarasvatī has been described as the queen of the serpents.[91] The *Vājasaneyi Saṃhitā* legend of the revitalising of Indra by the Aśvins and Sarasvatī recurs in the *Śatapatha Brāhmaṇa*.[92] Elsewhere in the same text Sarasvatī is described as the goddess of wealth.[93] In the *Atharvaveda* Sarasvatī is described as the goddess of wealth, vegetation and fertility.

Śrī and Lakṣmī occurs in the *Ṛgvedas*, though not in the sense of goddess.[94] However, both as the names occur in the Śrī-sūkta which is a supplement of the *Ṛgveda* composed in a later period. The later attributes of both Śrī and Lakṣmī are foreshadowed in this hymn. That Lakṣmī was originally the goddess of agriculture is attested by the evidence of the Śrī-sūkta. It appears that originally Śrī and Lakṣmī were different goddesses. In the *Vājasaneyi Saṃhitā* both the goddesses are described as the two wives of Āditya.[95] Later they became identical. Among other goddesses of abundance, bearing on the characteristics of Śrī-Lakṣmī, Puraṃdhi occurs about nine times in the *Ṛgveda*. She is nearly always mentioned with Bhaga, twice with Puṣan and Savitṛ and once with Viṣṇu and Agni. Another goddess of abundance is Dhiṣaṇā mentioned nearly a dozen of times in the *Ṛgveda*.

Ilā is the personification of the offering of milk and butter, thus representing plenty derived from the cow. As a personification she generally appears in the *āprī* hymns in which she usually forms a triad with Sarasvatī and Mahī or Bhāratī. Owing to the nature of offering Ilā is called butter-handed and butter-footed.[96] Agni is once called the son of Ilā and so is Purūruvas.[97] The name of the goddess Bṛhaddivā occurs four times in hymns to the Viśvedevas. She is called a mother and is mentioned with Ilā, Rākā and Sarasvatī.[98] Rākā is mentioned only twice in the *Ṛgveda* as a rich and bountiful goddess.[99] Sinīvālī is a sister of the gods, broad-hipped, fair-armed, prolific and is implored to grant offspring. She is invoked with Sarasvatī, Rākā and Guṅgu.[100] In the *Atharvaveda* Sinīvālī is called the wife of Viṣṇu.[101] Rākā and Sinīvālī and also Kuhū of the later Saṃhitās and Brāhmaṇas, as we have already had the occasion to remark in the preceding chapter in connection with their supposed Austric origins, are connected with phases of the moon. Pṛṣṇi, the mother of the Maruts, presumably represents the mottled storm cloud.[102] Saraṇyu occurs only once in the *Ṛgveda* as the name of Tvaṣṭṛ's daughter married to Vivasvat.[103] Āpaḥ, the Waters, deified as goddesses, are lauded in four hymns of the *Ṛgveda* as well as a few scattered verses.[104] These goddesses cleanse and purify the effects of moral guilt, violence, cursing and lying, bestow remedies and long life, watch over man's health, and dispose of boons and wealth. As mothers they mix their milk with honey.[105] They are the producers of Agni, one of whose forms is called 'Sons of Waters'.[106]

VI

It is generally held that the position of the goddesses in the age of the

Ṛgveda was subordinate and insignificant and that this inferior position was evidently due to the patriarchal outlook resulting from a purely pastoral economy. But in view of what has been stated above it is clear that although the Ṛgvedic pantheon was male-dominated, the female deities were not ignored. There can be no denial of the fact that a good number of the Ṛgvedic tribes were pastoral. That is why some scholars have argued that the general character of the *Ṛgveda* reflects a class society. Expanding their argument they say that the growth of private ownership in pastoral societies was more rapid than that in the agricultural because wealth in the form of cattle was durable, easy to steal or exchange, and could be increased by raids and wars. Thus among the pastorals, the leadership was military. The leaders and his followers received the lion's share of the spoils and the wealth thus amassed promoted social inequalities. The character of the pastoral war-leader and his followers is reflected in the *Ṛgveda* by that of Indra and his associates. Although they represented the forces of nature, most Ṛgvedic gods were modelled after the pastoral warriors. Hence male domination of the Vedic pantheon was inevitable.[107]

There is undoubtedly some truth in this assertion. But certain other factors are not also to be overlooked. The *Ṛgveda* was not composed in a single day. It took so many centuries to get the whole work compiled. Secondly, the Vedic literature in general and the *Ṛgveda* in particular do not represent a homogeneous culture. Apart from the Austric or Dravidian speaking tribes who formed an important part in the populace of Ṛgvedic India, the Aryan-speaking tribes also did not belong to a single race. They were multi-racial and multi-cultural. Though quite a good number of Vedic tribes—whether Aryan-speaking or non-Aryan-speaking—had pastoralism for their economic subsistence and patriarchy for their social organisation, there were others who depended on hunting or agriculture. Not all Vedic tribes were patriarchal. We have also references to matrilineal clans in the Vedic literature. In the *Ṛgveda* Dīrghatamas is designated as Māmateya after his mother's name.[108] Names of the teachers such as Ātreyiputra, Ārtabhāgiputra, Ālambiputra, Kautsīputra, Gārgīputra, Gautamīputra, Jayantīputra, Prāśnīputra, Pārāśarīputra, Paingīputra, Bāḍeyiputra, Bhāradvājīputra, Bhālukīputra, Māṇḍukīputra, Mauṣikīputra, Vaidabhutīputra, Śāṇḍilīputra, Śaunikīputra, etc., show that matriliny was not uncommon.[109] Some of these names have totemic significance as well.

The deities of the *Ṛgveda* were mostly personifications of natural phenomena under which the herders had to live. Even this was a new religion gradually adopted by the hunting tribes coming into pastoral stage. But could they give up the religious practices of their pre-pastoral life? In fact they could not. They propitiated the deities of pastoral religion with pre-pastoral rituals, of which animal sacrifice was obviously the most important. Two of the Ṛgvedic hymns,[110] later used to be recited in the Aśvamedha sacrifice, show the real nature of the early Vedic rituals. The animal, to be killed, was identified with some deities. It was anointed and then cut to pieces. Its flesh was then cooked and a lump was offered to fire. Then it was eaten up by the participants of the sacrifice in the midst of such utterings as *āghu, yājyā, vaṣaṭkārā.*

The sophisticated forms of the Vedic *yajñas* have some philosophical significance, but their incipient forms, both in theory and in practice, do not differ very much from the magical beliefs and practices, as has been shown by eminent Vedic scholars.[111] The hunting rituals of the primitive Vedic tribes, through which they endeavoured to establish efficacious relation with the awe-inspiring surroundings and conditions of nature, underwent a qualitative change when hunting led to the domestication of cattle. Pastoral peoples all over the world have two grades, the lower and the higher. Higher pastoral stage is achieved when cattle-rearing is supplemented by agriculture.[112] Although the Vedic economy was predominantly pastoral, the Vedic tribes must have been in the higher pastoral stage as is indicated by the variety of their rituals based upon fertility magic.

> So long as they have pasture, cattle feed and breed of themselves, but by comparison with cattle-raising the work of tilling, sowing and reaping is slow, arduous and uncertain. It requires patience, foresight, faith. Accordingly, agricultural society is characterised by the extensive development of magic.[113]

It should not be forgotten in this connection that important Vedic goddesses such as Aditi, Uṣas, Pṛthivī, etc. have been connected with vegetation and fertility. This also holds good in the case of minor goddesses such as Ilā, Mahī, Puraṃdi Dhīṣanā, Rākā, Kuhū, Sinīvālī, Pṛṣṇi, Saraṇyu, Lakṣmī, Oṣadhi,[114] Āpyā,[115] Gandharvi,[116] Niṣṭigṛ[117] and so forth, some of them being of Austric and Dravidian origin. But the typical goddess of agriculture in the *Ṛgveda* is Sītā who is also mentioned in *Atharvaveda* and later Vedic texts.[118] The hymn of the *Ṛgveda* (IV.57) dealing with Sītā contains eight verses. In the Gṛhyasūtras it is stated that every verse of this hymn is to be uttered before ploughing. The presiding deity of the first three verses is Kṣetrapati, the lord of the field who is invoked to bestow water for cultivation. The presiding deity of the fourth verse is Suna and of the fifth and eighth is Sunāsīra. According to Yāska Suna is Vāyu and Sīra is Āditya. Mahīdhara commenting on the *White Yajurvada,* XII.68 says that the original meaning of Sīra is ploughshare (*sīrāṇi halāni*). The presiding deity of the sixth and seventh verses is Sītā, literally the furrow. We have the following invocation to the goddess.

> Auspicious Sītā, be present. We glorify you so that you may bestow us abundant wealth and yield abundant fruit (or the reward of our toil). May Indra take hold of Sītā, may Puṣan guide her. May she, will fertilised with water yield as milk harvest year after year.

In the *Ṛgvedas* Sītā is simply the furrow which bears crops for men, and she is connected with Indra. The root of the *Rāmāyaṇa* story may be traced to these Ṛgvedic verses, and it is likely that the Vedic Indra was converted into the epic Rāma. In the *Rāmāyaṇa* Sītā is said to have sprung from Mother Earth and in the end she disappears again into her womb.[119] The derivative meaning of the word Rāma is also associated with cultivation and procreation. It is ritual that sustains myth: from the ancient agricultural rituals developed the myths of Sītā, and one of such myths was rendered into a form of epic by the great poet Vālmīki. The similarity of Demeter-Persephone myth with the main story of the *Rāmāyaṇa* is too striking to be ignored. The heroine of the epic is born of a field-furrow, abducted by a Pluto of the underworld, and after all her adventures she returns to the earth. The story of the quest of Sītā by Rāma and his troops resembles that of Demeter's quest for Persephone or that of the quest of Isis for the body of Osiris. The figure of Sītā, as Keith observes "naturally has more life in the Sūtras which deal with the operation of agriculture".[120] The *Gobhila Gṛhyasūtra*[121] invokes Sītā along with a few other goddesses at the rituals of furrowing, sowing and reaping the harvest. So does the *Pāraskara Gṛhyasūtra*[122] which invokes Sītā along with Urvarā, Yajā, Samā and Bhūti in connection with agricultural operations.

With their initiation into the agricultural way of life the Vedic tribes not only inducted some powerful goddesses like Ambikā, Umā, etc. from various sources into their pantheon but also adopted numerous rituals designed to secure the fertility of the fields, some of which were sexual in character. In the *Śatapatha Brāhmaṇa* we come across numerous passages in which sexual union is identified with sacrifice.[123] The conception of productive pairs[124] and fruitful semen[125] occur in many passages. In the *White Yajurveda* we come across a hymn which clearly shows that sexual union was employed to promote agricultural production.[126] The legend describes an agricultural rite in which the queen (Vāvātā) and the priest (Udgātā) had to make sexual intercourse in the presence of a number of persons. In all the verses sexual union is brought in relation to agricultural operations. Originally this ritual was a part of the Aśvamedha sacrifice in which the priest, as it seems, was probably killed after his ceremonial intercourse with the queen. Later on, beasts like the horse, were supplied as substitutes for men in such rituals, and the sexual scene used to be mimed.[127] In the Vāmadevya Sāman of the *Chāndogya Upaniṣad*[128] (the term reminds us of Vāmācāra) we come across the following:

> One summons; that is a *hiṃkāra.* He makes request; that is a *prastāva.* Together with the woman he lies down; that is an *udgītha.* He lies upon the woman; that is a *pratihāra.* He come to an end; that is a *nidhāna.* He comes to a finish; that is a *nidhāna.* This is the *vāmadevya sāman* as woven upon copulation. He who knows thus this *vāmadevya sāman* as woven upon copulation, comes to copulation, procreates himself from every copulation, reaches a full length of life, lives long, becomes great in offspring and in cattle, great in fame. One should never abstain from any woman. That is his rule.[129]

In many scattered passages of the Upaniṣads, the woman is conceived as the sacrificial fire, her lower portion as the sacrificial wood, the genitalia as the flames, the penetration as the carbon and the sexual union as the spark.[130] The *Bṛhadāraṇyaka Upaniṣad* says that the lower portion (*upastha*) of a woman is to be conceived as the sacrificial alter (*vedī*), the pubic hairs (*lomāni*) as the sacrificial grass, the outer-skin (*bahirścarman*) as the floor for pressing the Soma plants (*adhisavana*) and the two labia of the vulva (*muṣkau*) as the in most fire. He who remembers this during copulation gets the reward of the Vājapeya sacrifice.[131]

What is Vājapeya? In its sophisticated form Vājapeya is one of the principal ceremonies of royal inauguration which bestows upon the performer a superior kind of monarchy called *sāmrājya.* But originally it is an agricultural ritual employed as a productive technique to obtain food and drink. The most simple meaning of Vājapeya is *annapeya,* 'food and drink' and in this sense the term is explained in five big chapters of the *Śatapatha Brāhmaṇa.*[132] And it is very interesting to note that in the *Śatapatha Brāhmaṇa* food-production is conspicuously associated with the Female Principle of creation in connection with the chariot race in which the king is supposed to be the winner.

> That chariot, seized by the pole, he turns (from left to right) so as to make it stand inside the Vedī with 'in the winning of wealth, the Great Mother'—Wealth means food: in the winning of food, the Great Mother.[133]

This Great Mother is Aditi. The chariot itself is conceived as Indra's thunderbolt which is seized by the pole and turned from left to right with *mantras* (*Vāj. Saṃ.,* IX.5 ff) addressed to Aditi. Dyāvāpṛthivī is also invoked in this connection:

> May gain of wealth come to me; Wealth means food: he thus says: May gain of food come to me: May these two Heaven and Earth, the all-shaped come to me; for Prajāpati is Heaven and Earth.[134]

VII

In the post-Ṛgvedic literature we come across a different situation. The great gods of the *Ṛgveda* like Indra, Varuṇa, Mitra, Puṣan and others began to sink into oblivion. In the age of the later Saṃhitās and Brāhmaṇas the powerful Vedic gods were subordinated to the ritualistic principle of *yajña* and in the age of the Upaniṣads and Sūtras to the metaphysical principle known as Brahman. Among the Ṛgvedic goddesses, Uṣas went completely out of sight. Aditi was still invoked as the mother of the Ādityas[135] but she had already become a declining figure, being made the wife of Viṣṇu in the *Vājasaneyi Saṃhitā*[136] and still later the wife of the sage Kaśyapa in the Purāṇas. Pṛthivī or Earth Goddess was invoked in a hymn of *Atharvaveda* and her marriage was described in the *Aitareya Brāhmaṇa*[137] but later she was identified with the wife of Viṣṇu in the *Mahābhārata.*[138] It is said that when Mother Earth became burdened with excessive pressure of population, she sank down a hundred *yojanas* and sought the protection of Viṣṇu. Thereupon Viṣṇu took the shape of a boar and lifted her to her own place. Many of her attributes were absorbed by Sītā who as a deity presided over agriculture was mentioned once in the *Ṛgveda*. The name of Pṛthivī was diversified and she came to be known as Bhū, Vaiṣṇavī, Medinī, Mādhavī, Dharaṇī and so forth in later literature. There is nothing to show that Sarasvatī was anything more in the *Ṛgveda* than a river goddess, but we find her identified in the Brāhmaṇa literature with Vāc or speech, mentioned elsewhere in the *Ṛgveda*, and in post-Vedic mythology she had become goddess of eloquence and wisdom, invoked as a muse and regarded as the wife of Brahmā.

In the post-Ṛgvedic literature, just as the earlier nature gods have been replaced by more concrete divinities like Prajāpati etc. endowed with creative faculties, so also we come across a set of new goddesses like Ambikā, Umā, Durgā, Kālī and others who have been able to exert greater influence in the subsequent religious history of India. The names of these goddesses appear to have originally indicated different tribal deities who were afterwards identified with the wife of Śiva Paśupati, the pre-Vedic god who is supposed to have been worshipped by the Harappans. Again, these names have characterised the Supreme Being of the Śāktas. Ambikā is called Rudra's sister in the *Vājasaneyi Saṃhitā*.[139] The same is also said in the *Taittirīya Brāhmaṇa*[140] while in the *Taittirīya Āraṇyaka*.[141] Ambikā is described as the spouse of Rudra. In the Vedas Ambā is used in the sense of mother and there is little difference between Ambā and Ambikā.[142] Durgā is invoked in the *Taittirīya Āraṇyaka* as 'having the colour of fire who is illuminated by the power of austerity, who is Vairocanī, and worshipped for the consequence of action' (*tāmagnivarṇaṃ tapasā jvalantiṃ vairocaniṃ karmaphaleṣu juṣṭām*).[143] Durgā is also called Vairocanī. The word *virocana* means sun or fire. So Vairocanī is the daughter of Sūrya or Agni. In the same *Taittirīya Āraṇyaka*[144] there is a Durgā-Gāyatrī in which the goddess is also known as Kātyāyanī and Kanyākumārī (*kātyāyanāya vidmahe kanyākumārī dhīmati, tanno durgiḥ pracodayāt*). Umā, the daughter of Himavat, is mentioned in the *Kena Upaniṣad* (*sa tasminne-vākāśe striyamājagāma bahuśobhamānāṃ umāṃ haimavatim*).[145] Śaṅkara commenting on this *mantra* says that *haimavati* has two meanings, 'like one appearing as wearing, golden ornaments' and 'one who is the daughter of the Himalaya'. According to Jacobi she was an independent goddess of the Himalayan region who was later identified with the wife of Śiva Paśupati.[146] There is a *mantra* in the *Taittirīya Āraṇyaka*: *ambikāpataye umāpataye paśupataye namo namaḥ.*[147] This indicates that already in the age of the said Āraṇyaka both Umā and Ambikā were identified with each other and regarded as the wife of Śiva Paśupati. The name Umā seems to be of non-Sanskrit origin which was originally associated with Mā (cf. the goddess Ma of Cappadocia) or Amma denoting 'mother'. Amma or Umma was also an epithet of the Chaldean Mother Goddess who was identified with Ishtar.

> The Babylonian word for Mother is Umma or Uma, the Akkadian Ummi, and the Dravidian is Amma. These words can be connected with each other and with Umā, the Mother Goddess.[148]

It is perhaps due to her Upaniṣadic epithet Haimavatī that in later works she has been identified with Pārvatī or Durgā. The names of these goddesses emphasise their relation with inaccessible mountain regions inhabited by tribes known in Indian tradition as Kirātas, Niṣādas, Śabaras, Pulindas, etc. Kālī, Karālī, Bhadrakālī etc. were originally fearful goddesses of the dark-skinned peoples. Bhadrakālī is mentioned along with Śrī in the *Sāṅkhāyana Gṛhyasūtra*[149] in which it is said that while offering oblations to all gods Śrī is to be offered on the head of the bed and Bhadrakālī on the side. The *Muṇḍaka Upaniṣad*[150] refers to Kālī as one of the seven tongues of Agni, others being Karālī, Manojabā, Sulohitā, Sudhumravarṇā, Sphuliṅginī and Viśvaruci.

VIII

To recapitulate. The worship of the Female Principle was originally connected with agricultural communities and was as varied as the degree of culture attained by separated communities of mankind all over the world. It does not, however, mean that the concept of the Female Principle was unknown in more primitive societies subsisting on hunting and food-gathering, because in primitive thought the woman was the symbol of generation and life-giving power which made the Mother Goddess the central figure of religion and ritual. Even in pastoral societies which were basically patriarchal, this primitive legacy of the life-producing mother, her organs and attributes, thought to be endowed with generative power, was maintained, though side by side we come across the emergence of powerful male deities

Archaeological evidence found in the ruins of Harappa and Mohenjodaro suggests that in the pre-Vedic religion of India a great Mother Goddess, the personification of all the reproductive energies of nature, was worshipped, probably under different names but having substantial similarities with her Western Asian counterparts in regard to myths and legends and that associated with her was a secondary Male Principle of creation, both functioning as the precursors of the later Sāṅkhya conceptualizations of Prakṛti and Puruṣa and also of the Tantric cosmogony which connects the mysteries of nature with those of the human body suggesting that the birth of the universe is the result of the same or similar process as the birth of the human beings. The ritualistic aspects of this sexual dualism found expression in the real or imitative union of the human sexes for the sake of thereby ensuring the fruitfulness of the ground and in the increase of men and beasts as we find in the later Saṃhitās and Brāhmaṇas as well as in the *vāmadevya sāman* of the Upaniṣads.

There is no reason to suppose that the Vedic tribes with their initial pastoral economy and patriarchal social system effaced all traces of the pre-Vedic Great Mother and her male consort, because religious or cultic intolerance in the Semitic sense was never a feature of the religious life of India, South-East Asia and China. But there was of course a change in religious outlook and perspective. In all probability the Harappan Male Principle was inducted in the Ṛgvedic pantheon as Rudra who was transformed in post-Ṛgvedic literature into Śiva and later became the Supreme Being of different sects of Śaivism. Although the Vedic tribes created many nature-gods, mostly male deities, in the imagery of pastoral warriors, they also created some female deities representing suitable natural and abstract phenomena. The Harappan Magna Meter was probably reflected in their conception of Aditi, the mother of the gods, thought of to be a goddess of yore, even in the *Ṛgveda* itself. In the age of the later Saṃhitās and Brāhmaṇas the nature-gods of the *Ṛgveda* were overshadowed by more concrete and personalized deities, and owing to greater emphasis on agriculture the pre-Vedic Female Principle was resuscitated, in new forms under the motherly appellation of Ambikā, Umā etc. Goddesses like Durgā, Kālī, etc. also came into existence during this period, and these goddesses absorbed some qualities of Indra, Agni and other Vedic deities.

The pastoral economy of the Vedic tribes when supplemented by agriculture led to the production of surplus which prepared the ground for the rise of urban settlements. Trade was facilitated in which cattle served as the best means of exchange. The new condition did not encourage the destruction of cattle wealth. In the Vedic age cattle had to be killed on numerous occasions. In the case of the Aśvamedha sacrifice alone as many as 600 bulls were killed for the purpose of feeding the assembled guests and visitors. The Vedic attitude towards trade was not helpful. The Buddhist and Jain emphasis on the doctrine of the *ahiṃsā* or non-violence thus assumes a new economic significance in this context. It is perhaps at this stage of development that cow became identified with the Mother Goddess and beef eating became a taboo. This identification was not confined to India alone. In the late Predynastic Egypt her Hathor or cow form was worshipped.[151] The goddess Neith was also conceived as a cow[152] while Isis was simply a cow-goddess.[153] At Al-Ubaid on the Enphrates the cow-goddess later known as Nin-Khursag was the mother of all beings.[154]

References

1. For detail see my *AIHCTP,* 19-26.
2. I.23.15; 117.21; II.14.11; IV.57.1-8; V.33.13; VI.6.4; VIII.20.19; 22.6; 78.10; X.34.13; 48.7; 83.37; 94.13; 101.3-4; 117.7; 146.6.
3. II.11.
4. VI.50.11.
5. VII.32.22; 106.1; IX.22.2; passim.
6. I.154.6; VII.36.1.
7. Winternitz, *HIL,* I.64-65.
8. Briffault, *M,* II.251-52.
9. Farnell, *GB,* 96.
10. Macdonell, *VM,* 124-25.
11. Max Müller, *SR,* 52.
12. *RV,* I.101.3.
13. *RV,* II.156.4.
14. *RV,* II.38.9.
15. *SBE,* XXXII.241.
16. *SPD,* s.v. Aditi.
17. *RV,* X.63.3.
18. *RV,* II.27.1; passim.
19. *RV,* IV.55.3; VIII.27.5.
20. *RV,* I.50.2; II.17.1; III.4.11; VII.47.9; 85.4; VIII.18.3; 25.3; 47.9; 56.11; 90.13; X.36.1-3; 72.8-9; 13.26.
21. *RV,* I.136.1; II.40.6; V.46.6; VII.40.4; VIII.67.12.
22. *RV,* VII.87.7.
23. *RV,* I.94.15; 162.22.

24. *RV*, I.42.2; 113.19; IV.25.3; VII.40.2; VIII.82.10; 18.6; X.36.1.
25. *RV*, IX.26.1; 71.5; 96.15.
26. *RV*, I.89.10.
27. V.5.
28. *RV*, I.153.3; VIII.90.15; X.11.1; *VS*, XIII.43; 49.
29. *AV*, III.8.3; VI.4.1; VII.6.2; VIII.9.21; XI.1.11; XIII.1.38; *VS*, XXI.5.
30. *RV*, X.72.45.
31. *Nirukta*, X.4; XI.23.
32. Macdonell, *VM*, 122.
33. Apte in *VA*, 371.
34. Max Müller in *SBE*, XXXII.256.
35. *RV*, V.62.8.
36. *RV*, IV.2.11.
37. *RV*, VII.15.12.
38. *ZDMG*, VI.71.
39. Muir, *OST*, V.42.
40. *AV*, XV.18.4; XVI.7.6; *VS*, XVIII.22.
41. *AV*, VII.7.1.
42. The 20 hymns in which Uṣas is extolled are *RV*, I.48; 49; 113; 123; 124; III.51; 52; 61; V.79; 80; VI.64; 65; VII.75-81; VIII.172.
43. Muir's trans.
44. *RV*, IV.30.12-15, 20-22.
45. *RV*, I.113.19.
46. *RV*, I.113.2-3; 124.8; X.127.3.
47. *RV*, X.127.
48. II.74-77.
49. Cf. *Matsya*, CLIV; *Skanda*, M/K, XXII; passim.
50. Farnell, *CGS*, III.184.
51. *RV*, 159.2; 160.2; 185.1; passim.
52. *RV*, VII. 97.8.
53. *RV*, X.2.7.
54. *RV*, I.160.2; 185.7; IV.56.3; VI.70.1-2.
55. *RV*, I.159.1; 160.1; VI.56.2; 70.6; X.36.2.
56. *RV*, I.155.3; 159.2; III.3.11; VII.53.2; IX.85.12; X.1.7; 35.3; 64.14; 65.8; 110.9.
57. *RV*, I.159.2; III.3.11; VII.53.2; X.65.8.
58. *RV*, I.155.3; IX.85.12; X.1.7; 35.3; 64.14.
59. *RV*, X.110.9.
60. *RV*, I.89.4; 90.7; 159.2; 160.2; 185.11; IV.1.10; V.42.16; 43.2, 15; VI.51.5; 70.6; 72.2; VIII.92.2; X.53.4; 88.15.
61. *AV*, II.28.4; III.23.6; VI.4.3; 120.2; VIII.7.2; XII.1.10.
62. *VS*, XIX.47.
63. *RV*, I.185.1.
64. *RV*, X.37.7; 81.2-4.
65. *RV*, III.30.5; 32.8; 34.8; 44.3; VI.17.7; 30.5; VIII.6.5; 36.4; X.29.6; 54.3; 55.1.
66. *RV*, II.40.1; VI.72.2; IX.82.7; 98.9; X.121.9; 190.3.
67. *RV*, III. 59.1; IV. 53.2; VI. 70.1; 72.2; VII. 86.1; VIII. 42.1; IX. 87.2; X. 90.14; 110.9; 121.5; 149 1.
68. Macdonell, *VM*, 22.
69. *RV*, X.18.10.
70. *RV*, II.15.2.

71. VII.1.5.
72. I.1.3.5.
73. *RV*, V.84.
74. *AV*, XII.1.
75. *RV*, X.125.
76. V.5.
77. XI.27.
78. *SB*, III.2.4.1-6.
79. *AB*, I.27.
80. On I.11.
81. *SB*, III.5.1.21.
82. *RV*, VII.96.2; VIII.21.18; X.64.9; 75.5.
83. *RV*, II.41.16; V.43.11; VI.61.11-12.
84. *RV*, II.41.17; VII.95.2; VIII.21.17; X.18.42.
85. *RV*, II.30.8; III.54.13; VII.9.5; 39.5; 40.3; X.131.5.
86. *VS*, XIX.94.
87. *VS*, XIX.12.
88. *SB*, III.9.1.7; *AB*, III.1.
89. II.77.
90. *AV*, VII.68.1.
91. *SB*, IV.6.9.17.
92. *SB*, XII.7.1.11-12, 14.
93. *SB*, XI.4.3.16.
94. *RV*, V.57.6; X.71.2.
95. *VS*, XXXII.12.
96. *RV*, VII.16.8; X.70.8.
97. *RV*, III.29.9-10; X.95.18.
98. *RV*, II.31.4; V.41.19; 42.12; X.64.10.
99. *RV*, II.32.7; V.42.12.
100. *RV*, II.32.6-7; X.184.2.
101. *AV*, VIII.46.3.
102. *RV*, I.23.10; VI.66.1-3; *AV*, V.21.11.
103. *RV*, X.17.4
104. *RV*, VII.47; 49; X.9; 30.
105. *RV*, I.23.16-22; X.9.3-11.
106. *RV*, X.91.6; *AV*, I.33.1.
107. Bhandarkar, *VS*, 142; Crooke in *FL*, XXX. 284 ff.; Kosambi in *JBBRAS*, XXVI, 68 ff.; Chattopadhyaya, *L*, 242-46.
108. *RV*, I.147.3; 152.3; 158.6; IV.4.13.
109. *SB*, XIV.5.5.30-33.
110. *RV*, I.62-63.
111. Keith, *RPV*, 258-59; Winternitz, *HIL*, I.184; Macdonell in *ERE*, VIII.312.
112. Hobhouse et al., *MCSISP*, 16.
113. Thomson, *AA*, 21-22.
114. *RV*, X.1.4; 97; 145.
115. *RV*, X.10.4; 11.2.
116. *RV*, X.11.2.
117. X.101.22.
118. *RV*, IV.57; *AV*, III.17.
119. *Rām*, I.66.13-14; VII.110.14-16.

120. Keith, *RPV,* 186.
121. IV.4.29; *SBE,* XXX.113.
122. II.17.10; *SBE,* XXIX.234.
123. *SB,* I.9.2.7; VI.3.1.28; 4.3.7; 6.2.8; passim.
124. *SB,* II.4.4.21; 5.1.11; V.1.3.19; 2.5.8; VI.3.1.30; 3.3.38; VII.5.1.6; passim.
125. *SB,* I.7.2.14; 9.2.7; II.3.1.32; VI.3.3.18; VII.4.2.24; passim.
126. *VS,* XXIII.22-31.
127. For details see my *AIRTSC,* 1-24.
128. II.13.
129. Hume's trans.
130. *Ch U,* V.18.1-12; *Bṛ U,* VI.2.13.
131. *Bṛ U,* VI.4.6-7.
132. *SB,* V.1.1.1-5; 2.1.
133. *SB,* V.1.4.4; Eggeling's trans.
134. *SB,* V.1.4.26.
135. *AV,* VII.2.15; VIII.9.21; IX.1.4; XIII.2.9; *TB,* I.1.9.1; *SB,* III.1.3.3; VI.1.2.8; XI.6.3.8; passim.
136. XIX. 60; cf. *TS,* VII.5.14.
137. *AV,* XII.1; *AB,* IV.27.
138. III.141.
139. *VS,* III.57.
140. *TB,* I.6.10.4-5.
141. *TA,* X.18.1.
142. *RV,* II.41.16; X.86.7; 97.2; *VS,* VI.36; XI.68; *TS,* IV.1.9; VI.4.4.
143. *TA,* X.1.65.
144. *TA,* X.1.7.
145. III.12.
146. *ERE,* II.813.
147. *TA,* X.18.1.
148. Dikshit, *MG,* 59.
149. II.15.14.
150. I.2.4.
151. Hornblower in *JEA,* XV.39.
152. Levy, *GH,* 116.
153. Frazer, *AAO,* 106, 300, 319.
154. Gadd in *UE,* I.142 ff.

The Formative Period
(*c.* 600 BC-AD 300)

The varied religious and ritualistic contents of the Vedic literature and those later systems which claim to have based their doctrines on the Vedas are generally characterised by scholars as Brahmanism or Brahmanical religion which is, however, a misnomer. The popular view that Buddhism or Jainism as well as the later monotheistic creeds like Vaiṣṇavism, Śaivism and others were in constant conflict with the adherents of the orthodox Brahmanical religion is also fallacious. There was no such Brahmanical religion in Indian history, though there was no dearth of Brahmanical authority and influence on most religious systems including Buddhism and Jainism. In fact the renowned Buddhist and Jain teachers and theoreticians were mostly Brāhamṇas and they gave to these systems a new orientation through the process of Sanskritization.

From about the sixth century BC with the increasing detribalisation, growth of organised statehood, sharpening of social divisions, changes in the system of production, manifold development of trade and commerce, introduction of money economy, new systems of distribution and exchange and the growth of urbanism, the earlier forms of religious beliefs and practices began to lose their relevance, and need was felt to make them time-befitting with new ideas and interpretations. Already in the Upaniṣads we come across a new line of thinking, sponsored mostly by the Kṣatriya nobility, which insists on the identity of the individual self with the universal self.

> The Brahman, the power which presents itself to us materialized in all existing things, which creates, sustains, preserves and receives back into itself again all worlds, this eternal, infinite, divine power is identical with the *ātman,* with that which, after stripping off everything external, we discover in ourselves as our realmost essential being, our individual self, the soul.[1]

Apart from the Upaniṣadic thinkers that were others. The Buddhist and Jain accounts mention five philosophers—Pūraṇa Kassapa, Pakudha Kaccāyana, Ajita Keśakambalim, Sañjaya Belaṭṭhiputta and

Gośāla Maṅkhaliputta.[2] Specifically their views are different, but generically they belong to the same category as those of the Buddha and Lord Mahāvīra. It was due to the fact that they belonged to the same age and the same region and they responded and reacted, in their own ways, which were more or less similar, to the same stimuli arising out of the socio-political transformation which was taking place in their time.

Buddhism and Jainism were basically thought complexes which insisted on the concept of suffering and its extinction. This concept of suffering had obviously some material basis. The great transformation in social, economic and political life which took place in India about the sixth century BC was not an unmixed blessing. Both the teachers had to face the dual requirement of their age, and this alone explains why a considerable number of contemporary aristocrats formed their front-rank associates. Both the Buddha and Lord Mahāvīra gave moral support to the interests of the trading class. The Buddha accepted the new social requirements in which debtors and slaves could not run away from their obligations, animals could no longer be killed indiscriminately and private property could not be appropriated. At the same time both the teachers offered to the oppressed peoples a suitable illusion of ancient tribal equality which was already trampled and undermined in reality. Class society, in spite of all its ugliness, was an historical necessity, and what the Buddha could do under such a condition was to boost up some of its progressive features in public life and rescue some of the beneficial aspects of tribal life in a class society.[3]

The Buddha and Lord Mahāvīra did not found any new religion. They set forth a way of life based on ethical principles. Although their teachings later assumed a religious character, their original purpose was different. It should also be noted in this connection that while Lord Mahāvīra set forth certain ethical principles to be followed both by the monks and by laymen, those prescribed by the Buddha were meant exclusively for the monks. He had no concern for ordinary persons. Not only did he successfully build up his Saṅgha on the model of tribal society, but he took great care to see that the members therein—the *bhikṣus* within the Saṅgha, lived a perfectly detached life, i.e. detached from the great historic transformation going on in the society at large.

Buddhism and Jainism belonged to the same intellectual-cultural complex and the religio-philosophical terminology is almost the same in both cases. Though they had some functional difference with the Vedic systems and their sectarian offshoots, which subsequently came to be known as Hinduism, from the viewpoint of religio-philosophical terms and concepts the basic similarity underlying all these systems cannot be overlooked or ignored. This may be sufficiently demonstrated with reference to such concepts as *duḥkha, nirvāṇa, mokṣa, karma,* etc. The logical, epistemological and metaphysical terms and concepts, as also those pertaining to the functional aspects of religious life, originated from one primary source and these were subsequently adapted in all the religio-philosophical systems in India with necessary modification. An in-depth study in religious and philosophical terminology is therefore expected to demonstrate sufficiently that hitherto in the studies on Indian religion the so-called difference in various systems have been over-emphasised by most scholars and their basic unity has been ignored. When Mādhavācārya in his *Sarvadarśanasaṃgraha* dealt with Buddhism and Jainism he considered them merely as different schools of thought belonging to the same category as the Mīmāṃsā or the Sāṅkhya or the Vedānta.

It is wrongly said that Buddhism and Jainism are anti-Vedic systems. The evidence of the Buddhist and Jain texts suggests that both the Buddha and Lord Mahāvīra did not consider Śruti or the Vedas as the only source of valid knowledge. The Buddha did not reject the Vedic gods. Surprisingly enough, all the Ṛgvedic nature-gods have a place of honour in Buddhism. Even the legends pertaining to them occur in Buddhist mythology. Just as in the later Saṃhitās and Brāhmaṇas the Ṛgvedic gods were subordinated to the ritualistic principle called *yajña* and in the Upaniṣads to the idealistic principle called Brahman, so also in the Buddhist texts the Ṛgvedic gods were subordinated to the Buddha.[4]

To stigmatise the Vedic *yajñas* as the cunning devices of the priestly class and the Buddha's disapproval of these as a mark of protest against the degradation of the Vedic religion is fallacious. The Buddha could not have been unaware of the Vedic formulations and their interpretations regarding the efficacy of the *yajña* rituals. Rather he did not fail to observe how *yajña* was elevated into a world-principle, why the whole world was conceived of in terms of *yajña,* why Prajāpati typified *yajña* in his cosmogonic activities and why even the parts of the *yajña* rituals were invested with cosmic significance. The Buddha even used the term *yajña* to denote the principles he stood for. A careful scrutiny of the passages relating to the *yajñas* in the Buddhist texts shows that the Buddha's objection was concerned mainly with the question of animal slaughter involved in certain forms of the ritual. The contents of the *Kuṭadanta Sutta* clearly indicate that the Buddha tried to give a new interpretation to the concept of *yajña,* eliminating on the one hand the aspect of animal slaughter and adding on the other some ethical principles. The Buddha said that there were even better forms of *yajña* which could be performed by making regular gifts to the meritorious persons, by constructing vihāras, by taking refuge to *triśarana,* by adopting the *śikṣāpadas,* by absorbing into four forms of meditation, by acquiring knowledge and by abstaining from worldly desires.[5]

This new interpretation of *yajña* by the Buddha in terms of the ethical doctrine preached by him was also foreshadowed in the Vedic texts.[6] The concept of the Yajñakratus came into existence which was outside the purview of the normal ritual and consisted of recitation in forest of specific *mantras* required for the *yajñas* without corresponding oblations or offerings but with elaborate symbolic identifications of the various elements in the *yajña* with the phenomena of the physical and intellectual worlds. Renewed emphasis was laid upon what the *Bhagavadgītā*[7] aptly calls Svādhyāya, Jñāna and Dhyāna *yajñas* (pertaining to scripture, knowledge and meditation) in the place of Dravyamaya *yajña* (pertaining to material desire). Thus while the earlier *yajñas* seem to have been related somehow with the working of the secret causes underneath the surface of things and of the subtle correspondences that knit together the multiform personal and impersonal, animate and inanimate, small and great potencies of nature, the new-fangled interprpetations of them were conducive to the concepts of penance and asceticism, transmigration, metempsychosis and search for liberation. The Buddhist concepts of *nāma* and *rūpa* might also have been adopted from the same concepts found in the later Saṃhitās and Brāhmaṇas meant for qualifying the earlier Vedic gods relegated to the position of associated deities in connection with the *yajñas.*[8]

In the beginning of this chapter we have said that under the new socio-economic and political set up the Buddha and his contemporaries tried to 'modernise' the Vedic system in terms of some broad-based ethical principles so that the peoples, even by adhering to their traditional cults and rituals, could transgress the limits of tribal narrowness and come under a bigger fold of socio-ethical relationship. Other thinkers, who openly asserted their commitment to the Vedas, also did the same—a point which is generally missed by the historians. For example, Manu, who is almost universally regarded as 'the champion of Brahmanical orthodoxy' also thought in the same line as was done by the Buddha and Lord Mahāvīra. In fact the entire spirit of the *Manusmṛti* conforms so profoundly with the various aspects of the Vedic tradition that Śaṅkara or Kumārila did not hesitate to regard it as authoritative as the Vedas. Though Manu has condemned Buddhism and Jainism, his own interpretation of the Vedas is in striking agreement with that of the Buddha and Lord Mahāvīra. According to Manu, there are four means of defining the sacred law. They are Śruti or the Vedic texts. Smṛti or the legal treatises, Sadācāra or virtuous conduct and Ātmanastuṣṭi or self-satisfaction. The third and fourth sources basically insist on a person's individual sense of morality and judgement rather than an absolute dependence on codified and customary laws.[9] What could have been the cause of including these two categories within the purview of Vedic knowledge? Was it a fact that Manu wanted to reinterpret Vedas in the line of some new-fangled principles which were influencing the life and morals of the people belonging to his age?

That Manu tried to give a new orientation to the Vedas in accordance with the changing demands of time is attested by the fact that he was not very much interested in Vedic rituals.[10] He had a greater preference to the realization of the concepts of identity of *Brahman* and *ātman* as enumerated in the Upaniṣads as the *summum bonum* of the Vedic knowledge.[11] Though he had referred to a few *yajñas*, he was less inclined to their efficacy as is significantly proved in his following observation.

> The four Pākayajñas and those sacrifices which are enjoined by the rules of the Veda are altogether not equal in value to a sixteenth part of the sacrifice consisting of muttered prayers.[12]

Manu's *ahiṃsā satyamasteyaṃ śaucamindriyanigraha*[13] is frankly a restatement of the teaching of Lord Mahāvīra. In regard to the doctrine of *ahiṃsā* Manu is no less vociferous than the exponents of Buddhism and Jainism. In his own words:

> He who injures innoxious beings from a wish to (give) himself pleasure, never finds happiness, neither living nor dead. He who does not seek to cause the sufferings of bonds and death to living

creatures (but) desires the good of all (beings) obtains endless bliss. He who does not injure any (creature) attains without an effort what he thinks of, what he undertakes, and what he fixes his mind on. Meat can never be obtained without injury to living creatures, and injury to sentient beings is detrimental to (the attainment of) heavenly bliss; let him therefore shun (the use of) meat. Having well considered the disgusting origin of flesh and the (cruelty of) fettering and slaying corporeal beings, let him entirely abstain from eating flesh.

Abstention from injuring (creatures) veracity, abstention from unlawfully appropriating (the goods of others), purity, and control of organs, Manu has declared to be the summary of the law for the four castes.[14]

So the post-Vedic thought-ferment—whether of the so-called non-Brahmanical heterodoxy or of the so-called Brahmanical orthodoxy—yielded the same or similar ethical principles of universal application which formed the substrata of the functional aspects of all the subsequent sects and cults. There were also other forms of commonness in regard to the intellectual and emotional viewpoints. The Buddha and Lord Mahāvīra, as well as most of their contemporaries, did not believe in the existence of any creator God. Apart from the Nyāya-Vaiśeṣikas, other schools of Indian thought, such as the Mīmāṃsakas, the Sāṅkhyas and the Cārvākas, did not also subscribe to the theory of the existence of any creator God. Almost the same was the approach of the Śaṅkarite school of Advaita Vedānta which was to a great extent theoretically based upon the Śūnyavāda and Vijñānavāda schools of Buddhism. The main line of their argument is that if God be taken as a free agent he cannot have the desire to create and if taken as an agent under bondage he cannot have the capacity to create. Every real entity is a cause and also an effect, but the first cause as an effect has no cause and as such it is no effect. The changing and impermanent world cannot be the effect of an eternal and changeless cause. According to the Sāṅkhyas and the Mīmāṃsakas, as well as to the Buddhists and Jains, perception, inference and scripture do not prove God. God cannot act as the supervisor of *dharma* and *adharma*, since he cannot have any knowledge of them. The universe having neither beginning nor end does not require any creator.

So far as the emotional aspects are concerned there is also an unity among various sects which flourished in the post-Vedic period. And the point of unity is the doctrine of *bhakti*. It was based on Lokāyata or popular sentiments in which the idea of an all-powerful Supreme Being capable of bestowing grace on the devotees is found. Instead of raising questions concerning the origin, inner nature and purpose of the universe, or creating a framework of concepts and relations in satisfactions of some emotional or intellectual drive, the concept of an all powerful personal God controlling everything of the world was put forward. The association and identification of the human faculties with those of nature, often seeking the source of unity behind all diversities was also a contributory factor to this concept. The earliest expressions of such a concept is found in the *Bhagavadgītā* which says that complete devotion and absolute surrender to the will of God is the only goal of life. Needless to say that such an idea became popular among the masses as a result of which numerous cults insisting on the absolute devotion to the personal God bestowing grace and ignoring human frailties and blemishes came into existence which eventually culminated into more popular cults of Viṣṇu, Śiva, Śakti, etc. Behind such a conception popular sentiment seeking consolation in the wonder-working power of the superhuman entity was a driving force. The influence of local and tribal deities, either identified with the Supreme Being or regarded as its incarnation or regional form, was also by no means insignificant.

The concept of absolutism in politics and society might have some bearing on the development of monotheistic and devotional ideas in the sphere of religion. In the *Bhagavadgītā* the Lord says to Arjuna that he is the king among men which finds parallel in the Buddhist *Suttanipāta*.[15] The Buddha has also been described as Cakravartin in the image of the universal monarch. Manu says that "even an infant king must not be ignored and considered as a mere mortal, because he is a great deity in human form."[16]

But it appears more likely that belief in one personal all powerful God capable to bestow grace (*prasāda*) is a feature of human psychology. This *bhakti* element also influenced Buddhism and Jainism. The followers of Buddhism and Jainism felt it necessary to give their system a *bhakti* oriented theistic turn. The founders of these systems were elevated to the level of the Supreme Being and became objects of extensive cults in images and symbols.

II

It is against this background that we are to evaluate the historical role of the Female Principle in the aforesaid religious systems and also in post-Vedic Indian life. Unfortunately literary evidence helps us very little in this matter. We do not know what were the original tribal religions of the dynasties that ruled over the Magadhan empire and other adjoining kingdoms. Both Buddhism and Jainism claimed Bimbisāra and Ajātaśatru, the Haryaṅka kings of Magadha, as their followers. The same probably held good in the case of other kings. It is possible that the kings and the nobles in their personal life followed their own domestic or dynastic or tribal religion and at the same time they patronised the newly preached ideas according to their individual choice. This was the cause of the survival of the old religious beliefs and practices and also of their making room into the new religious systems. Religion in the modern sense of the term did not bother the ancients, and just as a modern Santal after embracing Christianity does not hesitate to worship their traditional Bonga, so also the ancients did not give up their traditional cults and rituals despite their attraction to new religious or ethical ideas. Moreover, a man's inclination to a particular system did not mean that all the members of his family, his sons and successors, should follow the same line. The Mauryan king, Candragupta patronised Jainism; his grandson Aśoka patronised Buddhism and his grandson Daśaratha patronised Ājīvikism. At the same time it was also the custom of the ancient kings to pay homage to the gods and rituals of the lands they would conquer. This was a very effective means of earning goodwill of the conquered peoples.

The Vedic religion did not perish due to the advent of Buddhism and Jainism. Men still followed the old rituals prescribed by the Sūtras. Goddesses of the later Vedas—Ambikā, Durgā, Kātyāyanī, Śrī, Bhadrakālī, etc., whose cults became very popular in subsequent ages and many of whom later made their way into the Buddhist and Jain systems—must have been widely worshipped. The popular influence of the Female Principle had already been reflected in the cult of Prajāpati-Brahmā. In fact, from the later Vedic age down to the age of the Mauryas and Śuṅgas, the cult of the Female Principle had a steady growth. It appears that the original tribal religion of the Maurya kings was that of the Mother Goddess. This we suggest on the basis of Lama Tāranātha's account of King Ásoka, according to which the king was not only the worshipper of Umādevī the Mother Goddess, but also he actually encouraged the sexual rites connected with her cult, and thus came to be known as Kāmāśoka.[17] Tāranātha, while writing his history of Buddhism must have depended on some authentic tradition, although, unfortunately, all of his source-books have not yet been traced.

All that we have said in the preceding paragraphs regarding the cult of the Female Principle is based upon negative evidence. But some positive evidence is not altogether lacking. A small gold tablet representing a naked woman standing on her legs in symmetrical rigidity, with exaggerated hips and sexual organs, heavy and clumsy ornaments and in a rigidly angular composition, was dug out of a tomb near Lauriya.[18] It was identified by Bloch as the iconic representation of the Earth Goddess and was ascribed by him to about the 8th or 7th century BC. According to Rowland, some of the terracotta figurines of the Mother Goddess of pre-Maurya date are closely related stylistically and iconographically to the gold plaque from Lauriya, having the same flatness and frontality and the same emphatic display of the attributes of fecundity—the heavy breasts and the enormously exaggerated sexual organ—characteristic of the earlier representations of the Mother Goddess found all over the ancient Near East.[19] A small gold tablet similar to that found at Lauriya and a small gold figure, forming part of the relics from the ruins of the Piprahwa stūpa and belonging to a period not earlier than that of the Mauryas, and also some of the oldest terracotta pieces recovered by Marshall from the ruins of Bhita prove the continuity of the cult of the Female Principle.[20]

III

The political condition of Northern India till the fifth and fourth centuries BC was not that of an empire of any considerable extent, but it was that of separate and small independent states and kingdoms under a king or tribal chief. It was only towards the third quarter of the 4th century BC that the ideal of an empire was partially achieved by the Nandas. Then under the Mauryas Magadha became the mistress of extensive dominions stretching from beyond the Hindu Kush on the west to Bengal on the east, and from Kashmir on the north to Karnataka on the south. The concept of absolutism in politics and society, as we have stressed elsewhere in this chapter, had a close bearing on the development of monotheistic ideas in the sphere of religion. From about the end of the third century BC Vaiṣṇavism began to flourish as a distinct creed. The *Mahābhārata* upholds the idea of the political unification of India under a Cakravartin, the human prototype of the divine Viṣṇu, mastering over the universe. As we have stated above, the *Bhagavadgītā*, a part of the *Mahābhārata*, composed about the second century BC, equates the king with god and demands total submission of the individual to the divine will. In this respect the *Gītā* supplements the *Arthaśāstra* which stands for the interest of newly developed values supposed to integrate the monopoly of state power. Even to a stark atheistic system like Buddhism, a monotheism in the form of the Buddha as the Supreme Being and controller of the universe was prefixed, and this form of Buddhism, we know from history, served a very useful purpose in China in consolidating the state power. Śaivism as a distinct monotheistic religion flourished from about the beginning of the Christian era.

Soon after the Buddha's death about 486 BC, his scattered sayings relating to Dhamma and Vinaya were put together in the First Council, and about a century thereafter, in the Second Council held at Vaiśālī, the Buddhist church was divided into two groups—the Sthaviras and the Mahāsaṅghikas. The former became gradually divided into eleven sects and the later into seven. All the eighteen sects were fundamentally Hīnayānists, keeping the system confined exclusively among the monks. The common people were, however, allowed to take the *triśaraṇa*, observe a few moral precepts and offer gifts to the Saṅgha, but there was no provision for organised worship and ritual. But a few sub-sects of the Mahāsaṅghika group already introduced new doctrines paving the way for Mahāyānism which probably originated in its full form about the first century in the Andhra country. It became a recognised form of Buddhism at the time of Kaṇiṣka and then it spread all over northern India in the first and second century AD. From this time Mahāyāna Buddhism came under the grip of the existing cults of the Female Principle. The cult of the Female Principle also influenced the Jain religion in the same way about the beginning of the Christian era. Although the Bhāgavata sect, worshipping Vāsudeva, was known to Pāṇini and Megasthenes, it was not so prominent before the third century BC. The identification of Vāsudeva with Viṣṇu is not recognised even in the earlier parts of the *Mahābhārata*. Although the inscriptions from Besnagar (second century BC), Ghosundi and Nanaghat speak of a steady growth of Vaiṣṇavism, iconographic representation of the god Viṣṇu Vāsudeva cannot be traced much earlier than the beginning of the Christian era. The association of Viṣṇu and Vaiṣṇavite deities with goddesses took place about the same period.

So we find that from about the beginning of the Christian era the popular cults of the Female Principle were gradually becoming the driving force even in Buddhism, Jainism and Vaiṣṇavism. We exclude Śaivism, because it had always been a popular religion, and so it had the greatest potentiality of absorbing the Mother Goddess elements, which we shall see later. The lists of the existing religious sects and cults, as found in the *Aṅguttara Nikāya* (fourth-third centuries BC) and in the *Mahāniddesa* and *Cullaniddesa* (second-first centuries BC), demonstrate the existence, side by side with well known sects, of a bewildering variety of primitive faiths and cults—Ājīvika, Nirgrantha, Jaṭilaka, Parivrājaka, Aviruddhaka, Muṇḍa-Śrāvaka, Māgandika, Traidaṇḍika, Gautamaka and Devadharmika, along with the worshippers of the elephant, horse, cow, dog, crow, Vāsudeva, Baladeva, Pūrṇabhadra, Maṇibhadra, the Yakṣas, the Nāgas, the Asuras, the Gandharvas, the Mahārājas, Agni, Candra, Sūrya, Indra, Brahman, Deva and Dik.

One of the interesting features of the aforesaid list is the cult of the Yakṣas. The Yakṣas and Yakṣiṇīs were malevolent deities of primitive tribal conception and were worshipped in every village. Later they held a very important place in Buddhist, Jain and Purāṇic myths, legends and religions. The Yakṣas and Yakṣiṇīs were conceived as having a physical form of large proportions and huge bulk, and since they owed their existence to tribal primitive imagination, they had a heavy earthly character of form, as is found in their sculptural representations assigned to the first century BC. A study of the extent Yakṣa and Yakṣiṇī images shows that the later images of the gods and goddesses were shaped after them. Of the earliest Yakṣiṇī sculptures influencing the iconographic conceptions of the Female Principle of contemporary and later religious systems mention must be made of the Alakanandā and Sudarśanā Yakṣiṇīs of Bharhut and also their Buddhistic partners Sirimā Devatā, Mahākokā Devatā and Culakokā Devatā belonging to the first century BC. To the same period (*c.* 50 BC) is assigned the Besnagar Yakṣiṇī, the modelling, the linear rhythm and the feeling for human form which are far in advance of Bharhut. J.N. Banerjee was inclined to identify this image with the goddess Śrī. The Didarganj Yakṣiṇī which is the best of the series from the artistic point of view is not very much earlier than the first century AD.

IV

The period about the beginning of the Christian era may thus be regarded as a turning point of Indian religious history. Buddhism and Jainism and also Vaiṣṇavism incorporated a large portion of the tribal cults all of which were cleverly woven in the texture of intellectual and rational scheme of their doctrines. As a result, the old religious cults made their appearance in new and sophisticated garments. In view of this changed set up the cult of the Female Principle had also acquired a new significance. Now let us see what the available data suggest in this respect.

The facts we have obtained from the *Aṅguttara Nikāya* and the *Niddesa* commentary may be supplemented by those found in the *Mahābhārata* (between 400 BC and AD 400) and the *Rāmāyaṇa* (between 200 BC and AD 200). In both the epics we notice Vaiṣṇavism and Śaivism becoming more prominent and widespread than other cults and dividing between them the allegiance of great masses of men. But the association of the Female Principle with Viṣṇu is less prominent in the *Mahābhārata* than that with Śiva. The only goddess who is brought in connection with Viṣṇu is Pṛthivī or Mother Earth. In the 'Durgāstotras' (hymns addressed to the goddess),[21] although the goddess is described as the younger sister of Kṛṣna, 'eldest-born in the family of the cowherd Nanda', 'born in the womb of Yaśodā', 'the favourite of Nārāyaṇa', 'the consort of Nārāyaṇa', etc., her Vaiṣṇavite association does not prove strong. On the other hand, it is in Śaivism that the ideas centering round Śakti or Female Principle have found a soil most favourable for their expansion. The history of Śaivism in many of its stages is not different from that of Śāktism, as we shall see later from the evidence furnished by the *Mahābhārata.*

It should, however, be stated in this connection that both Durgāstotras seem to be later interpolations. The critical edition of the *Mahābhārata* does not contain these two hymns in the body of the text. Raghu Vīra, the editior of the critical edition of the Virāṭaparvan, says that the hymn addressed to the goddess by Yudhiṣṭhira does not occur in most manuscripts. The hymn of the Bhīṣmaparvan, addressed to the goddess by Arjuna, however, occurs in the manuscripts from Bengal, Tanjore, Baroda and Poona. In Nīlakaṇṭha's commentary both the hymns find place. Though these hymns do not belong to the genuine portion of the great epic, they are not very late interpolations. As a commentator Nīlakaṇṭha was very critical and he consulted various manuscripts as is attested by his words. So, despite their later inclusion in the great epic the Durgāstotras belong to a fairly early period.

In some early coins, sculptures and relief carvings we have representations of Gajalakṣmī, the goddess of wealth being anointed with water by two elephants standing on her either side. Four such representations are met with in Bharhut. Lakṣmī in the sense of plenty occurs in the *Ṛgveda*, while in the *Vājasaneyi Saṃhitā* Lakṣmī and Śrī are described as co-wives of some god, and this tradition of their identity and difference continued down the ages. The cult of this goddess of wealth was taken up by the Buddhists, because it supplied a suitable means of worship to the trading class laity. Accordingly, the goddess was conceived in Buddhist mythology as the daughter of Śakra. The Sirimā Devatā of Bharhut recalls Siridevī or Lakkhī mentioned in the Jātakas. With the growth of her popularity, Lakṣmī became Nagara-lakṣmī, the protectress of cities, and then Rājalaksmī, fortune of the king. Popular stories about her departure from the city or kingdom were also invented. In literature reference is made to the city-goddesses. The 'city-goddess and Indian bull' was the type of the Puṣkalāvatī coins. It appears that the cult of Śrī and Lakṣmī was popularised before the beginning of the Christian era and that she was not originally linked with Viṣṇu. Besides the Gajalakṣmī type, the goddess seated or standing on a lotus or standing with a lotus in hand, in some cases surrounded by flowering stems, are found inscribed on coins belonging roughly between the second century BC and the second century AD.

The figures of a goddess with two elephants on either side anointing her appears on the coins from Kauśāmbī (first century BC), Ayodhyā and Ujjayinī (first century BC to first century AD).[22] Coins of Vāyudeva and Viśākhadeva (all of Ayodhyā) show the goddess standing while on those of Śivadatta she is shown seated. Such was the popularity of this device that many alien rulers of Northern India like Azilises (AD 28-40), Rañjuvula and Śoṇḍāsa (AD 15) adopted it on their coins.[23] Coins of Maues (20 BC-AD 22), Azes I (5 BC-AD 30) and Azes II show a female figure standing between trees. Marshall, following Whitehead[24] says that the coins of Maues and Azes I depict Bachante among Vines (Maenad according to Gardner)[25] while those of Azes II represent Demeter with Cornucopia.[26] Coomaraswamy thinks that the said figures represent a Hellenised version of the Padmavāsinī or Kamalālaya type of Lakṣmī.[27] The same deity again, without the attendant elephants, either seated on a full-blossomed lotus or standing with a lotus in her hand, very often appears on the Mathura coins like those of Gomitra, Dṛdhamitra, Sūryamitra, Viṣṇumitra, Puruṣadatta, Kāmadatta, Uttamadatta, Balabhūti, Rāmadatta and Śivadatta. She also appears on the coins of the Śaka Satrapas, of the Rājanya Janapada, and of the Pañcāla kings. The Kuninda coins illustrate a stag on the right of the goddess.[28] These coins can collectively be dated from the second century BC to the first century AD, and some of the figures found therein may even stand for Durgā.[29] The lotus on which a few of these goddesses are made to stand is not the characteristic of Lakṣmī alone. It is probable that the goddess who appears in the coins of Azes is Pārvatī or Durgā. References should also be made in this connection to several unidentified goddesses of Hellenic character appearing on the copper and silver coins of Maues and Azes. The Babylonian Mother Goddess Inanna, worshipped in Syria as Nanaia or Nana in Chaldea Nane and in parts of India as Nani, Naini, etc. occurs in the coins of the Kuṣāṇa king Kaṇiṣka (close of the first century AD).[30] On some of the coins of Huviṣka Śiva (Oeso or Bhaveśa) is depicted in company with this goddess described as Nana. Another goddess, Uma (Ommo), appears on the coins of the same king with Śiva, holding a cornucopia, instead of a lotus, like Demeter, Tyche and Ardokhso. Coins of the Kuṣāṇa king Vāsudeva represent a throned goddess, whose right hand holds a fillet and left a cornucopia, bearing the Greek legend Ardokhso.[31]

V

Numismatic evidence thus shows the great popularity of the goddess-cult before and after the beginning of the Christian era, and what is derived from the coins may be substantiated by literary and sculptural evidence. A large number of stone discs, belonging to the period between second century BC and first century AD, found from Taxila, Kosam, Patna and other historical sites, depict nude figures of the goddess of fertility.[32] To the same period of time have been assigned a few terracotta figurines collected from such widely separated sites as Sārnāth, Basarh, Bulandibagh, Kumrahar and other places round about the old sites of Pāṭaliputra, Bhita, Nagari, Samkisa, Kosam and Taxila. They represent females with heavy and exaggerated hips, round and prominent breasts and clearly marked navel and abdomen and seem to be associated with the primitive conception of the Mother Goddess.[33] A few specimens from Bhita, and Kasia belonging to the first century AD, display the Mother Goddess.[34] Two figurines from Mathura[35] (now in the Boston Museum and in the Bombay PW Museum respectively) representing the Mother Goddess have been assigned by Kramrisch to the Mauryan period, but they really belong to a somewhat later date.

Numerous votive plaques with figures of deities found from the Bhir mound, Taxila, form a class of antiquities of the second century BC. In one very frequent type the goddess is shown with full-flowing skirts, in another she is depicted as holding a bird in her hand while in a third she carries a child.[36] A small female statuette, nude save for a shawl, which falls over the left arm and below the hips in front, assigned to the first century BC, comes from Sirkap. The figure appears to be derived from the Greek Aphrodite type, but much Indianised, probably representing the goddess holding lotus in her hand as portrayed in some coins mentioned above.[37]

A Gajalakṣmī representation occurs in the doorway of Ananta-gumpha, an Orissan cave which belongs to a period not earlier than the first century BC.[38] Such figures, described by some as the nativity of the Buddha, or Gajalakṣmī in the Brahmanical specimens, or Śrī Devī or Padma Śrī of the Jains, a frequent numismatic device at the same time, are found in abundance in different historical sites. An interesting specimen Basarh, belonging to the first century BC, shows a winged goddess flanked on two sides by lotus stalks. The same site also yields a similar fragmentary specimen.[39] The winged goddess is again found in a bronze specimen from Dheri Akhun, in a stone relief from Mathura, and in a stūpa-bracket at Sirkap, all belonging to the first century AD. Images of Hāritī, the Buddhist goddess conceived as the protectress of children, belonging to the first century of the Christian era and later date have been found in abundance.[40] The earliest representation of Mahiṣamardinī is said to be offered by certain terracotta plaques discovered at Nagar near Uniyara in Tonk district, which are now preserved in the Amber Museum. One of these has been assigned to the first century BC or first century AD. Sambhar has also yielded a terracotta plaque of white clay of Mahiṣamardinī believed to be of first century AD. The head of the plaque is broken. Excavations at Rairh in Rajasthan have yielded a very large number nude and semi-nude Mother Goddesses not earlier than the first century AD. Excavations at Kankali Tila, Mathura, have revealed some Jain Specimens which offer an interesting study along the Buddhist and Brahmanical finds from other sites of the same place. Referring to an interesting headless statue of the goddess Sarasvatī discovered from the excavations of the Jain stūpa, Smith observes:

> The goddess is shown sitting squatted with her knees upon a rectangular pedestal, holding a manuscript in her left hand. The right hand which was raised has been lost. The figure is clothed in very stiffly executed drapery, a small attendant with hair dressed in rolls stands on each side. The attendant on the left wears a tunic and holds a jar—the attendant on the right has hands clasped in adoration.[41]

The pedestal bears an inscription relating to the dedication of the image in 54th year of Kaṇiṣka. The sculpture thus can be dated in the first half of the second century AD.

VI

What we get from coins and sculptures is corroborated by literary evidence. Here we shall depend mainly upon the *Mahābhārata* which is said to have been composed between *c.* 400 BC and AD 400. It appears that sectarian religious ideas began to find their way into the Great Epic some time before the beginning of the Christian era.

The tribal basis of the Mother Goddess cult, her association with the hunting peoples, evidently survived in the days of the *Mahābhārata,* as it does survive even today. The Great Epic thus refers to the goddess residing in the Vindhyas (*vindhye caiva nagaśreṣṭhe tava sthānaṃ hi śāśvatam*),[42] the goddess who is fond of wine and meat (*sīdhumāṃsapaśupriyā*) and worshipped by the hunting peoples. In the Kirātārjuna episode,[43] Umā, the divine consort of Śiva, is described as a Kirāta woman. In early Indian literature, the term Kirāta denotes a Himalayan people, but in a wider sense it seems to denote the hunting tribes in general.

The Dakṣa-*yajña* story as enumerated in the *Mahābhārata* indicates that the orthodox followers of the Vedic religion did not count Śiva and Devī in their pantheon. According to the *Mahābhārata,* Dakṣa arranged for a horse-sacrifice at Hardwar which was attended by all the gods. The sage Dadhīci happened to notice that Maheśvara (Rudra Śiva's, the consort of Pārvatī, was not present in the assembly and when he asked Dakṣa the reason of Śiva absence, the latter replied that there were eleven Rudras with matted hair and holding spear, and he did not know who was Maheśvara among them. This insult made Pārvatī angry, and in order to please her Śiva created Vīrabhadra. Mahākālī, also called Bhadrakālī, born of Devī's wrath, followed Vīrabhadra to the place of Dakṣa's sacrifice, and they destroyed the sacrificial materials.[44] The destruction of this sacrifice brought Dakṣa to his senses, and he was advised by Vīrabhadra to propitiate Śiva. Dakṣa prayed to Śiva, and having moved by his fervent appeal Śiva appeared on the spot and consoled Dakṣa delivering a brief lecture on his own religious views.

> It should be noticed, that the Śiva whom Dakṣa ignored in his sacrifice was not the Vedic Rudra but the Śiva worshipped by the Pāśupatas. This legend of Dakṣa's sacrifice indicates that the Pāśupata conception of Rudra of Śiva arose outside the pale of Vedism and the orthodox followers of the Veda could not persuade themselves to acknowledge them readily. No share of sacrificial food is claimed on behalf of Śiva's consort, Durgā.[45]

H.C. Raychaudhuri[46] thinks that the Epic Śiva finds a closer parallel in the deity called Teshup worshipped by the Hittites in Western Asia. Teshup was the spouse of the Great Mother Goddess venerated as Ma in Cappadocia.[47] The word Umā is intimately associated with Ma or Amma, as we have seen above, and her connection with Śiva recalls that of Ma with Teshup. The consort of Teshup stands on a lioness or a panther like the Cretan Rhea or the Phrygian Cybele or the Syrian Atargatis. The consort of Śiva is also *siṃhavāhinī,* having the lion for her vehicle.

> The Father God at Boghaz-Keui, meeting the Mother Goddess on her lioness, is attended by an animal which according to the usual interpretation is a bull, and that the bull itself was worshipped, apparently as an emblem of fertility, at Euyuk near Boghaz-Keui; that at Tarsus and Boghaz-Keui, as at Hierapolis-Bambyce, the Father God and the Mother Goddess would seem to have had as their sacred animals or emblems the bull and the lion respectively.[48]

In the Svayamvaraparvādhyāya of the *Mahābhārata* Draupadī is compared with Umā.[49] Along with her consort she is again mentioned in the Sabhāparvan as a member of the court of Kuvera,[50] and twice in the Kirātaparvādhyāya.[51] Arjuna having returned from pilgrimage informed his brothers of his meeting with Śiva and Umā.[52] She is mentioned in relation to Skanda's birth[53] and Jayadratha's Śiva worship and also as the presiding deity of the northern quarters. In Arjuna's Durgāstotra,[54] Umā occurs as a Mother Goddess and elsewhere she is mentioned along with Aditi, Hri, Śrī, Svāhā, Sarasvatī and others. In the Dakṣa-*yajña* episode and also in a section entitled Śiva-Umā Saṃvāda, Umā is frequently mentioned.[55]

Ambikā and Rudrāṇī or Rudrapatnī of the later Vedic texts occur in the *Mahābhārata*. The hill association of the goddess is indicated by such names as Śailaputrī, Śailarājasutā, Girisutā, Girirājatanayā, Parvatarājakanyā, Mandaravāsinī, etc. Gaurī, Kālī, Mahākālī, Bhīmā, Mahābhīmā, etc. are also referred to in the *Mahābhārata*. It is, however, in the Durgāstotras of the Great Epic that the Devī is first revealed in her true character. The said hymns (IV.6; VI.23), although belong to a later period, are significant because they reveal the process through which numerous local goddesses combined into one in terms of an all-powerful Female Principle.

Elsewhere we have seen that in the *Mahābhārata* it is for the first time that Mother Earth is brought in relation to Viṣṇu. It is said that when she became burdened with excessive pressure of population, she sank down for a hundred *yojanas* and sought the protection of Viṣṇu who in his turn took the shape of a one-toothed boar and lifted her above. A rudimentary form of this legend is found in the Ādiparvan in which the over-burdened Earth goes to Brahman and seeks his protection.[56] In the *Mahābhārata*[57] we come across the city goddess of Magadha, called Rākṣasī Jarā, who was also the protectress of children. Her legend, as found in the Great Epic, has a significant bearing on the evolution of the cult of the goddess Ṣaṣṭhī and that of the Buddhist Hāritī. The city goddesses of the Semitic world was also protectress of children. A number of protectress Mothers were also associated with the birth of Skanda. They were known as Kākī, Halimā, Mālinī, Vṛnhilā, Āryā, Palālā and Vaimitrā. Evidently these were local goddesses. Skanda's wife Devasenā was also known by such names as Ṣaṣṭhī, Lakṣmī, Āśā, Sukhapradā, Sinīvālī, Kuhū, Satvṛtti and Aparājitā which proves that she absorbed a good number of Vedic goddesses.[58]

A more concrete idea of the popularity of goddess cult in the first three centuries of the Christian era may be formed from the evidence furnished by the Tīrtha-yātrā section of the Vanaparvan of the *Mahābhārata*,[59] which refers at least to three holy places associated with the *yoni* (sexual organ) and *stana* (breast) of the Devī. These are the Yonikuṇḍas at the Bhīmāsthāna near the Pañcanada (Punjab) and on the hill called Udyatparvata, and the Stanakuṇḍa on the peak known as Gaurīśikhara. The name of the Gaurīśikhara (literally the peak of Gaurī, the Mother Goddess) probably connects the peak with the Himalaya. The Stanakuṇḍa may be brought in relation to Jalandhar which later became a *mahāpīṭha* were the breast of Satī fell. The Bhīmāsthāna, literally, the resort of Bhīmā, a form of the Mother Goddess, was situated on the Karamar not far from Shahbazgarhi in the Peshawar district.

> It should be pointed out that hills or mountain peaks roughly resembling a human phallus were regarded in ancient times as the *svayambhū* (natural) *liṅga* of Śiva. There is reason to believe that the tanks or pools of a particular shape were often conceived as the *yoni* of the Mother Goddess. A pair of hills or peaks of the shape and position of female breast appear sometimes to have been likewise regarded as the *stana* of the goddess.[60]

The Tīrtha-yātrā section also speaks of other holy places—Mātṛ-tīrthas or Devī-tīrthas—connected with the goddess cult. Of these, Puṣkara and Kurukṣetra were associated with the goddess Sāvitrī or Gāyatrī, and Śākambharī-tīrtha with the great goddess Śākambharī of the Purāṇas, mentioned in the *Mahābhārata* also as Suvratādevī. Other holy places like Kālikā-saṅgama, Lalitā, Campā, Dhūmāvatī, etc. seem to be associated with the cult of the Female Principle.

VII

The *Rāmāyaṇa* was composed between the second century BC and the second century AD. It appears that Sītā, the heroine of the epic, was originally an earth goddess. In the ancient hymns of the Vedas, as we have seen above, Sītā is simply the furrow which bears crops for men.[61] In the *Arthaśāstra* of Kauṭilya[62] the goddess Sītā is conceived as residing in seeds and plants. Referring to the vegetative aspects of the Devī, the *Harivaṃśa*[63] says that she is Sītā to the ploughmen.

The present form of the *Rāmāyaṇa*, especially its seventh book, was composed under Vaiṣṇavite influence. The Female Principle is generally worshipped by the Vaiṣṇavas as the consort of Viṣṇu in the form of Lakṣmī or Śrī. There are many passages identifying Rāma with Viṣṇu, and in one such passage,[64] Sītā, Pṛthivī and Śrī are described as the wives of Rāma. Śrī, the goddess occurring frequently,[65] is sometimes mentioned with Hrī, Kīrti, Lakṣmī, Bhūti and others,[66] goddesses associated with Durgā in the *Mahābhārata* and the *Harivaṃśa*. Sometimes Śrī and Lakṣmī are differentiated.[67] Bhū or Mother Earth, identified with Vaiṣṇavī in the *Mahābhārata* and traditionally regarded as the second wife of Viṣṇu, also occurs in the *Rāmāyaṇa*[68] variously designated as Medinī, Mādhavī, Dharaṇī etc. The rivers Sarasvatī and Ganges are deified.[69]

The *Rāmayaṇa* also betrays some Śaivite passage in which we have references to Umā, sometimes called Pārvatī, mentioned as the younger sister of Gaṅgā, born of Menā by Himalaya.[70] She lengthened the life of Sukeśa, the deserted offspring of the demon Vidyutkeśa and granted a boon to the demons (Rākṣasas) that their children would get the age of their mothers immediately after their birth.[71] The legend shows that Umā had a soft corner for the non-Vedic peoples, her original worshippers. Even Rāvaṇa was not deprived of Śiva's grace.[72] More beautiful than Śrī,[73] Umā was not in good terms with other gods.[74] Once while she was uniting with Śiva for the purpose of a son, the gods disturbed them, and thereupon she cursed the gods that they would never beget children. She also cursed the Earth who absorbed the seed of Śiva that she would be the wife of many and never be happy with her children.[75]

Four Vedic goddesses viz. Diti, Aditi, Sacī and Rātri occur in the *Rāmāyaṇa*, though not in their original character. Devi Laṅkā,[76] the protectress of the city of Laṅkā, recalls the Semitic city-goddesses Surasā,[77] the serpent-mother, came from tribal religion. No goddess of a purely Śākta character is mentioned in the *Rāmāyaṇa*. Only Kālikā is mentioned once.[78]

VIII

The *Harivaṃśa*, a supplement of the *Mahābhārata*, composed not earlier than the first century AD, contains two Āryāstavas[79] in which the goddess is invoked by numerous names and epithets. Such names as Kālarātri, Nidrā, Kātyāyanī, Kauśikī, Vīrūpā, Virūpākṣī, Viśalākṣī, Mahādevī, Kaumārī, Caṇḍī, Dakṣā, Śivā, Kālī, Bhayadā, Vetālī, Śakunī, Yoginī, Bhūtadhātrī, Kuṣmāṇḍī, etc. later became popular as names of the Tantric goddesses. A few of her epithets like Hrī, Śrī, Kīrti, Lajjā, Prabhā, Dayā, Mati, etc. refer to abstract qualities and these may be traced to the Vedas. The *Harivaṃśa* refers to the association of the goddess with the non-Vedic hunting peoples like the Śabaras, the Barbaras and the Pulindas. Her association with the animals is also indicated. The work was composed by the worshippers of Viṣṇu who could not avoid the increasing influence of the popular cult of the Female Principle. Thus the virgin goddess Kauśikī, the supposed sister of Indra, residing in the Vindhyas and worshipped with animal sacrifice, was taken into the Vaiṣṇava pantheon and conceived as the daughter of Yaśodā and the consort of Nārāyaṇa.

IX

The currency of the cult of the Female Principle in South India in the early centuries of the Christian era is amply indicated in early Tamil literature, the Sangam Classics, in which occur such goddesses as Amarī, Kumārī, Gaurī, Samarī, Śūli, Nīlī, Aiyai, Sayyavaḷ, Koṛṛavai, Nallāl, Kaṇṇī, Śaṅkari, etc. Of the goddesses, Kumārī, the virgin goddess Kanyākumārī of the *Taittirīya Āraṇyaka* who gave her name to the southernmost point of India, is mentioned in *Periplus*.

> Beyond this there is another place called Comari at which are the Cape of Comari and a harbour; hither come those men who wish to consecrate themselves for the rest of their lives, and bathe and dwell in celibacy and women also do the same; for it is told that a goddess here dwelt and bathed.[80]

Next important goddess in Koṛṛavai, the great mother of Muruga[81] identified with Malaimagal,[82] daughter of the mountain, i.e., Pārvatī. Her dance was known as *tunaṅgai*. According to the *Tolkappiyam*, the earliest Tamil grammatical work, Koṛṛavai was the goddess of the region of Pālai. This goddess is frequently mentioned in early Tamil literature, as we shall see later.

The story of the deification of a human being called Kaṇṇaki into Pattanikaḍavul, the goddess of chastity, is met within the great Tamil epic *Śilappadikāram* (second century AD). This lady destroyed the city of Madura by fire to avenge the execution of her husband Kovalan. Kosar, the king of Kaṅgu, Gajabāhu, the king of Laṅkā, Perunkkilli, the Cola king, and the Cera king Senguttuvan erected temples and instituted festivals in her honour. The Bhagavatī temple of Cranganore in Kerala, dedicated to Bhadrakālī whose wrath is supposed to be the cause of all epidemic diseases, is said to have been founded between the years AD 115-25 by Senguttuvan Perumal to commemorate the tragic end of Kannaki, the heroine of the *Śilappadikāram*.[83] The goddess enshrined at Cranganore, according to the popular tradition, goes by the name of Oṛṛaimulaicci, i.e., goddess with one breast.

Kaṇṇaki is said to have cut off one of her breasts when she cursed the city at the death of Kovalan.

How and when the Kannaki cult was assimilated with and finally absorbed into the Kālī or Bhagavatī cult cannot be said at our present state of knowledge. In the *Śilappadikāram.*[84] we have references to the worship of Kālī. On their way to Madura, Kaṇṇaki and Kovalan stopped at a Kālī temple where they witnessed a weird dance of the priestess of Kālī who, attired like the dread goddess, stood up in the village common and trembling all over as if she was possessed by a devil declared in terrific tones that the goddess Kālī was angry, as the Maṛavar had not offered any sacrifice at her temple for sometime past.

In the *Śilappadikāram* also occur such goddesses as Aryāni, Aiyai Kumārī, Āpya, Antari, Bārati, Pitāri, Māyaval, Koṛṛavai, etc. Aryāni is the Tamil name of Indrāṇī. Aiyai-Kumārī is the goddess worshipped by the Vaḍuvar or Maṛavar and she is known by different names. Pitari or Cāmuṇḍā is conceived as one of the seven Lokamātās or divine mothers. We have already referred to the goddess Koṛṛavai, known as the goddess of victory. The Eyinor of Palai worshipped her and sacrificed buffaloes at her temple. According to the *Śilappadikāram,*[85] peacocks and parrots, fowls, sandal, grains and oblations of rice with flesh and blood were offered tc her. Her hair was matted. She was clad in skins of tiger and cobra while a stag was her vehicle. She was so much dreaded that when once the doors of her shrine could not be opened, the Pāṇḍya king felt that it was due to the divine displeasure and sought her mercy by the grant of the revenue of two villages for her worship.[86] According to the *Kalittogai,*[87] the she-devils taught her how to dance while the *Kuṛuntogal*[88] calls her Śūlī, i.e., wielder of the trident.

The idea that Lakṣmī, Sarasvatī, Pārvatī, etc., represent different aspects of the same power is evident from the *Venba* is canto XXII of the *Śilappadikāram.* The cult of Durgā is also found in the *Veṭṭuvavari* of the same epic. Durgā is described as "having a body, the colour (dark blue) of which resembles that of a flower of the *kaya* (Memecylon edule), lips red like the coral, teeth white and neck dark, with a third eye on the crescent like forehead, holding the discuss and conch, sword and *śūla* (spear) and the bow which was the *meṛu* (*neḍumalai*) strung with the snake Vāśuki as its *ñān* (bow-string), wearing the skin of a tiger and a belt (*mekalai* of lion's skin), a *kaḷal* (hero's calf-band) on one leg and *śilambu* (woman's anklet) on the other, with a coiffure of *jaṭā* adorned by a serpent and the crescent moon, covering herself with the hide of the elephant as *uttarīya* (*ékāśam,*) wearing a snake as her breast-band (*kaccu*), carrying a standard of lion (*āḷikkodi*).[89] The goddess standing on the cut off head of a buffalo, a frequent sculptural representation of South India, is found in the epic which also describes her fight with the Asuras, her killing of Dāruka and Mahiṣāsura. The worship of Maṇimekalai, the chief guardian deity of the sea, is seen throughout in the south in the epics, especially in the *Maṇimekalai* (second century AD). In the said epic, she acted as the guide of the heroine who was her namesake.[90] Another goddess who is mentioned with special importance in the *Maṇimekalai*[91] is Cintā Devī who is said to have given a cup, which was never empty, to Aputra, a pious youth of obscure origin. The *Maṇimekalai* also refers to a forest-goddess called Kāḍamarśelvi[92] who was also known as Kāḍuraikaḍavuḷ, Moti, Karitāy etc. She is described as standing with a beggar's bowl and generally worshipped in temples adjacent to the burial grounds.

X

The ultimate triumph of the Female Principle did really happen. At least its progress during the period before and after the Christian era is testified by the sporadic evidence furnished above. The cause of the increasing popularity of the Female Principle was evidently connected with the changing social patterns arising out of the new economic conditions resulting from changes in the mode of production, expansion of internal and external trade, centralised state authorities and the growth of urbanism. The agriculturists and other professionals, apart from the priestly, warrior and trading classes, did form the majority of the population, and it was the religion of this majority, the Mother Goddess of the agriculturists, that found its way into the higher levels of society under diverse historical conditions. Even the ethical systems like Buddhism and Jainism, in order to get themselves popular among the masses and widely preached, had to make compromise with the existing cults and beliefs, and this was one of the processes through which female divinities of the lower strata of society could have easy access therein. Goddesses in considerable number came from the tribal proples who, unable to maintain themselves by their traditional mode of production, had to come in contact with the advanced peoples and were put in different social grades on the basis of the quality of services they offered to the existing caste society. Thus the tribes subsisting on war and plunder could easily become Kṣatriyas by offering their war-services to the king, while those depending on lower occupations (*hīnaśilpas*) formed sub-castes of the Śūdra category. Such a process, of tribes coming into the fold of caste system, had always been an important characteristic of Indian society, and its religious reflex was also of great historical consequence.

XI

In early Buddhism Lakkhi, also called Siri (Śrī), is the Pāli equivalent of Sanskrit Lakṣmī, both the names often found mentioned together.[93] Siri Lakkhi is regarded as the goddess of beauty and fortune. The *Abhidhānappadīpikā* says that Siri Lakkhi is a synonym of the goddess of beauty and property. The Jātakas describe her as the goddess of *parivāra-sampatti* (family property), *paññā* (wisdom) and luck or fortune.[94] The popularity of this goddess in early Buddhism was due to the Buddhist association with the interest of the trading communities—profit, property and security. Also success in profit-making depends on luck and as such she is the goddess of fortune. She does not forsake wise man who is grateful, tender, heart-winning, gracious, proves himself a good and steadfast friend, enjoys his own property with others, speaks smoothly and so forth.[95] She is also mutual and Rājya-siri, the goddess of kingdom and property[96] and Vīra Lakkhi, the goddess who gives success to the hero in the battle. The Buddha says that the wealth which one earns through hard labour can be earned by those who are favoured by Lakṣmī without any effort.[97] Her favour is the result of the merit earned by a person in previous births through virtuous deeds which enables one to obtain treasures. Siri Lakkhi loves the man who is energetic, enterprising, bold and free from jealousy.[98] Lakkhi comes down to earth through the air with raiment of golden hue and ornament of golden brightness diffusing yellow light.[99] She lives in four objects—a fowl, a gem, a club and a wife.[100]

As a goddess presiding over *paññā* or wisdom, Lakkhi has often been identified with Sarasvatī, the goddess of learning.[101] But Sarasvatī is a different goddess. The *Culavaṃsa*[102] mentions a Buddhist king who had erected a Sarasvatīmaṇḍapa in Śrīlaṅkā. The Buddha did not share the traditional belief that Lakṣmī and Sarasvatī could not live together, for he said that unless a person was favoured by the goddess of wisdom it was impossible for him to preserve wealth.[103] Among other goddess mentioned in the Pāli literature we have already had the occasion to refer to Maṇimekhalā (Maṇimekalai) in connection with the South Indian cults. She is the goddess of ocean who protects people suffering from shipwreck.[104] The conception of this goddess, taking station upon the sea, must have been due to the Buddhist encouragement to the sea-faring merchants. Her place was probably later taken by Tārā who was also the guardian of navigation. The goddess Kālakaṇṇi, also called Kālī and Caṇḍī, and often identified with Alakkhi, the opposite number of Lakkhi, is mentioned as a fearful goddess coming down to the earth through the air diffusing blue light who is the favourite of the hypocrite, wanton, morose, greedy and treacherous.[105] The Pāli literature also mentions some minor goddesses such as Bahusodarī, Birāṇī, Yaśuttarā, Jālinī, Lājā, etc.

References

1. Deussen, *PU,* 39.
2. For their views see my *JPHO,* 69-80.
3. Chattopadhyaya, *L,* 485.
4. For details see my *BHII,* ch IV.
5. Cf. the *Kuṭadanta* and *Tevijja Suttas* of the *DN: Yajña Sutta* of the *SN; AN,* II.205; *MN* (51), I.342 ff; *Bhuridatta Jātaka* (Cowell, VI, no. 54); passim.
6. *AB,* V.25; *SB,* XI.3.1.1 ff; *Ch U,* III.17.1 ff.
7. IV.28ff.
8. Cf. *KS,* VIII.9; *MS,* 1.6.7; *TB,* III.8.14; *AB,* V.23; *SB,* I.2.3.1-5; VI.2.1.1 ff.; *JUB,* III.6.4; passim.
9. *Manu,* II.6.
10. Ibid., II.4; cf. *Bhagavadgītā,* II.42-44, XVII.11-13.
11. Ibid., XII.88-91.
12. Ibid., II.86; Bühler's trans.
13. Ibid., X.63.
14. Ibid., V.45-49; VI.75; X.63; cf. XI.223; XII.83.
15. *BG,* X.27; *Suttani,* 121.
16. Manu, VII.8.
17. Chattopadhyaya, *HBT,* 53.
18. Bloch in *ASIAR,* 1906-7, 122ff; Bachhofer, *EIS,* I, 14-15.
19. *AAI,* 23.
20. Ray, *MSA,* 6.
21. *Mbh,* IV.6.23; Vangavasi ed.
22. Allan, *CCAT,* 129-39, 148-58, 252.

23. Ibid., 1318 ff; Whitehead, *PMC*, I, 135.
24. *PMC*, I, 100-101, 122.
25. *BMC*, 70-71, 89.
26. *ASIAR*, 1914-15, 29-30.
27. *EA*, I, 175 ff.
28. Allan, *CCAI*, 159, 169-91, 194 ff, 210ff.
29. Banerjea, *DHI*, 108 ff.
30. See Mukherjee, *NL*.
31. *ASIAR*, 1910-11, 16.
32. *ASIAR*, 1927-28, 66; Marshall, *MIC*, I, 62-63; Banerjea, *DHI*, 158 ff.
33. Saraswati, *SIS*, 100-101.
34. *ASIAR*, 1911-12, 71ff.
35. Kramrisch, *AIA*, pl. VI.
36. Marshall, *GT*, 59.
37. Marshall, *BAG*, 21; *T.*, II, 701; III, pl. 211.
38. *CHI*, I, 638 ff.
39. Coomaraswamy in *IPEK*, 1928, 71, fig. XXV; *ASIAR*, 1922-23, pl. X.B.
40. *ASIAR*, 1903-4, 76-77, 133; 1911-12, 107, 137; Majumdar, *GSIM*, II, 100; Hargreaves, *HSPM*, 44, 50; Marshall, *BAG*, 84.
41. Smith, *JSAM*, 56, pl. XCVIV.
42. IV.6.18.
43. III.40-41.
44. XII.282-83; Cr. Ed., XII.274.23 ff, gives a different version.
45. Chanda, *IAR*, 129.
46. In *DRBV*, 301ff.
47. In her temple at Comana, women used to offer their bodies voluntarily, Frazer, *AAO*, 34.
48. Frazer, *AAO*, 131.
49. I.178.4.
50. II.10.20 ff.
51. III.40-41.
52. III.163.42.
53. III.220.10; 221.31; passim.
54. VI.23.4-16.
55. III.39.4; VII.78-40; 200.70; 201.92-93; X.7-46; XII.283.29; XIII.14.406; passim.
56. I.64.
57. II.17-18.
58. III.220 ff.
59. III.82 ff.
60. Sircar, *SP*, 8: cf. Kālidāsa's description of the Malaya and Dardura mountains in *Raghu*, IV.51.
61. *RV*, III.17 ff; IV.57; *YV*, XII.69-72; *Gobhila GS*, IV.4.27-30; *Pāraskara GS*, II.17.9-10; cf. Hopkins in *JAOS*, XVIII, 85n; Keith, *RPV*, 186; *VBYS*, 306; *SBE*, XXIX, 334; XXX, 113-14.
62. I.24.
63. *Viṣṇu*, III.14 (LVIII).
64. II.4.17.
65. II.70.72; 79.15; VI.111.89; 113-21; VII.9.9; 47.9.
66. III.46.17; VII.5.31.
67. II.44.19; VI.33.14; 91.68; VII.47.8.

68 II.1.34; VIII.72.42, 52; 110.14-16, 19.
69. II.52.85-91; VII.10.46; 18.28.
70. II.35.19-23.
71. VII.4.28-31.
72. VII.17.
73. VII.42.30.
74. I.36.6-25.
75. I.18.12; II.15.22; 25.35; 93.22; IV.1.119; VII.11.14-16.
76. V.3.21-51.
77. V.1.139-64.
78. VI.35.28.
79. *Viṣṇu*, III; CXXII (LVIII; CLXXVII).
80. Schoff, *PES*, 46.
81. *Perumbaṇāṟṟuppadai*, 457 ff.
82. *Tirumurugāṟṟuppadai*, 258 ff.
83. *IHO*, II.621-22.
84. XI-XII.
85. XII.22-29.
86. XIII.113-25; XX-37-40.
87. LXXXIX. 8.
88. CCXVIII.1.
89. *JMU*, XXXII.152.
90. VI-X.
91. XIII-XIV.
92. Cf. Ahananūru, 345.3-7.
93. *Jāt*, III.262, 442; V.112.
94. Ibid., III.306, 443; IV.281-82.
95. Ibid., V.146.
96. *Dh A*, I.17; II.17.
97. *CV*, LXII.101, 112; LXXVI.233.
98. *Jāt.*, II.411-14.
99. Ibid., II.257, 258, 262.
100. Ibid., II.415.
101. Ibid., III.306, 442-43.
102. LXXIII.86.
103. *Jāt.*, VI.356-62.
104. Ibid., IV.15-21; VI.135.
105. Ibid., III.259 ff; IV.378; V.112-13; VI.349.

4

Rise of Śāktism: The Gupta Age and After (AD 300-700)

The political history of the Gupta empire which made its start about AD 320 carries us to the middle of the sixth century. But the cultural history of this age began much earlier. The Sanskritised pan-Indian culture, made of diverse ethnic, linguistic and religious streams, which for the sake of convenience may be described as Hindu, was gradually coming under an orderly framework since the beginning of the Christian era when the north-western and parts of northern India were being ruled by the Kuṣāṇas, the western by the Śaka Kṣatrapas, the Deccan by the Sātavāhanas, the Kaliṅga region by the Cedis and the Far South by the Colas, Pāṇḍyas and Ceras.

The Maurya empire which brought about the political unity of India left a rich legacy behind it. For the first time after the fall of the Mauryas there was a vast Kuṣāṇa empire which not only embraced nearly the whole of north India, but also considerable territories outside it as far as Central Asia. India was thus brought into close contact with the outside world. The new social and economic set up of the period from 150 BC to AD 320 led to a cultural unity which manifested itself through the development of a uniform type of language, literature, art and religion all over India which left a deep impress on the subsequent Gupta age. The period witnessed an all-round development of agriculture, industry and trade. This was due partly to private enterprise and partly to state-control and state-management. The latter aspect is delineated in Kauṭilya's *Arthaśāstra*. One of the most remarkable features of the period was the introduction of a regular coinage in business. The Graeco-Roman coins and the large influx of Roman coins profoundly influenced those of the Śakas, Parthians and Kuṣāṇas and other Indian rulers. Inland trade was facilitated through various highways such as the Royal Road leading from the North-West Frontier up to Pāṭaliputra, the routes from Śrāvastī to various directions such as Rājagṛha, Paithan and Sind, and so forth. The earlier centuries of the Christian era witnessed the growth of a brisk foreign trade between India and the

West, with the Roman Empire as its chief customer. Traces of this profitable sea-trade are left in hoards of Roman coins found at several places close to the south Indian coast on which also grew up several port towns.

This economic mobilization through trade and commerce contributed to the development of a kind of social and cultural integration. It was due to the fact that interdependence of communities in relation to production, distribution and exchange became imparative during the period under review. But in this integrated cultural phenomenon, owing to natural diversities, the ideal of absolute homogeneity was out of question. The races were many; despite Sanskritisation languages were numerous; customs varied from region to region. Consequently the social structure was a federated organisation in which there was a spirit of harmony which welded together the discordant elements. As a result, we find a tendency towards forming a social whole out of diverse and conflicting elements. A derivative of this social whole came into existence with hierarchical grades for diverse communities and with social duties and means of livelihood allotted to each of them. In this way the principle of equality was sacrificed, but in its place the lower orders received a guarantee for the protection of life and property and proper chances for the maintenance of life. The system had undoubtedly its defects but it did much to mitigate ethnic and other hostilities among different sections of peoples by the creation of economic compartments within the caste groups and entrusting each of these with a peculiar function and means of livelihood.

A process of historical determinism must have given a concrete shape to this system during the Kuṣāṇa and the Gupta period which came into existence as a result of a long social evolution extending over centuries. The working of this process, however, did not escape the notice of the ancient law-givers—the authors of the Dharmasūtras and Dharmaśāstras—who were eager to incorporate conflicting tribes of various cultural grades within the framework of an idealised four-fold social order and to rationalise their existence in the prescribed set up by inventing the theory of *varṇasaṅkara* or 'mixed castes' by which even the foreign tribes such as the Ābhīras, Yavanas, Śakas, Pāradas, Kuṣāṇas, Cīnas, etc. could be inducted into the scheme of the four-fold system. They tried to create a plural society by offering the detribalised castes special hereditary occupations and absolute cultural freedom to follow their traditional social practices, cults and rituals, laws and customs. But they were not ready to give them equality of status and position.

II

The Greeks, Parthians, Śakas and Kuṣāṇas who came as invaders were ultimately absorbed in the vast population of India. They were completely merged in Indian society and adopted the language, religion and customs of the land without retaining any trace of their foreign origin. Kadphises I, the first Kuṣāṇa king, was a Buddhist. His son Kadphises II was a follower of Maheśvara as is attested by the expression *mahīśvara* in his coins which represent Śiva with two arms, hair in spiral top-knot, and tiger's skin over the left arm, grasping combined trident and battle axe in right hand. The third king Kaṇiṣka was a Buddhist, but the reverse of his coin types represent Greek, Sumerian, Elamite, Iranian and Indian deities. Amongst these, special mention should be made of the Sumerian Mother Goddess Nana, Nanaia or Nane Shao (Inanna of the Ishtar-Astarte category; cf. (Bībī Nānī of Hinglaj in Baluchistan, Naīnā Devī of the Kulu valley, Nainī of Nainital, etc.). This diversity of the deities points to some sort of religious eclecticism and reflects the various forms of cults that prevailed in different parts of the Kuṣāṇa empire. Among the non-Indian Mother Goddesses found in the coins of Huviṣka mention may be made of Ardoksho, the goddess of abundance, and Oanao or Oaninda. Besides Śākyamuni Buddha, the Kuṣāṇa coins contain representations of Śiva, Viṣṇu, Umā and deities of the Skanda-Kārttikeya group. The issue of Vāsudeva mostly exhibit the figure of Śiva with his bull Nandin.

The Śaka Satraps were also foreigners who were completely Hinduised. Mahākṣatrapa Rudradāman was a great Sanskrit scholar and was reputed for his excellence of his compositions in Sanskrit. The spiritual quests which began under the shadow of the earlier Vedic and non-Vedic traditions eventually culminated in the formation of numerous theistic sects. Prominent among these were the cults of Viṣṇu, Śiva, Śakti, Gaṇapati, Sūrya, Skanda-Kārttikeya and other deities, each of whom was regarded as the Supreme Being by the distinctive sectarian devotees and thought of as capable of bestowing grace when approached with reverence and devotion. The ancient Vedic cults and rituals did not go out of vogue. The Nanaghat inscription refers to the Sātavāhanas as performers of the

Vedic sacrifices. The Gupta King Samudragupta is also known to have performed the Aśvamedha sacrifice. But the sectarian gods were coming to the forefront. The coins of Huviṣka refers to the cults of Skanda, Kumāra, Viśākha and Mahāsena besides those of Viṣṇu and Śiva. The said Nanaghat inscription of the Sātavāhanas begins with an adoration to the gods Dharma, Indra, Saṅkarṣaṇa and Vāsudeva, the Moon and the Sun, and the four Lokapālas, viz. Yama, Varuṇa, Kubera and Vāsava. This shows that the position of some of the major Vedic deities have been lowered to the rank of the Lokapālas while new cults such as those of the Vṛṣṇi heroes were coming into prominence.

Buddhism, Jainism, Ājīvikism and a few other systems approached the problems of life and the universe from a non-theistic point of view and insisted on a moral renaissance. The influence of all these systems on the masses varied both in extent and in degree. Despite functional differences, all these systems had many points in common. All accepted the same basic concepts and their representative terms, the same logical system and the same fixed points of metaphysical speculation. The goal was also the same—*mokṣa* or liberation. To a follower of Viṣṇu or Śiva or Śakti, the Buddhist or Jain monks and their monasteries were objects of respect and veneration, while lay followers of Buddhism and Jainism were attracted by the doctrine of *bhakti* which was an easier way to get rid of worldly suffering, and the worship of image. The Jains did not hesitate to allow image worship of the Tīrthaṅkaras and also of gods of the existing systems as idealised human beings. They erected temples as well, and appointed priests who were mostly Brāhmaṇas. In Buddhism, the elaborate growth of Mahāyānism was a triumph of the *bhakti* cult. The Buddhist and Jain deities were also worshipped by the non-Buddhists and non-Jains, despite obligations to their own sectarian cults. On a higher plane, the Buddhist and Jain logicians and philosophers were held in high esteem by their non-Buddhist and non-Jain counterparts. In fact, Hindu logical literature was greatly influenced by the Buddhist and Jain logicians. Without the Mādhyamika and Yogācāra schools of Buddhism, there could not have been such an elaborate growth of the Vedānta in the subsequent history of Indian thought.

III

It is against this background that one has to understand the historical processes through which the development of Hinduism in its modern sense took place from the Gupta period onwards. In the shaping of the mass-adaptability of heterogeneous religious elements the importance of the Purāṇas is most significant. In fact, the Purāṇas as well as the two great epics

> afford us for greater insight into all aspects and phases of Hinduism—its mythology, its idol worship, its theism and pantheism, its love of God, its philosophy and its superstitions, its festival and ceremonies and its ethics, than any other works.[1]

The Purāṇic legends pertaining to different cults and sects, which were by nature very interesting and instructive had a greater appeal to the masses. Various ideals thus preached through the Purāṇas, wonderfully blended with entertaining episodes, prepared the substratum of what is known as popular Hinduism. The basic ground on which most of the Indian religious systems met comprised concept of suffering and liberation, worldly fetters, the doctrine of *karma* and rebirth, recognition of all accepted cults belonging to the people at various cultural levels, insistence on *bhakti* or devotion to the personal god (*iṣṭadevatā*), efficacy of temple and image worship and the way of life upheld by the Smṛti texts. Since most of the religious systems subscribed to all these points—Buddhism and Jainism being no exception—there was no difficulty in the development of that catholicity and spirit of tolerance by which Hinduism still stands unique. Buddhism being basically a monkish system did not offer any social code to its lay followers who were free to observe the traditional social rules later regularised by the Smṛtis. So the lay worshipper of Avalokiteśvara or Tārā, the personal deities who bestow grace like Viṣṇu or Śiva, was otherwise a Hindu, following the Smārta-Purāṇic way of life. And this was one of the reasons for the metamorphosis of Buddhism in India.

IV

By the end of the third century AD Jainism could become one of the principal religions of India. It was popular in Kaliṅga, Mathura and Malwa, and also in parts of the Deccan and South India. The Gaṅga kings of Karṇāṭaka and the Kadamba rulers of Banavāsī were patrons of Jainism. About AD 512 the Second Jain Council was held at Valabhī where the Jain canon took its present shape. The Khandagiri caves of Bhuvaneswar contain some standing and seated Jain images of the later Gupta period. The Satghara cave, the northernmost of the Khandagiri group, contains two rows of carvings on its rear wall. The upper row represents seven Tīrthaṅkaras and the lower seven female figures guarded by Gaṇeśa. It is the Jain version of the existing Saptamātṛkā concept showing that the Jains had by this time adopted the cult of the Divine Mothers as a submission to the demands of the lay followers of the creed. The female figures are variously depicted, ten-armed, four-armed, and two-armed, the first five of which reminds us of Brahmāṇī, Vaiṣṇavī, Indrāṇī, Māheśvarī, and Kumārī, as is suggested by their emblems, while the sixth and the seventh stand probably for Padmāvatī and Ambikā, the Jain counterparts of Manasā and Durgā. All of them, except the first, sit in *lalitāsana*, while the fourth, fifth and seventh carry a small child in their arms. According to B.C. Bhattacharyya,[2] the fifth cannot be identified while the others stand for Cakreśvarī, Ajitādevī, Duritāri or Prajñapti, Gaurī or Mānavā, Padmāvatī and Ambikā respectively. Another section of the same cave contains two rows of figures, the upper showing the 24 Tīrthaṅkaras, the lower 24 female figures, the corresponding Śāsanadevatās of the former. Jain texts like *Uttarādhyayana Sūtra*, *Ācāra Dinakara*, etc. show in their classification of Jain goddesses that many of them were adaptations from the existing cults. The Śāsanadevatās or goddesses are regarded as devoted adherents of the Jinas and they were to be worshipped with specialised rituals. Their names are as follows: Cakreśvarī, Ajitabalā, Duritāri, Kālikā, Mahākālī, Śyāmā, Śāntā, Bhṛkuṭi, Sutārakā, Aśokā, Mānavī, Caṇḍā, Viditā, Aṅkuśā, Kandarpā, Nirvāṇī, Balā, Dhāriṇī, Dharaṇapriyā, Naradattā, Gāndharī, Ambikā, Padmāvatī, and Siddhāyikā. Of other Jain goddesses, mention must be made of Śrī-Lakṣmī, the Mātṛkās and the Vidyādevīs. The Vidyādevīs are sixteen in number, the goddess of learning *par excellence* being Sarasvatī, while others were known by such names as Rohiṇī, Prajñapti, Vajraśṛṃkhalā, Kālī, Mahākālī, Gaurī, Mānavī, etc. The cult of the sixty-four Yoginīs was also adopted by the Jains.

But the process of the transformation of Buddhism was more rapid. The older form of Buddhism lost its hold upon the people giving way to a new movement, the Mahāyāna. The followers of the Mahāyāna regarded the Buddha as eternal, without origin and decay, and as such beyond any description whatsoever. They indulged in certain speculations regarding the Buddha's body and gave currency to the *trikāya* conception which was further elaborated with the rise of a regular Mahāyāna pantheon. The latter came into being with five Dhyānī Buddhas, viz. Vairocana, Akṣobhya, Ratnasambhava, Amitābha and Amoghasiddhi who were said to have issued out of Ādi-Buddha (the Original Buddha) through contemplation. Each of these Buddhas was associated with a Bodhisattva and a goddess, called Tārā. A being destined to attain *bodhi* (knowledge) and become a Buddha in the long run was evidently a Bodhisattva, and as such every Mahāyānist was a potential Bodhisattva, but a few became more distinguished and ranked almost as gods. These Bodhisattvas—Avalokiteśvara, Mañjuśrī, Vajrapāṇi, Samantabhadra, Ākāśagarbha, Mahāsthāmaprāpta, Bhaiṣajyarāja and Maitreya—were highly advanced in spiritual perfection and could easily have attained Buddhahood, but refrained from doing so for the cause of the suffering humanity. The cults of Avalokiteśvara, the embodiment of compassion, and Mañjuśrī the personification of wisdom, flourished in the Gupta age and survived for so many centuries. The former was associated with the goddess Tārā, the personification of knowledge (*prajñā*) while the latter with Lakṣmī or Sarasvatī or both. Subsequent Buddhism came under the complete grip of the Tārā cult which was evidently a force from outside. But who was this goddess? According to the Mahāyāna conception she is the primordial female energy, the consort of Avalokiteśvara, who enables her devotees to surmount all sorts of dangers and calamities. A mere prayer to this goddess is sure to remove the eight *mahābhayas* (great dangers). She is also known as the goddess Prajñāpāramitā, as it is by the fulfilment of this *pāramitā* that a Bodhisattva reaches the goal. Sometimes she is conceived as the Supreme Being, 'the mother of all the Buddhas and Bodhisattvas.' She became a very popular deity in India, during the early centuries after Christ when the Mahāyāna pantheon was developing rapidly, and passed out of India to Tibet and China. In Tibet, where her cult developed about the seventh century she was known as Sgrol-ma (Dol-ma) and conceived under quite a large variety of subsidiary forms.

Tārā was evidently admitted to the Mahāyāna pantheon from the older religions. The conception of this goddess is very primitive, and it is quite possible that in course of her conceptual development she had absorbed within herself a number of divinities representing different aspects of the Female Principle. The epithets Tārā Tārinī, attributed to the Devī in the *Mahābhārata* and the Purāṇas, may be traced to the *Yajurveda* in which the term *Tāra*, meaning 'the saviour' is an appellation of the god Śiva. Then there is the Sanskrit word *Tārā* or *Tārakā* meaning a star (cf. Persian *Sitārā*, Greek 'Aster', Latin 'Stella' and English 'Star' and also the names of such foreign goddesses as Ishtar, Astarte, Atargatis, Astaroth etc.) and the word might easily give the names of a goddess dwelling among the stars. Many such streams later culminated into the conception of Tārā whose cult was established in different parts of India by the sixth century AD. A good number of sculptural representations testifying the popularity of this goddess are found in the Buddhist caves of western Deccan such as Ellora, Aurangabad, Kanheri, Nasik and others and also at Sirpur in Madhya Pradesh, but very few of them can chronologically be assigned to a period earlier than the sixth century AD. The earliest literary reference to a Buddhist worshipper of Tārā is found in Subandhu's *Vāsavadattā*[3] which was also composed about the sixth century AD. From the seventh century onwards, the influence of the Buddhist Tārā began to be felt upon the religious systems of India and abroad. The significant changes which the Tārā cult brought in the Chinese way of religious life will be dealt with in the next chapter. In India, the development of the Śākta religion received a great momentum from the Tārā cult of the Buddhists. The Śākta Tārā, also called Ugratārā, Ekajaṭā and Nīla-sarasvatī is undoubtedly an adaptation of the Mahāyāna Buddhist goddess of the same name.

V

One of the most important features of Vaiṣṇavism in the Gupta period was the conception of Lakṣmī or Śrī as Viṣṇu's wife. In Kālidāsa's *Raghuvaṃśa*[4] we have a description of Viṣṇu lying on the great serpent in the ocean of milk, with Lakṣmī rubbing his feet. As usual, she bore the name Śrī, and the traditional epithets Hrī (modesty), Medhā (talent), Dhṛti (patience), Puṣṭi (growth), Kṣānti (forgiveness), Lajjā (bashfulness), Kīrti (fame), Bhūti (prosperity), Rati (love) etc. were attributed to her. Her figure appears in the lintels of Viṣṇu temples at Badami and Aihole. As the wife of Viṣṇu Lakṣmī is mentioned in the Junagarh inscription of Skandagupta[5] and the Sārnāth inscription of Prakaṭāditya,[6] while Śrī is mentioned in the Aphsad inscription of Ādityasena.[7] A Kadamba record of *c.* AD 500 begins with an adoration of Bhagavat with Śrī on his breast.

Lakṣmī continued her function as the guardian angel of kings (Rājalakṣmī) and cities (Nagaralakṣmī). The Gajalakṣmī motif, used as a coin-device by both indigenous and foreign rulers a few centuries earlier, was adopted as a symbol for the administrative offices by the imperial Guptas, who styled themselves Paramabhāgavata, and also by other rulers belonging to the Gupta age and later, as is evident from numerous device portrayed on terracotta and copper seals from Madhya Pradesh (Eran, Arang, etc.), Uttar Pradesh (Bhita, Rājghāt, Kauśāmbī, etc.) and Bihar (Basarh and Nālandā).[8] The Ardoksho-Lakṣmī type, the former probably identified with the latter by the Kuṣāṇas, holding a cornucopia instead of lotus, continued to be copied by the foreign successors of the Kuṣāṇas, viz. the Kidara Kuṣāṇas and the white Huṇas (Toramāna, Mihirakula and some other Ephthalite kings), influenced the initial issues of the Guptas, but the artistic sense of the age freed the goddess shortly from the crude and stereotyped representation, and very soon she became a full-fledged Indian Lakṣmī, traces of which can be noticed on the early issues of Samudragupta. The identification of a goddess on the reverse of certain types of the Gupta coins has aroused some controversy because of her association with the lion and the lotus at the same time, e.g. the coins of the Candragupta-Kumāradevī type and of the Lion-slayer type of Candragupta II.

Originally Śrī and Lakṣmī, regarded as two personalities, were described as the two wives of Āditya. Later tradition made Śrī and Mahāśvetā the two wives of Sūrya, one on either side of the sun image. This was followed by the still later conception of Lakṣmī and Sarasvatī as the two wives of Viṣṇu. In a few inscriptions e.g. in the Chastu inscription of Bālāditya,[9] Lakṣmī, as in the Kāvyas and Purāṇas, is a co-wife of Sarasvatī, jealously guarding her husband's attention. In the *Vikramorvaśīya*[10] of Kālidāsa, Lakṣmī and Sarasvatī are represented as rivals, jealous of each other. In the *Kāmasūtra* of Vātsyāyana[11] we are told that the wealthy citizens used to flock every fortnight to the temple of the goddess Sarasvatī to enjoy dramatic performances, etc. Skanda's wife Devasenā had Lakṣmī as one of her names, and Kubera, too, claimed her as wife at a later time. A second wife of Viṣṇu was supposed to be the Earth, called Vaiṣṇavī in some epigraphs, e.g. those of the Śarabhapura kings. Lakṣmī as the divine consort of Viṣṇu and also as the eternal Female Principle is mentioned in the writings of the Tamil Āḷvars. It is interesting to note that the *gopī* element in Vaiṣṇavism, which is the forerunner of the later conception of Rādhā as the Eternal Female associated with the Supreme Being Kṛṣṇa, is met with in the devotional songs of the Āḻvars. Āṇḍal or Kodāi, daughter of Periyāḻvār, saw herself as one of Kṛṣṇa's *gopīs,* and approached the god, her beloved, in that spirit.

The Gangadhar inscription of AD 423 speaks of a worshipper of Viṣṇu building a temple, full of the Ḍākinīs, in honour of the Divine Mothers "who utter loud and tremendous shouts in joy and stir up the ocean with the mighty wind rising from the magic rites of their religion.[12] This no doubt points to the influences of Śāktism upon the Vaiṣṇavas. The cult of the Divine Mothers, as we have seen above, made its way into the Jain religion. The early Cālukya rulers of Badami, whose family god was Viṣṇu, also worshipped the Seven Mothers associated with Kārttikeya.

But the influence of Śāktism was greater upon the Śaiva religion. We have stories of the resurrection of Satī, the first wife of Śiva, as Umā, her austerities to win her husband again, the marriage of Śiva and Pārvatī, their domestic life on the Kailāsa, and so on. Kālidāsa, the great Sanskrit poet and playwright, was probably a devotee of Śiva. His *Kumārasambhava* tells us the story of the birth of Kumāra, but the whole work centres upon Śiva and Pārvatī, the hero and the heroine. The two characters appear again in the *Kirātārjunīya* of Bhāravi, composed about the sixth century, in which the *Mahābhārata* story of the combat between Arjuna and Śiva in the garb of a Kirāta finds expression. Śiva and Umā occur, as the Male and Female Principles, sometimes identified with the Sāṅkhya concepts of Puruṣa and Prakṛti, in the devotional hymns of the Śaiva Nāyanārs of south India. In the Ardhanārīśvara figures Śiva and Umā are blended together. There is an interesting type of this composite figure, the right half possessing all the iconographic features of Śiva and the left half those of Umā, in a Gupta seal found at Bhita. A number of sculptures depicting this theme, to be dated from the Gupta to the medieval period, have been found in different parts of India. The Badami Ardhanārīśvara stone panel is a good representative of such figures. Particular interest attaches to an image of Śiva and Pārvatī from Bhita, assigned to the Gupta age, showing the god and the goddess seated side by side on a throne.[13] The Śiva-Pārvatī image from Kosam, also assigned to the Gupta age, and an earlier sandstone relief of the same god and goddess, now preserved in the Mathura museum, deserve special mention in the connection. The Kosam stone image inscription of Bhīmavarman stands on a broken vase which constitutes a standing group of Śiva-Pārvatī sculpture.[14] Pārvatī or Umā also appears in a terracotta plaque of the late Gupta period found among the ruins of an ancient Śiva temple of Ahicchatra.[15] Two pillars from Chandimau, belonging to the Gupta period, depict in each the image of Śiva and Pārvatī and the Kirātārjunīya story respectively.[16] The cites of Kosam also yield several terracotta reliefs of Śiva and Pārvatī.

The relation between Śiva and Devī became more intimate in the Gupta age, as is suggested by the evidence of the earlier Purāṇas. The story of Dakṣa's sacrifice must serve as a good example. We have already seen that the *Mahābhārata* contains a Dakṣa-*yajña* story, according to which Śiva and Devī, not being invited at the sacrifice of Dakṣa, due to the ignorance of the latter of Śiva's existence, destroyed in anger the sacrificial materials through their agents Vīrabhadra and Mahākālī, which brought Dakṣa to his senses, who thereafter propitiated Śiva and was taught by the latter the mysteries of his cult. This story has further been developed in the Purāṇas. The *Vāyu Purāṇa*,[17] composed between the third and the fifth centuries AD, holds that Satī, the oldest of the eight daughters of Dakṣa, was married to Śiva, but the latter did never care to salute his father-in-law or conceal his roughness. Satī's death and the destruction of Dakṣa's sacrifice are described in the *Vāyu Purāṇa* in two episodes. The first says that Satī, the wife of Śiva, having received a cool reception from her father became very much shocked and destroyed her body whereupon Śiva cursed Dakṣa. On the other hand, Satī was reborn as Umā in the house of Himalaya and was married to Śiva. The second story describes the event of Dakṣa's sacrifice which occurred when the Devī was no longer the daughter of Dakṣa. The *Matsya Purāṇa*[18] composed about the seventh century AD, says that Rudra or Śiva was not invited because Dakṣa thought him a malevolent spirit unworthy of a rank among gods. Further developments of the story of Dakṣa's sacrifice, found in subsequent Purāṇic literature, will be discussed later. The Dakṣa-*yajña* story, as enumerated in the earlier Purāṇas, points to the alliance of the Female Principle with Śiva, and it is not difficult to determine the process of such an alliance. While in the *Mahābhārata* the goddess appears indifferently as the wife of Nārāyaṇa and of Śiva, her later associations became increasingly Śaivite.

In the *Viṣṇu Purāṇa* (fourth century AD) the Female Principle is regarded as Mahālakṣmī who is the consort of Viṣṇu. Even there are passages in the *Mārkaṇḍeya Purāṇa* which describe the goddess as Viṣṇumāyā, the *śakti* or energy of Viṣṇu, and Nārāyaṇī, the wife of Nārāyaṇa. In spite of all this, Vaiṣṇavism was not very successful in bringing Śāktism in close alliance with it. This was due to the fact that Vaiṣṇavism failed to embrace within itself all the tribal elements associated with the Mother Goddess cult which Śaivism could do on account of its popular character. The fearful forms of the goddess, the cults of blood and wine, the rituals of sex, and many other allied practices did not suit the Vaiṣṇavite religious approach, and hence they were satiated only with the primary material of her composition, her feminine nature and the patent provision of maintenance proceeding from her.

VI

So long we have dealt with that which may be called 'dependent Śāktism', i.e. the cult of the Female Principle under the garb of Vaiṣṇavism, Śaivism, Buddhism and Jainism. But 'independent Śāktism' had already made its appearance in the Gupta age. The Śākta principles find expression in the Devīmāhātmya section of the *Mārkaṇḍeya Purāṇa* (composed between the third and fifth centuries AD) in which the goddess is invoked thus:

> Thou art the cause of all the worlds. Though characterised by three qualities even by Hari, Hara and other gods thou art incomprehensible. Thou art the resort of all; thou art this entire world which is composed of parts. Thou verily art the sublime original nature untransformed.... Thou art Medhā, O goddess; thou hast comprehended the essence of all scriptures. Thou art Durgā, the boat to cross the ocean of existence, devoid of attachments. Thou art Śrī who has her dominion in the heart of the enemy of Kaiṭabha. Thou indeed art Gaurī who has fixed her dwelling in that of the moon-crested god.[19]

The Śākta Devī in her developed form absorbed within herself innumerable goddesses representing different streams. The invocation, quoted above, mentions a few goddesses, who stand by themselves as independent deities, though the poet knew them only as forms of the great goddess unto whom they were absorbed. In the concluding portion of the Devīmāhātmya of the *Mārkaṇḍeya Purāṇa* the Devī assures the gods by granting them the boon that she will always become incarnate and deliver the whole world whenever it is oppressed by the demons. In the Vaivasvata-manvantara, when the demons Śumbha and Niśumbha will become too powerful, she, born as the offspring of Yaśodā and dwelling in the Vindhyas will destroy them both. Again, having become incarnate in the very horrible form of Raktadantikā she will slay and devour the demons of the Vipracitti lineage and her teeth will become red, like the inside of a pomegranate. And again, after a period of a hundred years during a drought she will appear as Śatākṣī at the invocation of the sages. Then she will nourish the whole world with the life-sustaining vegetables, which will grow out of her own body, and thus will be famous as Śākambharī. At that time she will slay the great Asura named Durgama and become famous as Durgā. And again, assuming the terrible form of Bhīmādevī she will kill the Rākṣasas on the Mount Himavat. When the demon Āruṇākṣa will become a terror in the three worlds, she will slay him as Bhrāmarī.[20]

Gaurī, Śatākṣī, Śākambharī, etc. of the above list were undoubtedly developed forms of rudimentary Earth and Corn Mothers. In Rajasthan, Gaurī or Īśānī is the Corn Mother whose cult resembles that of Isis in Egypt, Demeter in Greece and Ceres in Rome.[21] She is also called Vāsantī since her festivals are held in spring. A prototype of the Earth Goddess Śākambharī is found in a terracotta seal from Harappa in which the goddess is shown upside down with her legs wide apart and a plant issuing from her womb. A terracotta relief of the early Gupta age, found by Marshall from the ruins of Bhita, also shows a nude female figure, upside down with legs wide apart, and with a lotus issuing out of her neck instead of her womb. Śākambharī is also known as Annadā or Annapūrṇā, the goddess who bestows food to all. Śākambharī is still worshipped in a *pīṭha* of the same name near Saharanpur. She is the presiding goddess of the Sambhar lake and tutelary deity of the Cauhans. A reference to this goddess and her resort is found in the *Mahābhārata*.[22] Raktadantikā, the goddess who is red all through according to the *Mūrtirahasya* also called Raktacāmuṇḍā and Yogeśvarī,[23] is definitely a survival of the primitive Mother Goddess representing the age when red was considered to be the symbol of new life.[24] Bhīmādevī was an important goddess of north-western India whose shrine at Shahbazgarhi was visited by Hiuen Tsang in the seventh century.

> About 50 *li* (nearly 8 miles) to the north-east of Palusha was a great mountain which had a likeness of Maheśvara's spouse Bhīmādevī of dark blue stone. According to the local accounts this was a

natural image of the goddess; it exhibited prodigies and was a great resort of devotees from all parts of India; to true believers, who after fasting seven days prayed to her, the goddess sometimes showed herself and answered prayers. At the foot of the mountain was a temple dedicated to Maheśvaradeva in which the ash-smearing *tīrthikas* performed much worship.[25]

The *Mahābhārata*, as we have seen above, refers to the Yonikuṇḍas at Bhīmāsthāna (place sacred to the goddess Bhīmā) near the Pañcanada (Punjab). Likewise the goddess Bhrāmarī is worshipped in Kashmir as Bhramaravāsanī.[26] A goddess named Bhramarāmma is popular in the south.

The second stream leading to the monotheistic Śāktism is represented by the Umā-Pārvatī group which developed under the garb of Śaivism. Umā of the *Kena Upaniṣad* and that of the *Kumārasambhava* or the Purāṇas are not the same. The epithet Haimavatī (daughter of Himavat) was responsible for her identification with Pārvatī and Durgā. The latter, as we have previously remarked, was associated with inaccessible regions, and it is also possible that she was originally conceived as the protectress of forts (*durga*). A fanciful explanation of Durgā was, however, invented on etymological ground by associating her with the slaying of a demon called Durgama. Whether a demon-slayer or saviour, Durgā is equipped with arms, a feature which is totally absent in the conception of Pārvatī-Umā who is extremely homely as the daughter of Himavat, wife of Śiva, mother of Kumāra. It is interesting to note that of the earlier Purāṇas the *Vāyu, Brahmāṇḍa* and *Matsya* and of the later the *Kūrma, Śiva, Garuḍa, Brahma,* etc. do not insist upon the demon-slaying conception of the goddess and her terrible forms. This also holds good in the case of Kālidāsa's *Kumārasambhava.* It is in the *Mārkaṇḍeya* and *Vāmana* Purāṇas, and also in the later Devī-oriented Purāṇas that we have her terrible demon-slayer form which is represented by Caṇḍikā or Kauśīkī and further developed by Kālī. The goddess Kauśīkī was probably associated with the Kuśika tribes, and later came to be identified with Caṇḍikā. According to the Devīmāhātmya of the *Mārkaṇḍeya Purāṇa,* Kauśikī emerged from the muscles of Pārvatī, and the latter turned black and became known as Kālikā dwelling in the Himalayas. According to another conception of the same text, Kālī emerged from the forehead of Caṇḍikā with the purpose of killing the demons Caṇḍa and Muṇḍa and having accomplished the task she got the epithet Cāmuṇḍā. From a grammatical point of view, however, Cāmuṇḍā cannot be derived from Caṇḍa-Muṇḍa, and hence Cāmuṇḍā and Kālī were different goddesses. Kālī is referred to in the *Raghuvaṃśa*[27] and in the *Kumārasambhava*[28] she is described as a Divine Mother.

Kauśikī, Caṇḍikā, Kālī, etc. were evidently adopted in the Śākta pantheon from the surviving tribal divinities. Kālī in Kālañjara mountain, Caṇḍikā in Makarandaka and Vindhyavāsinī in the Vindhyas are mentioned in the *Matsya Purāṇa*[29] as the different manifestations of the supreme goddess, and her particular interest for wine and meat is found in the *Viṣṇu Purāṇa.*[30] Aparṇā, a name by which Kālī is sometimes identified, signifies a deity 'without her leaf-cloth'. This naked goddesses must have originally been worshipped by a tribe such as the Nagna-Śabaras (the naked Śabaras) of the *Bṛhatsaṃhitā,* just as the Buddhist deity Parṇaśabarī was undoubtedly associated with the Parṇa-Śabaras (the leaf-clad Śabaras) of the same work. Bāṇabhaṭṭa, in whose time (seventh century AD) Śāktism became more or less an established religion, as is proved by his own poetry on the goddess, mentions in his *Kādambarī* the goddess cult of the wild Śabaras and the cruel rites involved therein. Also in his *Harṣacarita* he refers to the destructive character of the goddess. In Subandhu's *Vāsavadattā* the blood-thirsty goddess Kātyāyanī or Bhagavatī of Kusumapura is mentioned. The *Gauḍavaha*[31] of Vākpati, composed about AD 725, describes a vivid picture of the aweful atmosphere of the temple of Vindhyavāsinī, the goddess who was worshipped by the Śabaras with human sacrifice. It also deals with the slaying of the buffalo-demon, the association of the goddess with the peacocks and her blood-thirsty character. In the *Mālatīmādhava* of Bhavabhūti, we find that near Padmāvatī there was a temple of the goddess Cāmuṇḍā who was worshipped with regular human sacrifices. Aghoraghaṇṭa, a Kāpālika, kidnapped the heroine with a view to sacrifice her at the altar of the goddess.[32] This eighth century authority not only testifies to the prevalence of human sacrifice before the goddess, but also to the interesting fact that the Kāpālikas were followers of the goddess cult. In the *Mattavilāsa-prahasana* (attributed to Pallava Mahendravarman I *c.* AD 600-685) detailed account of the Kāpālikas and their cults are described.

VII

The Purāṇas, as we have them now, were written at different periods.

Of the earlier Purāṇas, the *Vāyu, Brahmāṇḍa, Viṣṇu* and *Bhāgavata* mention the Guptas among the royal dynasties, and hence they cannot be regarded as finally compiled before the fourth century AD. The *Vāyu Purāṇa* is mentioned in the *Harṣacarita* and was therefore earlier than the seventh century AD. The same holds good in the case of the *Mārkaṇḍeya Purāṇa,* because it is difficult to ignore the influence of its Devīmāhātmya section upon Bāṇa's *Caṇḍīśataka* and Bhavabhūti's *Mālatīmādhava.* However, for the present work, we are inclined to follow the chronology suggested by Prof. R.C. Hazra according to which principal portions of the *Mārkaṇḍeya, Brahmāṇḍa, Vayu* and *Viṣṇu* Purāṇas were composed before the fifth century AD, those of the *Bhāgavata* within the sixth century and of the *Matsya* between the sixth and seventh centuries.

In the *Mārkaṇḍeya Purāṇa,* the Devī is primarily conceived as the war-goddess who not only confers victory and success on her worshippers in the battlefield but also actually participates in the war to deliver the world whenever it is oppressed by the demons. According to the Devīmāhātmya section of the said Purāṇa, the gods oppressed by the demons Śumbha and Niśumbha, went to the Himalayas and worshipped the goddess, whereupon Śivā or Kauśikī appeared from the *kośa* (frame or muscle) of Pārvatī and said that it was she whom the gods were invoking for killing the demons. This Kauśikī is also identified with Kātyāyanī, Vindhyavāsinī, Caṇḍikā and Nandā. The name Kauśikī, as we have already pointed out, was connected with the Kuśika tribe, and the legend of her coming out from the *kośa* of Pārvatī was evidently invented to rationalise the role of the tribal goddess into the framework of the Śākta conception of the Devī. The same also held good in the case of Kātyāyanī, who probably belonged to the Kātya tribe, but it is stated that a mass of energy produced from the flames of the gods' anger caused by the misdeeds of Mahiṣāsura, was thrown into the hermitage of the sage Kātyāyana who nourished it to create the goddess. The goddess thus produced came to be known as Kātyāyanī whom Śiva gave his trident, Viṣṇu his disc, Varuṇa his conch, Agni his dart, Yama iron rod, Vāyu his bow, Sūrya his quiver and arrows, Indra his thunderbolt, Kubera his mace, Brahmā his rosary and pot, Kāla his sword, Viśvakarmā his sword, Himavān his lion, and other gods their various weapons. Vindhyavāsinī, as the name implies, was a regional deity who came to be identified with Caṇḍikā, Kauśikī and Kātyāyanī, and especially with Nandā, the offspring of Yaśodā in the house of Nandagopa, who was made responsible for the slaying of Śumbha and Niśumbha.

Of all the major achievements of the Devī, the story of her fight with Mahiṣāsura became most popular as is proved by numerous Mahiṣamardinī sculptures. The Mahiṣāsura episode of the Devī-māhātmya suggests in itself a nice outline of the Śākta conception of the Devī as the embodiment of an all-pervading power. The gods being defeated and driven out of the heaven by Mahiṣāsura hastened for the protection of Viṣṇu and Śiva. Having heard their grievances, Viṣṇu, Śiva, and other gods emitted flames of anger from their eyes, and this was transformed into a mass of intense energy which, shortly afterwards, took the shape of an exquisite lady, called Caṇḍikā, whose face was made by Śiva's energy, hair by Yama's, arms by Viṣṇu's, breasts by Moon's, waist by Indra's, legs by Varuṇa's, hips by the earth's, feet by Brahmā's, toes by Sun's, hands and fingers by the Vasu's, nose by Kubera's, teeth by Prajāpati's, eyes by Agni's, and ears by Vāyu's. This conception of the goddess, her creation from the energy of all the gods, became popular with the Śāktas, and it was further elaborated in the later Purāṇas.

The Mātṛkās or Divine Mothers play a very important role in the Devī legends. In the *Mahābhārata* we come across numerous Mātṛkās associated with Skanda,[33] and they had also access in Jainism and other religious systems. In the Purāṇas, they are regarded as the offshoots of the goddess Kauśikī or Caṇḍikā, some of them like Vaiṣṇavī, Kālikā, etc. often identified with the Devī herself. There are different versions of the origin of the Mātṛkās in the Purāṇas. (1) When Śiva's spear pierced the heart of the demon Andhaka, each drop of the latter's blood created a demon. This enraged Śiva and from his body emerged the goddess Yogeśvarī, and at the same time Vaiṣṇavī, Brahmāṇī, Kaumārī, Indrāṇī, Māheśvarī, Cāmuṇḍā and Vārāhī appeared from the bodies of Viṣṇu, Brahmā, Kumāra, Indra, Maheśvara, Yama and Varāha respectively. They drank and drained all the blood that fell from Andhaka's body and the purpose of the gods was served. (2) When the Asura Śumbha sent Raktabīja to fight against the Devī, the latter uttered a fearful war-cry when Brahmāṇī, Māheśvarī, Vaiṣṇavī, Kaumārī, Vārāhī and Nārasiṃhī emerged out of her mouth. The seventh, viz. Caṇḍamārī or Cāmuṇḍā had already sprung from the Devī's body when the latter was engaged in war with Ruru, a general of Śumbha, and each drop of blood that fell from the body of Raktabīja was drunk by Cāmuṇḍā alone.[34]

VIII

The *Bṛhatsaṃhitā*[35] refers to the worship of the Divine Mothers by the *mātṛ-maṇḍala-vidaḥ* or *maṇḍala-kramavidaḥ*. The first means those who know fully the circle of the Divine Mothers. As to the second, the word *krama* means 'custom or rule sanctioned by tradition'. The word *maṇḍala* has different meanings—'the magic circle', 'group' etc. A passage, *mātṛnām loka-matṛnām maṇḍalam,* occurs in a sixth century inscription from Udayagiri in Jhansi district, U.P. It records the construction of a temple of the Divine Mothers.[36] The *mātṛmaṇḍala* referred to in this inscription recalls the *mātṛgaṇa* or the 'group of Divine Mothers' mentioned in the records of the early Kadamba kings.[37] These rulers claimed to have been favoured by Kārttikeya and the Divine Mothers. The early Cālukyas of Badami are stated to have been nourished by the Seven Mothers described as *sapta-loka-mātṛ,* often interpreted as 'the Seven Mothers of Mankind' though its real meaning seems to be 'the Mothers of the Seven Worlds'.[38] The reference in all these cases seem to be the collective worship of the Divine Mothers regarded as seven in number and probably known as the Circle of Seven.

It seems therefore that in different parts of the country, at least in the age of the Guptas, the Great Goddess was worshipped in her individual aspects as well as collectively in a Circle of Seven. The Bihar Stone Pillar inscription of Skandagupta mentions the Divine Mothers, the Mātṛs.[39] We have already had occasion to refer to the Gangadhar stone inscription of Viśvavarman[40] which refers to the temple of Divine Mothers as the terrible abode full of Ḍākinīs or female ghouls and the goddesses themselves are represented as uttering loud and tremendous shouts of joy and stirring up the very oceans with the winds rising from the *tantra* or magical rites. The Deogarh rock inscription of about the sixth century AD refers to another early temple of the Divine Mothers.[41] The Aulikara inscription of AD 423 records the construction and consecration of a temple of the Divine Mothers.[42]

Gaurī is mentioned in the Sārnāth Stone inscription of Prakaṭāditya[43] while the Mandasore Stone Pillar inscription of Yaśodharman[44] records Kṣitidharatanayā which evidently refers to Umā or Pārvatī. The Khoh Copperplate inscription of Samkṣobha[45] states that at the request of a certain person named Coḍugomin of the village of Opani, the king installed a temple for the goddess Piṣṭapuri and made an endowment for its maintenance. This goddess also occurs in two copperplates of Sarvanātha.[46] The Nāgārjuni Hill Cave inscription of the Maukhari chief Anantavarman records the installation in the cave of an image representing Śiva in the form of Bhūtapati and his wife Pārvatī under the name of Devī. Another Nāgārjuni Hill Cave inscription of the same king refers to the installation of an image of the goddess Pārvatī, under the name of Kātyāyanī, and also the grant of a village to the same goddess under the name of Bhavānī. This inscription also stresses upon the Mahiṣamardinī form of the goddess.[47] A stanza in adoration of the same form of the goddess is found at the beginning of an inscription from the Bhramaramātā temple near Choti Sadri not far from the Neemuch station on the Ajmer-Khandwa railway line.[48] The epigraph records the construction and consecration a temple of the Devī in AD 491. The Kalahandi Copperplate grant of Tuṣṭikera[49] (5th or 6th century AD) refers to the cults of Stambheśvarī, the family-goddess of the Śulkis.

IX

It is difficult to identify the goddess depicted on the Gupta coins.[50] More suggestive are the numerous terracotta seals, mostly belonging to the early and late Gupta period. Durgā and Śiva are depicted on a few seals from Bhita.[51] The same site yields the seals of Śivamagha and Bhīmasena in which a female figure, probably Durgā, appears by the side of a bull. The goddess facing a lion found on many seals hailing from Bhita and Basarh can only be explained in terms of the goddess Durgā. Several Rājghāt seals bear on them interesting figures of a goddess. An oval seal of sun-burnt clay bears a two-armed goddess, and the name of the deity, written below in Gupta characters, is Durggah (Durgā).

Some of the finest sculptures of the Gupta and later periods, as we have seen above, represent Vaiṣṇava, Śaiva, Buddhist and Jain goddess. Images of popular river goddess like Gaṅgā, Yamunā, Sarasvatī, etc., are also met with.[52] But it was the Mahiṣamardinī form that became most popular. A very important Gupta image is found in a relief carved on the facade of a cave at Udayagiri near Bhilsa, Madhya Pradesh, which shows the goddess killing Mahiṣāsura, the buffalo-demon. Here the goddess is twelve-armed, and the sculpture can be referred to the beginning of the fifth century AD. A terracotta plaque of Mahiṣamardinī from Bhadrakālī in the Ganganagar district of Rajasthan, belonging to the early Gupta period, shows the Devī in the act of killing the buffalo-demon with a *triśūla* which she holds in her upper right hand. The upper left hand is broken. With the lower left hand she holds the head of the buffalo demon. There is no shield or lion. The goddess in the act of killing rides on the buffalo-demon.[53] This plaque is now in the Bikaner Museum. In a beautiful plaque of the Amber Museum, the goddess holds a rectangular shield in her upper left hand and a *vajra* in the upper right. With her lower left hand she holds the tongue of the buffalo-demon. There is also a small lion at the foot of the goddess. In another of the same museum, the buffalo-demon is shown between the legs of the goddess who is seen pressing the horns of the buffalo.[54]

The structural temple of the goddess Durgā at Aihole was erected by the Cālukya kings who reigned between AD 550 and 642. The Aihole relief shows the eight-armed goddess piercing the upturned neck of the buffalo-demon. The chief Cālukya monument is the series of the cave temples of Badami, the pillared balcony of which give some of the finest figures of the goddess in her different forms. The monumental relief of Mahiṣamardinī in the Rāmeśvara cave at Ellora probably belongs to *c.* AD 650. The same cave contains figures of Pārvatī and the Saptamātṛkā which also occur in other caves. One of the most beautiful and delightful Pallava specimen is the Mahiṣamardinī of Mamallapuram, assigned to the seventh century AD, which shows the goddess Durgā mounted on the lion, hands armed with bow, sword, club, conch, axe, gong, etc., the demon represented with the head of a buffalo holding a club and a sword.

The form of Durgā standing on the severed head of a buffalo is described in the *Śilappadikāram*[55] while in the story of Sakkravāḷakkoṭṭam in the *Maṇimekalai* we hear a temple of Durgā. From this it appears that even in the pre-Pallava days temples for Durgā were built. Of the Pallava monuments, the Kodikālmaṇḍapam at Mahābalipuram and the Yāli-maṇḍapam at Saluvankuppam appear to be intended for Durgā as may be gleaned from the bas-relief sculptures of the *dvārapālikās* flanking on the shrine entrances in the case of the first and from the facade of the cave in that of the second. That the Draupadī-ratha was originally intended for Durgā is evident from her carved image in the hind wall of the shrine. Besides her own temples, Pallava sculptures of Durgā are found in the rock-cut caves. The Pallava Durgā does not reveal any iconographic rigidity, standing either on the severed head of a buffalo as at Singavaram, the Ādivarāha and Trimūrti caves or simply on a *padmapīṭha*, as in the Varāhamaṇḍapa and in the hind wall of the shrine in the Draupadī-ratha.

X

The wide distribution of the Mahiṣamardinī sculptures, the popularity of the concept of the goddess slaying the demons, must have a social significance. While dealing with the political, economic and social changes in India before and during the time of the Guptas, we have seen that from about the beginning of the Christian era, a plural society based on functional interdependence came into existence with the increase of the state power, warfare for wealth, commercial enterprises, agricultural development, specialisations in the field of occupations, detribalisation and other socio-economic factors. While these factors led to a general economic progress and social mobility conducive to multifarious activities in different walks of life, they could not remove oppression and injustice, social and economic inequalities, the tensions and frustrations of the common men, the toiling masses who were really responsible for the production of social wealth, the benefit of which was enjoyed only by the ruling class and the upper echelon of society. The Devī's fight with the demons, symbolising the ultimate triumph of good over evil, must have provided the toiling masses with the illusion of a cherished reality, when the existing reality went against their hopes and aspirations. Though gods like Viṣṇu or Śiva are also said to have killed many demons to save the world from oppression and injustice, their legends failed to attract popular imagination. But in the case of the exploits of the Devī, the situation was different, because of the closest association of the Mother Goddess with the common people, with the facts of their daily life, in her capacity of being the goddess of vegetation and fertility, the producer of life and the protectress of the children, the healer of diseases, the mistress of cattle, the guardian of forests and wild life, the bestower of success and fortune and the trouble-shooter of all types. The association of the goddess with the hopes and aspirations of the common people since time immemorial must have given a new dimension to the Purāṇic Devī legends.

References

1. Winternitz, *HIL*, I.529.
2. *JI*, 24 ff.
3. Gray's tr., 97.
4. Canto X.
5. *CII*, III.56.
6. Ibid., 286.
7. Ibid., 200-208.
8. *ASIAR*, 1903-4, 107 ff; 1911-12, 52 ff; 1913-14, 129 ff; *MASI*, no. 66; Banerjea, *DHI*, 194 ff.
9. *EI*, XII.13.
10. V.24.
11. IV.27.33.
12. *CII*, III.72.
13. *ASIAR*, 1911-12, 76.
14. *CII*, III, 266.
15. Banerjea, *DHI*, 471.
16. *ASIAR*, 1911-12, 161 ff.
17. XXX.38-47.
18. XIII.12-15.
19. Pargiter's tr.
20. Cf. *Vāmana Pu*, LVI.67-70.
21. Tod, *AAR*, I.570 ff. A detailed account of the Earth and Corn Mothers of India is given in my *IMG*, 18-32.
22. III.84.
23. *Mālatīmādhava*, V; *Matsya Pu*, CCLXI.33-37; *Varāha Pu*, XCVI.
24. For the symbolism of red see my *IMG*, 17-18; *IPR*, 18, 98-99.
25. Watters, *YCTI*, I.221.
26. *Rājataraṅgiṇī*, III.394-431.
27. XI.15.
28. VII.39.
29. XIII.32ff.
30. V.2.84.
31. 285-347.
32. Act V.
33. *Supra.*
34. *Matsya*, CLXXIX, *Devī M*, VIII.12-21.
35. LX.19.
36. *IA*, VI.27.
37. *IA*, VII.74.164; XIII.138.
38. Cf. Sircar, *SS*, 239-40.
39. *CII*, III.49.
40. *CII*, 78.
41. *EI*, XVIII, 126 ff.
42. Sircar, *SI*, 284 ff.
43. *CII*, III.286.
44. Ibid., 142, 150; *IA*, XVIII.219, XX.188.
45. *CII*, III.112

46. Ibid., 132, 138.
47. Ibid., 225-28.
48. *EI*, XXX.120 ff.
49. Ibid., 274-78; *JKHRS*, II.107-10.
50. See Altekar, *CIG*, IV.31.
51. *ASIAR*, 1911-12, 51.
52. Zimmer, *AIA*, I.83.
53. *Lalita Kalā*, no. 8, pl. XXVI, 23.
54. See especially *Artibus Asiae*, XXI (2), 123-30.
55. XX.34-35.

5

The Period of Śākta Expansion (AD 700-1000)

The new social and economic set up of the Gupta age changed radically the whole religious outlook of India. The ceremonial worship of the images of Viṣṇu, Śiva and the Buddhist and Jain deities, along with their consorts, installed in numerous temples of magnificent proportions, became a very important feature of religious life, the installation of such temples and images being evidently due to the social surplus introduced by the new economic conditions. Aspects of the old Vedic religion were retained, but they were mostly used in a formal way, each system claiming a Vedic origin for the purpose of respectability. Some of the Śrauta and Gṛhya rites, as also the Vedic sacraments were, however, maintained. The Aśvamedha sacrifice was still popular among the kings. Even kings of the remote north-eastern region are said to have performed the Aśvamedha sacrifice as is evident from the inscriptions of Assam. Buddhism changed qualitatively from the pristine simplicity of an austere moral code to the most complex system of Mahāyāna. The progress of Jainism was slow in the process of transformation, while Vaiṣṇavism and Śaivism came in closer connection which was marked by the attempt to establish the unity of Viṣṇu and Śiva and to combine in a single iconographic motif the attributes of different Vaiṣṇavite and Śaivite deities. To Viṣṇu and Śiva was added Brahmā of the older pantheon, and they formed the official trinity. The influence of the cult of the Female Principle placed goddesses by the side of the gods of all systems as their consorts and symbols of their energy or *śakti.* But the entire popular emotion centering round the Female Principle was not exhausted. So need was felt for a new system, entirely female dominated, a system in which even the great gods like Viṣṇu or Śiva would remain subordinate to the goddess. This new system containing vestiges of hoary antiquity, varieties of rural and tribal cults and rituals and strengthened by new-fangled ideas of different ages, came to be known as Śāktism.

II

The crisis of the decline and fall of the Gupta empire made India once again divided into a number of independent states. In the seventh century Harṣavardhana was able to consolidate his power in northern India on the ruins of the Gupta empire, but the focal point of political history had already been shifted to the Deccan and South India where the Cālukyas and the Pallavas could establish powerful kingdoms of long duration. The defeat of Harṣa by the Cālukya king Pulakeśin was not merely a military defeat. It marked not only the end of Northern supremacy over the South but also the beginning of Southern supremacy over the North. Henceforth we have a series of Southern influx towards the North, political as well as cultural. From the seventh century onwards, religious movements of the South began to exert tremendous influence on the North. The prosperity of the South, as is revealed by her architectural greatness, was evidently due to the inter-oceanic trade of which the North was deprived. The disintegration and fall of the Roman empire acted severely upon the overland trade routes connecting north India with Rome. This natural flow of foreign trade when thus ceased abruptly, the North felt a grave economic crisis, ultimately leading to her political and cultural decline.

The middle of the eighth century AD saw the rise of three powerful dynasties—the Gurjara-Pratihāras in Western India, the Pālas in Eastern India and the Rāṣṭrakūṭas in the Deccan and South India. The Pratihāras derived their economic strength from the naval trade of the Arabian Sea and the Pālas from that of the Bay of Bengal. The economic and cultural relation with south-east Asia developed during this period. The Rāṣṭrakūṭas utilised both the Arabian Sea and the Bay of Bengal for the same purpose. That is why the Rāṣṭrakuṭas fought successfully not only with the Pallavas and other powers of the South Indian Peninsula and advanced even as far as Ramesvaram, but at the same time they defeated the Pratihāra rulers Vatsarāja and Nāgabhaṭa and the Pāla king Dharmapāla. Rāṣṭrakūṭa Dhruva carried his victorious campaign as far as the Doab between the Gaṅgā and the Yamunā and his son Govinda III overran the whole country up to the Himalayas. The South thus emerged effectively in the political life of the country, as it has already emerged in its religious and cultural life.

III

While the Gupta and post-Gupta ages were characterised by an apparently sophisticated approach towards religious beliefs and practices, as was manifested by a process of institutionalism in the way of establishing organisations, monastic or otherwise, erecting temples and buildings of gigantic structures, constructing of a bewildering variety of images and receiving generous endowments from the princes and the nobility, the concept of a non-formal and personal approach towards the divine was gaining ground among the masses. The Supreme Being whether approached in the first instance as Viṣṇu or Śiva or Śakti, was a beloved to be wooed with love and devotion. The concept was not new; it lay at the root of all theistic systems. However, this non-formal approach had been replaced by an elaborate growth of institutionalism, organised priesthood, rigid codification and sectarianism. But such overgrowths did not bother the people at large. To them a visit to the temple, performance of rites, offering a fee for worship, pilgrimage, and other allied religious duties were routine acts which thus believed would earn for them some spiritual dividend. All these they learnt from the recitals of the Epics and the Purāṇas which had imprinted in their minds the utility and sanctity of the personal and social codes prescribed by the Dharmaśāstras on the one hand, and the efficacy of the doctrine of *bhakti* on the other. But in the latter case there had always been an inconsistency, because pure *bhakti* implied sharp criticism and rejection of all external formalities in regard to religious practices and spiritual quests.

The concept of pure *bhakti* in the form of the experience of the Supreme Being, of any sect or cult, was revived by the Śaiva Nayanārs and the Vaiṣṇava Āḷvārs of South India. The collection of their priceless legacy of devotional poetry was possible because of the labour of the Śaiva saint Nāmbi-Āṇḍār-Nambi and the Vaiṣṇava saint Śrī Nāthamuni. Among the Śaiva Nāyanārs, Tirumular flourished in the sixth century AD. Appār, Sambandar and Māṇikkavacagar belonged to the seventh century while Sundarar to the first quarter of the eighth century. Their poems may be described as the quintessence of later Tamil Śaivism. The Vaiṣṇava Āḷvars flourished in the period between AD 500 and 800. The first three Āḷvars—Poykai, Bhūtattar and Periāḷvar—have contributed one hundred stanzas each in *venba* in praise of Tirumal. The fourth was Tirumaḷisai who sang of single-minded devotion, his chosen deity being Nārāyaṇa. Of the five Āḷvars of the second group Nammāḷvar is said to have poured the cream of the Vedas into his songs. Madhurakavi, Periyāḷvar, and the latter's daughter Āṇḍal were great composers. Āṇḍal in her poems saw herself as a *gopī* of Kṛṣṇa. Other celebrated Āḷvar poets were Kulaśekhara, Tiruppan, Toṇḍaradippodi and Tirumangai. Because of the Āḷvars, their successors, the famous Vaiṣṇava *ācāryas* of the south, were able to add new dimensions to later Vaiṣṇavism.

The contribution of the South to the integration of Śāktism was also by no means insignificant. Vedic and Āgamic ideas altered the old forms of worship in the Tamil country during the early centuries of the Christian era. Koṛṛavai, the Tamil goddess of war and victory, was easily identified with Durgā. The *Śilappadikaram* describes her as the three-eyed goddess whose feet rest upon the severed head of Mahiṣāsura. The *Maṇimekalai* refers to her worship with Tantric *mantras* by priests garbed as Bhairavas. The association of Durgā with the mercantile communities is attested by the fact that the members of the famous trading corporation known as the 'Nānādesíyatiśai-āyirattu-aiñ-ñūrruvar' were worshippers of Durgā in whose honour they erected temples in different parts of the Deccan and South India. In one such temple she is called Aiyāpolil Parameśvarī—the Parameśvarī of Aihole. To the Tamil members of this corporation Durgā was *kendaḷi*, a Tamil word meaning the Divine Principle, beyond form and name and transcending all manifestations. Durgā was also identified with the Bhagavatī of Kerala and the eternal virgin enshrined in Kanyākumārī. She was invoked in one or other of her nine forms (Navadurgā) or as Bhadrakālī. The Tamil tradition also associates her with Sarasvatī or Vāc, Cintā Devī and Kalaimagal, as also with Śrī and Lakṣmī. Thus in Durgā the devotee visualised the triple aspects of power, beneficence and wisdom. The larger temples of the Pallava and early Cola periods had shrines dedicated to the Sapta Mātṛkā or the Seven Mothers and Jyeṣṭhā.

From the earliest period the South had a rich tradition of the cult of the Village Mothers concerned with facts of daily life. We have already had the occasion to refer to these goddesses who were much dreaded and propitiated to ward off calamities. There were also other categories of the goddesses. Draupadī, for example, was a common deity of South India. A whole canto of the *Śilappadikāram* has for its theme the deification of Kannaki, the heroine of the great epic. These deities either in their individual capacity or in their collective spirit were identified with the Mātṛkās and other Purāṇic goddesses and came to be looked upon as representing the parts (*aṃśa*), the portion of parts (*kalā*), and the fragments of the portion of parts (*kalāṃśa*) of the Great Goddess symbolising the primordial energy. Some of the local goddesses such as Śrī Mīnākṣī of Madura, whose local legends contain influence of the *Sīlappadikāram* story and the Kannaki cult, or Śrī Kāmākṣī of Kanchipuram in whose praise Mūkakavi composed five hundred verses were identified with the Great Goddess herself.

The idea that Śakti is a not different from Śiva and that they present the two aspects of the same reality got a solid theoretical foundation in the South. Śiva or Kāmeśvara, is *prakāśa* or subjective illumination while Śakti, known as Kāmeśvarī, Śivakāmā, Kāmakoṭi, Lalitā and Tripurasundarī, is *vimarśa* or Śiva's objective experience of himself. The six forms of *Saguṇa* worship, said to have been approved and propagated by Śaṅkara, included the worship of the Devī. At Śringeri the presiding deity is Sāradā who is enthroned on a Śrīcakra, symbolising the highest knowledge, the knowledge of the self. Śrīcakra is the symbol of the universe, both macrocosm and microcosm, and its divine cause. There are in it two sets of triangles, one set composed of four male or Śiva triangles and the other of five female or Śakti triangles. These nine *cakras* are ruled over by Yoginīs presiding over forms of mind, sense and matter. Some of the holy shrines of the Tamil country such as Tiruvarur, Kanchi, Jambukeśvaram. Madura, Avadaiyarkovil and so forth symbolically represent these *cakras*. Later Vedāntists explain how the attributes of Brahman, through the play of its inherent Māyā assumed two froms—*dharma* and *dharmin*. While *dharmin* is static, *dharma* manifests itself both as male and female; and this manifestation is the material cause of the universe. Through this doctrine they emphasised the identity of Viṣṇu and his Śakti or Śiva and his Śakti which many centuries earlier had found expression in the hymns of the early Āḷvars and Nāyanars and in the iconography of the seventh century.[1]

IV

"The second half of the seventh and the first half of the eighth century AD," says Winternitz,[2] "was a period of lively philosophical disputes. Kumārila, the great Mīmāṃsā philosopher and representative of Brahmanical orthodoxy, attacked the Buddhist and Jinistic logicians, including among the last-named the prominent teachers Samantabhadra and Akalaṅka, whilst Prabhacandra and Vidyānanda defended their co-religionists against Kumārila". Here Winternitz echoes a popular but fallacious sentiment, Kumārila was never a champion of Brahmanical orthodoxy; the purpose of Mīmāṃsā philosophy was different. Kumārila's attack on Buddhist and Jain philosophy was indeed of some importance. His main target of attack was, however, the Nyāya-Vaiśeṣika conception of God and the Vedāntic conception of Brahman and Māyā. But, before dealing with the great intellectual dispute, occurring between AD 700 and 1000, we should have here a total picture of the philosophical arena.

The Sāṅkhya concept of Prakṛti, as we have seen in the introduction of the present work, evolved out of the primitive conception of a material Earth Mother and later became the strongest theoretical basis of Śāktism. We have also hinted that the origin of the Sāṅkhya system may be traced to a pre-Vedic stream which is likely to be matriarchal in nature while the other stream represented by the Vedic tribes is decidedly patriarchal. Reference to the Sāṅkhya system are found scattered not only in the *Mahābhārata* which considers it as authoritative as the Vedas but also in the Upaniṣads, the *Caraka Saṃhitā,* the *Manusmṛti* and the *Arthaśāstra* of Kauṭilya. Pre-Buddhist existence of the Sāṅkhya is indicated by the place name of Kapilavāstu, by the doctrines of Pakudha Kaccāyana who was a senior contemporary of the Buddha and by Buddhaghoṣa's claim that the preceptor of the Buddha was a follower of Sāṅkhya system.[3] But, in spite of numerous references to the Sāṅkhya in ancient literature, we know practically nothing of its original form. The well known *Sāṅkhyakārikā* of Īśvarakṛṣṇa which was composed between the second and the fifth centuries AD preserves only a fabricated form of the original system.

> The fact that Caraka (AD 78) does not refer to the Sāṅkhya as described by Īśvarakṛṣṇa and referred to in other parts of the *Mahābhārata* is definite proof that Īśvarakṛṣṇa's Sāṅkhya is a later modification which was either non-existent in Caraka's time or was not regarded as an authoritative Sāṅkhya view.[4]

The hypothesis of a non-Vedic authorship of the Sāṅkhya may be substantiated by the fact that (i) the Sāṅkhya conception of Prakṛti as the material cause of the universe is incompatible with the Vedāntic conception of Brahman, that (ii) greatest care is taken in the *Brahmasūtra* to refute the Sāṅkhya, and that (iii) there had always been conscious attempt to revise the Sāṅkhya in the light of Vedānta. According to Śaṅkara, Kapila's doctrine not only contradicts the Vedas but also the sayings of those peoples like Manu who follow the Vedic way (*Kapilasya tantrasya vedaviruddhatvaṃ vedānusārimanu-vacana-viruddhatvañca*). As regards Prakṛti, the Female Principle and the material cause of the world, Śaṅkara states:

> It is impossible to find room in the Vedānta texts for the non-intelligent *pradhāna*, the fiction of the Sāṅkhyas; because it is not founded upon scripture.[5]

It is interesting to note that in the *Brahmasūtra*, which consists of 555 *sūtras*, 60 are employed to refute the Sāṅkhya and only 43 to deal with others. According to Śaṅkara, by the refutation of the Sāṅkhya, which is the "most dangerous adversary", the conquest of the minor enemies (other schools) is virtually accomplished.[6]

Relics of the original anti-Vedic character of the Sāṅkhya are also found even in the present form of the Sāṅkhya texts. The grounds of the Sāṅkhya objection to the validity of the Vedas are explained by Gauḍapāda quite elaborately in the *Kārikā*.[7] In a verse of the *Saṅkhyasūtra*[8] it is stated that the Vedas cannot lead to the *summum bonum* because the fruits of the Vedic rituals have a beginning and therefore also an end. According to Dasgupta,[9] Śaṅkara's contention that the Sāṅkhya was non-Vedic is right because the apparent references to Śaṅkhya in the *Katha* and the *Śvetāśvatara* show that these ideas have no organic connection with the general Upaniṣadic scheme of thought, "Originally the Sāṅkhya must have taken up a position of direct opposition to the doctrine of the Brāhmaṇas, as is proved *inter alia* by its polemic against their ceremonial,"[10] says Garbe, who also holds that,

> the origin of the Sāṅkhya system appears in the proper light only when we understand that in those regions of India which were little influenced by Brahmanism the first attempt had been made to explain the riddles of the world and of our existence mainly by means of reason. For the Sāṅkhya philosophy is, in its essence, not only atheistic but also inimical to the Veda. All appeal to Śruti in the Sāṅkhya texts lying before us are subsequent additions. We may altogether remove the Vedic elements grafted upon the system and it will not in the least be affected thereby. The Sāṅkhya philosophy had been originally, and has remained up to the

present days in its real contents, un-Vedic and independent of Brahmanical tradition.[11]

The advocates of the Vedānta schools wanted to interpret the Sāṅkhya in terms of their own philosophical creed. There was a deliberate contamination of genuine Sāṅkhya with Upaniṣadic Vedānta and the Epic Sāṅkhya is a hybrid combination of the classical Sāṅkhya and Vedānta.[12] Vijñānabhikṣu in his introduction to the *Sāṅkhyasūtra* indicates that his real motive is to give Sāṅkhya a colour of Vedānta. That the *Sāṅkhyasūtra* is really burdened with Vedāntic elements has been demonstrated by Garbe.[13] Other commentators on the *Sāṅkhyasūtra*, Aniruddha and Mahādeva, were confirmed Vedāntists, and so was Gauḍapāda, the chief commentator on the *Sāṅkhyakārikā*, who did not hesitate to transform the original doctrine of the plurality of Puruṣa into that of the non-duality of the same, without which the underhand conversion of original Sāṅkhya into disguised Vedānta could not be complete.[14]

In spite of all this, the Vedānta itself could not get rid of the expanding influence of Śāktism. Even in its Advaita form, in which Brahman is one without a second, the conception of Māyā as a Female Principle gradually evolved. Thus Brahman could become the creator only when he was associated with Māyā, which was subsequently called his eternal energy (*nityā śakti*). While in the Vedāntic school of Śaṅkara it is the eternal Māyā or Śakti of Brahman that became responsible for the origin of the world of diversity, in the theistic schools of the Vaiṣṇavas and Śaivas this *Māyā* or *Śakti*, also identified with the older conception of Prakṛti, got greater personification and became identified with the wife of the supreme deity. The position of the Mīmāṃsā school was somewhat different. They rejected the conception of God absolutely[15] but, strangely enough, they adhered strictly to the Vedic ritualistic tradition. Their stark atheism on the one hand and inclination to ritualism on the other made them stand in a contradictory position, as is thought by scholars like Radhakrishnan, etc.[16] But there is no real contradiction. The nearest equivalent of the word *yajña* acceptable to the Mīmāṃsā standpoint was ritual, or more strictly magical ritual that had nothing to do with prayer, propitiation and worship. These were acts which, by their intrinsic efficacy, led to the designed results. The original form of Mīmāṃsā seems to be a sophisticated rationalisation of primitive empiricism, the contemplation, study and knowledge of nature, an enquiry about the origin of the universe not starting from the *terra incognita* of the hypothetical First Principle, but from the tangible and knowable concrete. It revealed the eternalness of nature, having no place for a creator. The philosophers of the Mīmāṃsā school were also in favour of the effectiveness of ancient tribal rites and customs. Unlike other philosophical systems, the Mīmāṃsā was concerned with social problems and devised a socio-legal system of its own.

V

In the preceding chapter we have seen that both Buddhism and Jainism recognised female deities side by side with the male Buddhas and Jinas and their emanations. The Buddhas and Jinas were regarded as gods, and their images were worshipped, along with those of their female consorts, in temples with devotional songs, accompanied by rites and ceremonies. From the seventh century onwards Śākta Tantric ideas began to influence all the major religious systems of India. Jainism alone withstood this new current and largely maintained its rigid orthodoxy. Between AD 700 and 1000, one-third of the population of the Deccan were in the Jain fold[17] but Jainism received a serious setback shortly afterwards owing to the rapid spread of the Liṅgāyata sect. In north India too, except in the west and perhaps Malwa, Jainism appears to have lost its hold during the period. In the Tamil area also Jainism faced a stage of decadence. The organised efforts to stamp out Jainism by the Śaiva Nāyanars, the conversion of Kūn Pāṇḍya by Sambandar and that of the Pallava king Mahendravarman by Appar led to the downfall of Jains in Tamil land about AD 750, as a result of which the Jains left the Pallava and Pāṇḍya kingdoms and migrated possibly to Koppaṇa, Śravaṇa Belgola and surrounding territory where they were patronised by the Gaṅgas and other rulers. But it is interesting to note that the great Jain teachers and philosophers understood their declining position very quickly and adopted possible measures to overcome the crisis. Akalaṅka Haribhadra, Vidyānanda and other philosophers did their best to defend Jainsim from the attacks of the rival schools. Important commentaries on the Digambara canon were composed. Literary output was also immense, not only in Sanskrit but also in Prakrit and Apabhraṃśa as well as in regional languages, especially in Kannaḍa language. To popularise the religion, the Jain teachers insisted on the doctrine of four gifts—learning, food, medicine and shelter.

This helped a great deal in winning the allegiance and devotion of the masses. It may be noted in this connection that the Āḷvars and Nāyanars, who led opposition against Jainism adopted the very methods of the Jains—the fourfold *dāna* in the forms of *āhāra, abhaya, bhaiṣajya* and *śāstra*—to gather followers. This orientation of religion to the primary needs of humanity was undoubtedly due to the awareness of the social realities. The introduction of theism in Jainism should also be taken into account in this connection. The Jinas came to be looked upon as gods. They were described as the Universal Spirit and identified with Śiva, Dhātṛ, Sugata and Viṣṇu.[18] Jainism of this period tried to save itself from the influence of the all-pervading Śāktism. But this attempt was not crowned with complete success. The names and iconographic features of the Śāsanadevatās, female attendants of the Jinas, distinctly indicate the Śākta association of many of them. The name and iconographic features of Ambikā or Kuṣmāṇḍinī, the Śāsanadevatā of Neminātha and consort of Gomedha, leave little doubt that she is a Jain adaptation of the Śākta goddess of the same name. Likewise Padmāvatī who is associated with snakes is a Jain adaptation of Manasā who is also known as Padmāvatī or Padmā. Images of Ambikā are found all over India, and her two, four, eight- and even twenty armed varieties are known. She is often represented with her symbol of a bunch of mangoes and a child or sometimes two children near her with her lion mount. Sometimes she is represented as seated or standing by her consort Gomedha or accompanied by the dancing Saptamātṛkās or seated underneath the spreading branches of a tree by the side of her consort with children in their laps. The cult of Jain Ambikā was especially popular in West Bengal.

VI

Tantric elements profoundly influenced Buddhism of this period and transformed it almost beyond recognition. While the philosophical teachings of Buddha received a new interpretation at the hands of the master-minds like Asaṅga, Nāgārjuna, Vasubandhu and Āryadeva and the great logicians like Candrakīrti, Śāntideva. Diṅnāga and Dharmakīrti, were guarding the front doors of Buddhist monasteries, Tantrism steadily made its way into Buddhism through the backdoors. It should be pointed out in this connection that Tantric ideas, generally regarded as the basis of the Śākta religion, also pervaded different religious sects and radically changed their views and practices. The reason behind the ultimate triumph of Tantrism is not easy to determine. "Tantrism", as S.B. Dasgupta observes, "is neither Buddhist nor Hindu in origin. It seems to be a religious undercurrent, originally independent of any abstruse metaphysical speculation, flowing from an obscure point of time in the religious history of India."[19] There is reason to believe that primitive Tantrism was a practical means to stimulate the generative powers in nature, and as such it was closely related to the Mother Goddess, the puissant and eternally active Śakti representing the forces of life in nature. We find a considerable degree of unity among men in different parts of the world in respect of such primitive beliefs. There are traces of Tantric rituals in the material remains of Harappa and Mohenjodaro.[20] In later Vedic literature also we come across sex-rites associated with agriculture[21] and this stream of thought and action did not cease to exist in the subsequent ages.

As a popular religion Mahāyānism, in course of its development, had to make compromise with peoples of widely different tastes and intellectual calibre. Heterogeneous elements of faith and customs thus began to crop up in the province of Buddhism. In course of time, elements like the *mantras* and the *dhāraṇīs* were introduced in Buddhism and in the *Tattvaratnāvalī*[22] we find Mahāyānism subdivided into two schools viz., Paramitā-nāya and Mantra-nāya. This Mantra-nāya or Mantra-yāna seems to be the introductory stage of Tantric Buddhism, from which other offshoots, like Vajrayāna, Kālacakrayāna, Sahajayāna, etc. arose in later times.

The earliest Buddhist literature which may be called precursor of Tantra was known as the *dhāraṇīs*. The growth of the *dhāraṇī* literature took place between the fourth and eighth centuries AD. The earliest works dealing with Tantric Buddhism are the *Mañjuśrīmūlakalpa* and the *Guhyasamāja,* composed about the fifth or sixth century AD. The former deals with the *mudrās* (finger poses) *maṇḍalas* (diagrams), *mantras* (spells), *kriyās* (rites) and *caryās* (duties) and also *paṭavidhāna,* i.e. directions for drawing pictures of the Buddhist gods and goddesses. The text also furnishes us with a list of holy places which later became the chief seats of Tantric Buddhism. The *Guhyasamāja* on the other hand is devoted to *yoga* and *anuttarayoga* and although it contains a few directions for *mantras* and *maṇḍalas,* it is practically the earliest text to the Vajrayāna form of Buddhism of which we shall refer to in the next chapter. The philosophy of Tantric

Buddhism as can be reconstructed from these texts may be summarised as follows: The gods and goddesses are the symbols of the Buddhist conceptions of four elements and five constituents of a being. Earth is represented by the goddess Locanā, water by Māmakī, fire by Pāṇḍaravāsinī and air by Tārā while the five constituents of a being are represented by the five Dhyānī Buddhas. Creation is due to the Śakti or female energy of the Ādi-Buddha, and as such the adepts should realise that the female sex is the source of all. The *Guhyasamāja*, while describing the different ceremonies in connection with initiation mentions *prajñābhiṣeka* or the initiation of the adept with Prajñā or Śakti.[23] The preceptor takes the hand of Śakti, a beautiful woman, and placing it on the hand of the disciple says that, as Buddhahood is impossible of attainment by any other means, this Vidyā should be accepted and never abandoned in life. The Vidyās were women of flesh and blood and later on they were deified. The *Sammoha Tantra* gives a list of the Vidyās whose worship was current in different parts of India.[24] Some of these Vidyās are well known names of Buddhist and Brahmanical goddesses.

In the earlier *dhāraṇīs* Bodhisattva Avalokiteśvara is the chief object of worship. The goddess Tārā occurs in the *Mañjuśrīmūlakalpa*[25] in her various forms like Bhṛkuṭi, Locanā, Māmakī, Śvetā, Pāṇḍaravāsinī, Sutārā, etc. She is described as Vidyārājñī who is full of compassion. Tārā is elevated to the position of the highest deity in the *Mahāpratyaṅgirādhāraṇī*, a fragment of which is found in Central Asia, in which she is described as a goddess of white colour wearing a garland of *vajras* and having the figure of Vairocana on her crown. From the seventh century onwards we find the exuberance of Tārā-*stotras* (cf. the *Sarangdharā-stotra* composed in praise of Tārā by the eighth century Kashmirian poet Sarvajñamitra) and the goddess is raised to the mothership of all Buddhas. It was from this time that her cult became popular in Tibet and China of which we had the occasion to refer to in the preceding chapter.

According to the *Sammoha Tantra*, Nīlasarasvatī or Ugratārā was born in a lake called *cola* on the western side of the Meru which was included in the Cīnadeśa. P.C. Bagchi[26] suggests that *cola* is connected with *kul*, *kol*, the common word for 'lake', which is found with names of so many lakes to the west of T-ien-shan. In China, Tārā became merged with the pre-Buddhist Mother Goddess Si-Wang-Mu, the representative of *yin* or the Female Principle. The two streams, thus assimilated, produced a new form of Tārā and a new set of rituals called *cīnācāra*, and these were recovered from China by the Indians. The *Tārārahasya, Rudrayāmala, Mahācīnācārakrama,* etc. categorically hold that the *Vāmācāra* practices, connected with the worship of the goddess Tārā, were brought from China by the sage Vasiṣṭha who was instructed by the Buddha himself. According to the legend, Vasiṣṭha actually performed the Tārā ritual at the shrine of Kāmākhyā, but failing to obtain his objective he was angry and frustrated, when the goddess herself manifested before him and asked him to go to Mahācīna which he did accordingly.

The cult of Tārā and her various forms was strong in Eastern India. Mahācīna-Tārā, also known in the Buddhist Tantras as Ugratārā, has been incorporated in the Śākta pantheon under the name Tārā, and is now regarded as one of the ten Mahāvidyās. She is described in the *sādhanās* as of terrific appearance, four-armed, standing in the *pratyālīḍha* pose on a corpse, and holding a sword, a chopper, a lotus and a skull in her hands and a miniature figure of Akṣobhya within the crown of chignon (*ekajaṭā*) on her head. The iconographic trait of *ekajaṭā* of Tārā gave rise to the conception of the goddess Ekajaṭā, and the cult of this new goddess became popular in Bhoṭa (Tibet). According to tradition Ārya Nāgārjuna recovered the Ekajaṭā cult from Bhoṭa. We come across five varieties of Tārā, classified according to colour,—green, white, yellow, blue and red.[27] In north and east of India images of Khadiravanī Tārā, also known as Śyāma Tārā who is an emanation of Amoghasiddhi, are found in abundance, though they belong to a subsequent age. Another variety of Tārā, described several times in the *Sādhanamālā,* is the Vajra-Tārā who is simultaneously an emanation of the groups of five or four Dhyānī-Buddhas. Her *maṇḍala* consists of several encircling attendant deities.[28]

Of other Buddhist goddesses, Parṇaśabarī is of great iconographic interest. Two extant images of this goddess found in East Bengal closely follow the textual description.[29] The *sādhanās* describe her as three-faced and six-armed, standing in *pratyālīḍha* pose and clad in leaf garments. Her very name associates her with the Parṇa-śabaras of the *Bṛhatsaṃhitā,* the leaf-clad aboriginal tribes. Vasudhārā, the consort of Jambhala, is the Buddhist counterpart of the Brahmanical Vasudhārā, Pṛthivī or Bhūdevī, the consort of Viṣṇu. Nairātmā, one of whose images is preserved in the Indian Museum, resembles the Śākta Kālī. She is shown dancing on a corpse, holding a short sword and a skull cup in her two hands.[30] Several images of Mārīcī have been found in eastern and northern India who is usually depicted as three-faced and eight-armed and attended by four goddesses Varttālī, Vadālī, Varālī and Varāhamukhī.[31] Special mention should be made in this connection to the eight-armed Mārīcī, now in the Lucknow Museum, which was originally found at Sārnāth. Mārīcī is invoked by the Lamas of Tibet about the time of sunrise. Of other Mahāyāna Buddhist goddesses Vajravārāhī, Prajñāpāramitā, etc. are specially important from iconographic point of view. The Buddhist Vajrayoginī reminds us of the Śākta-Tantric goddess Chinnamastā. Vajravetalī of the Buddhist Tantras reminds us of Vetāla Devī mentioned in Subandhu's *Vāsavadattā*. In the Devīmāhātmya section of the *Mārkaṇḍeya Purāṇa* we come across such goddesses as Māyūrī, Aparājitā, Vārāhī, Bhīmā, Kapālinī, Kauberī, etc. These goddesses also occur in the *Sādhanamālā*. The presiding deities of the Śākta Ṣaṭcakra, like Ḍākinī, Hākinī, Lākinī, Rākinī, Śākinī, etc., owe their origin to the Buddhist conceptions. The cult of Jāṅguli finds its Hindu counterpart in that of Manasā and Viṣahari.

Tantric manuscripts of seventh to ninth century have been found in Nepal. Buddhist Tantras were translated into Chinese in the eighth and into Tibetan in the ninth century AD. A Cambodian inscription refers to the fact that the Tantric texts were introduced there from India at the beginning of the ninth century AD.[32] As regards the Tantric practices, the *Guhyasamāja* and a few other early texts refer to meat-eating, union with females, and finger poses. It is generally held that some Taoist ideas and practices, especially the *vāmācāra* (also known as *cīnācāra*) rites came to India from China. Referring to the Chinese ideas about erotics and erotic practices, K.H. Van Gulik observes:

> "this (sexual) practice, again, has been the starting point of a secret Tantric-Taoistic ritual intended not only to increase the length of life, but even to win immortality for the adepts.... This ritual sheds a most significant light on certain obscure doctrines and practices of Indian and Tibetan mysticism, especially of Yoga, the Buddhist-Tantric Siddhācāryas and the Vāmācāra Śāktas."[33]

Further light on this *cīnācāra* has been thrown by Joseph Needham whose final conclusion is that although Tantrism at the first sight seems to have been an Indian export to China, a closer inspection leads to the conclusion that the whole thing was really Taoist.[34]

Interchange of ideas between Taoism and Tantrism might have taken place at their advanced stage of development, but at the initial stage they were developed independently. Sexual rites related to fertility magic are common to all forms of primitive religion. Erotic practices associated with the goddess cult are older than the Tantric and Taoist texts themselves. This also holds good in the case of the rites of wine and fish. Among many surviving primitive tribes of the world wine is connected with fertility and funeral rites and the concept of resurrection. Fish is also closely associated with matriarchal beliefs as a fertility symbol.[35] Aphrodite, the fish-goddess "was worshipped as the bestower of all animal and vegetative fruitfulness and under this aspect especially as a goddess of women."[36] The relation between fish and Mother Goddess is a very common feature of primitive religion.[37] Wilson[38] and Mackenzie[39] inform us that geometrical patterns, like the Tantric diagrams representing the female genitalia, were also well known in the Mesopotamian and Aegean world, and their appearances on the persons of certain goddesses like, Artemis, Hera, Demeter, Astarte, and the Chaldean Nana, suggests that these signs were employed as fecundity symbols.

VII

The primitive basis of the Tantric *pañca-makāra* or *pañca-tattva*—the use of *madya* (wine), *māṃsa* (meat), *matsya* (fish), *mudrā* (diagrams) and *maithuna* (sexual intercourse)—can thus be established on further investigations. This primitive undercurrent of ideas and practices profoundly influenced not only Buddhism but other religious systems as well. Many of the Vaiṣṇava Saṃhitās and Śaiva Āgamas are full of Tantric elements. The Vaiṣṇava Saṃhitā and Śaiva Āgamas agree on one point, namely, that a Female Principle representing *śakti* or energy must be associated with the ultimate reality, Viṣṇu or Śiva, and this *sakti* is not only the cause of manifestation, but is also responsible for differentiation of worldly objects including the finite individuals. The universe comes into being because of the association of the male and the female. Viṣṇu and his *śakti* or Śiva and his *śakti*, and at the end of a cosmic cycle the created universe returns to its source when *śakti* comes to repose in the Lord. Vaiṣṇava teachers of this age, like Nāthamuni of Śrīraṅgam, wanted to base the religion upon the doctrine of Vedānta. In the earlier stages of this process the *Māyā* element as the Female Principle and as the *śakti* of Brahman began to get importance, as we have seen above, but later it became a potent factor, the religious implication of which culminated in the conception of Rādhā.

In Vaiṣṇava sculptures of this age, Lakṣmī, Sarasvatī and Bhūdevī, associated with Viṣṇu, were still the most represented ones. The Gajalakṣmī motif was also prevalent. Reference to one eleventh century bronze figure of four-armed Gajalakṣmī, hailing from north Bengal, may be made in this connection. Independent figures of Sarasvatī were also common. While Vaiṣṇavite sculptures of this age were following the old traditional line, the Śaivite ones were marked by new innovations. It was due to the deep-rooted Śākta-Tantric influence upon Śaivism which enhanced its prestige and position as a popular religion. Some of the famous cave temples of India were dedicated to Śiva. The marriage of Śiva and Pārvatī, the peaceful householder's life of Śiva with Pārvatī and her children, Purāṇic episodes related to Śiva, etc. became the popular theme of sculpture of this period. Sculptures representing the marriage of Śiva and Pārvatī, usually described as Kalyāṇasundara-mūrti, are common in several parts of India, one of the most outstanding examples of which is the Elephanta relief. The numerous Śiva figures hailing from different parts of India, illustrative of various Śiva mythologies, are divided into two groups—gracious (*saumya*) and destructive (*ugra*). Among the different types of the terrific or *ugra* forms of Śiva mention may be made of his Bhairava, Aghora, Vīrabhadra and Virupākṣa forms. The Āgamic texts describe as many as sixty-four Bhairavas, divided into groups of eight, and they are the consorts of sixty-four Yoginīs referred to in the Tantric form of Śakti worship.

In Kashmir we get two schools of Śaivism, the Spanda and the Pratyabhijñā. The former was founded about the ninth century by Vasugupta to whom Śiva is said to have revealed the *sūtras*. His disciple Kallaṭa wrote *Spandasarvasva* in which he explained the meaning of the Śiva-*sūtras* as taught by his master. The important works of the Pratyabhijñā school are the *Śivadṛṣṭi* and the *Pratyabhijñā-sūtra* composed by Somananda and his pupil Utpala respectively in the beginning of the tenth century AD. The *Pratyabhijñāvimarśinī* of Abhinavagupta is a commentary upon the *Pratyabhijñāsūtra*. Abhinavagupta has also given us two more works of this school, the *Tantrāloka* and the *Paramārthasāra*. The Kashmir Śaivism has based its doctrines on the Vedānta system with emphasis upon the *Māyā* element regarded as the Śakti of Brahman (Śiva). This *Śakti* mainly divided into five categories,—*cit* (the power of intelligence), *ānanda* (the power of bliss), *icchā* (the power of will), *jñāna* (the power of knowledge) and *kriyā* (the power of action)—is not different from Śiva and is spoken of as his feminine aspect. With the opening out of *Śakti,* the universe appears and with her closing it disappears.

VIII

Now we shall deal with the independent development of Śāktism during the period under review. We have seen that the new religious sentiments of Vaiṣṇavism and Śaivism were directed to an ultimate reality united with his *Śakti* conceived as a Female Principle. It was an indirect triumph of Śāktism. That there had been a keen rivalry among the existing creeds can easily be made out from the Saṃhitā, Āgama and Tantra literature of the time, and this struggle helped Śāktism immensely to consolidate its position. The *Devī-śataka* of Ānandavardhana of Kashmir testifies the popularity of the Devī cult in the land of the Śaivas. In South India Śāktism received an impetus from Śaṅkarācārya. He was not a Śākta in the sectarian sense. In his commentary on the *Brahmasūtra* he gave a stout theoretical opposition to the Śākta tendencies of the doctrine of *Māyā.* He had also ruthlessly criticised the Sāṅkhya conception of Prakṛti as the material cause of the universe. Despite all this, it is interesting to note that he had a soft corner for Śākta religion, perhaps due to its popularity among the masses, and was in all probability the author of the *Saundaryalaharī* the well known ode to the goddess.

With the decline of the Pallava hegemony and the rise of the Cola empire under Vijayālaya (AD 850-70), the cult of Durgā entered a new phase in South India. The Tiruvalangadu Plates of Rājendra Cola says that Vijayālaya built a temple of Niśumbhamardinī at Tanjore, and this aspect of Durgā appears to have been popular during the early Cola[40] period. This representation is found even in miniature bas-reliefs of the temples of Punjai, Pullamangai and Tirukkarugavur, all in the Tanjore district. The early Cola Durgās are eight-armed in the Pallava fashion, but one belonging to the Nāgeśvarasvāmī temple of Kumbhakoṇam is found four-armed. The hands of Durgā could be two, four, six or eight, or even ten or twelve at a later time. The goddess is represented in Bengal sculpture with sixteen, eighteen, twenty and even thirty-two hands. Reference may be made in this connection to a twenty-armed image from Sirala in the Rajsahi district belonging to the tenth century which is now lost. A peculiar iconographic attribute of Durgā in Tamil land is her association with a stag which reminds us of Artemis and also the fugures in the Kuninda coins. Some of the literary descriptions like *Pāykalaippāvai* and *Kalaippariurdi* show that darting deer was her mount. Self-mutilation was probably a feature of the worship of the goddess during the Pallava and early Cola period, as is evident from several Pallava panels where the devotee is shown to offer his own head. This custom might have some bearing on the later conception of Chinnamastā. A late Pallava inscription upon a slab refers to a warrior who had offered his own head to the goddess, and the slab itself contains a relief of that act.[41]

As we have seen above, the *Mārkaṇḍeya Purāṇa,* while dealing with the exploits of the Śākta Devī, describes the Mahiṣamardinī episode in addition to some other accounts of the achievements of the goddess as also the promise of her periodic appearance whenever the demons would threaten the peace of gods. The Mahiṣamardinī theme was elaborated in later Purāṇas.[42] Other achievements of the Devī, like her slaying the demons Śumbha and Niśumbha,[43] Vetra and Rudra,[44] are described in the Purāṇas. It is generally believed that it was one goddess who in her different forms and manifestations killed all these demons, but the fact is that they were different goddesses later identified with the Supreme Being of the Śāktas. Numerous eight or ten-armed images of Mahiṣamardinī have been discovered in different parts of eastern India. An image which should be specially mentioned in this connection comes from a North Bengal village in the Dinajpur district portraying in a very interesting manner the nine Durgās (Navadurgā) with eighteen-armed Mahiṣamardinī as the central figure and with eight other sixteen-armed miniature figures of the same type grouped round it. Another interesting specimen is a stone image of the thirty-two-armed Devī engaged in combat with demons. This also comes from the same district.[45] Mahiṣamardinī also became popular in Rajasthan and we have already referred to some early specimens. The exterior of the main sanctum of the Ambikā temple at Jagat, about 34 miles from Udaipur (10th century AD) is studded with elegant sculptures of the eight-armed Mahiṣamardinī. The three niches on the three sides of the temple depicts Mahiṣamardinī in three different styles which is an exceptional feature.[46] The temple sculptures of Osian, Abaneri and Paranagar are also fine specimens of Durgā as Mahiṣamardinī.

The Purāṇas are also responsible for popularising the cult of the

Mothers, generally seven in number, who are the energies of different major gods and described as assisting the great Śākta Devī in her fight with the demons. In the Saptamātṛkā slabs they appear from left to right, with occasional variations here and there, in the following order—Brahmāṇī or Sarasvatī, Māheśvarī or Raudrī, Kaumārī or Kārttikeyānī, Vaiṣṇavī or Lakṣmī, Vārāhī, Indrāṇī or Mahendrī, and Cāmuṇḍā. Nārasiṃhī replacing Cāmuṇḍā, or Yamī replacing Vārāhī is not unknown. To the list is sometimes added Mahālakṣmī or Yogeśvarī, and sometimes Caṇḍikā herself, to make the eight. The *Varāha Purāṇa*[47] says that Yogeśvarī is the symbol of lust, Maheśvarī of anger, Vaiṣṇavī of greed, Kaumārī of attachment, Brahmāṇī of pride, Aindrī of jealousy, Cāmuṇḍā of depravity and Vārāhī of envy. According to their iconographic descriptions, Brahmāṇī is four-armed and four-headed, seated on a swan, bearing a rosary and a water-pot from which she sprinkles water with *kuśa*; Māheśvarī is seated on a bull wearing a *jaṭāmukuṭa* (locked hair dressed in a pyramidal form) and a crescent; Kaumārī is red-coloured and four-armed, carrying a *śakti* (weapon) and seated on a peacock; she looks like Kumāra, decked with red robe, necklace and *keyūra*, armed with *śūla* and *śakti* and surrounded by fowls; Vaiṣṇavī resembles Viṣṇu while Vārāhī a boar; her vehicle is buffalo and she is armed with a club and a wheel; Indrāṇī or Aindrī is many eyed, and she carries a thunderbolt, a spear and a club; her complexion is golden and her vehicle is elephant; Cāmuṇḍā is three-eyed, fleshless and bony; she is clad in tiger skin and seated on a corpse.[48]

The Saptamātṛkā figures are flanked on the left by Śiva or Skanda and on the right by Gaṇeśa. The growing importance of Śāktism brought them into greater prominence and distributed their cult far and wide. The colossi of the Eight Mothers from Muktimaṇḍapa near Jaipur and the Eight Mothers with Śivadūtī on the bank of the Vaitaraṇī indicate their popularity in the Orissa region. At present we have two sets of Mātṛkās at Jajpur. The one referred to above is the first set while of the second, two colossal figures of Vārāhī and Indrāṇī, survive. An inscribed image of Cāmuṇḍā also comes from Jajpur which was installed by queen Vatsadevī, probably of the Bhaumakara dynasty.[49] The Paraśurāmeśvara temple of Bhubaneswar contains a group of Saptamātṛkā carved in relief on the north-west corner of the northern wall of the *jagamohana*. The Vaitāla temple contains a terrific Cāmuṇḍā as its presiding deity and on the inner dark walls of its *jagamohana* we find a group of Seven Mothers, all of them sitting in *yogāsana* pose on full-blown lotus with their different attributes. In the Mukteśvara temple the presentation of Seven Mothers occurs on an eight-petalled lotus carved on the ceiling of its *jagamohana*. In Bengal some of the Mothers have been separately sculptured and Camuṇḍā of various forms, such as Rūpavidyā, Siddha-Yogeśvarī and Danturā, has found independent representation. An image of the last-mentioned aspect of Cāmuṇḍā, showing a two-armed goddess sitting on her haunches, found originally in a Burdwan village strikingly portrays the weird and uncanny "with its bare canine teeth, rounded eyes, ghastly smile, emaciated body, lean and pendulous breasts, sunken belly and peculiar sitting posture".[50] It is now in the collection of the Vaṅgīya Sāhitya Pariṣad Museum, Calcutta. Several other figures of Danturā have been found in north Bengal. The goddess Vaiṣṇavī is sometimes replaced by Vāgīśvarī whose figure in octo-alloy, with eight hands, is now in the Rajshahi Museum. Another inscribed four-handed image of Vāgīśvarī of AD 940 comes from Nālandā. In Rajasthan, Cāmuṇḍā is worshipped at Jodhpur, Jaswantpur, Bhinamal, Ajmer and other places, and a large number of Mātṛkā images found at Mandor, Nagda, Chitorgarh, Ramgarh, Kekinda, Phalodi, Osian and other places bear testimony to the popularity of their cult. Specially important is the group of Eight Mothers of Mandor. They are carved out of a single rock which carries an inscription of VS 742. Beginning from Gaṇeśa at the left, the Mothers have two and four hands alternately. Another group of Eight Mothers is found on the shrine door of the Nīlakaṇṭha Mahādeva temple of Kekinda which is modern Jasnagar near Merta city. The temple belongs to the tenth century AD where the Mothers are shown with children in their laps, a feature which is common also to some Mātṛkā sculptures of Orissa. To emphasise the Mother-aspect, these goddesses are sometimes shown as carrying a suckling baby on their laps, and the Ellora Saptamātṛkā panel is a striking example of this type of Mātṛkā images. The Seven Mothers were favourite deities of the early Cālukyas and their cult spread in Tamil land about the beginning of the eighth century AD.[51] The first sculptural representation of the Mātṛkās is found in the Kailāsanātha temple of Kanchipuram, and subsequently their sculptures are noticed in the Pāṇḍya and Muttaraiya cave temples at Tirugokarṇam, Malaiyadippatti, Kunnattur and Tirukkalakkudi. An inscription of Cola Rājakeśarī states that during the reign of the Pallava king Dantivarman, a temple of Saptamātṛkā was built at Alambakkam in the Tiruchirapalli district.[52] In an inscription of Pārthivendravarman reference is made to a temple of Mātṛkās at Velacheri in the Chingleput district.[53] From the ninth century onwards it became an established fashion to construct small shrines of the Mātṛkās in the temple enclosures.

The primitive Yoginī cult was also revived on account of the increasing influence of the cult of the Seven or Eight Mothers. Originally the Yoginīs were probably human beings, women of flesh and blood, priestesses who were supposed to be possessed by the goddess, and later they were raised to the status of divinities. By the usual process of multiplication their number increased from eight to sixteen and then to sixty-four or more. In Sanskrit literature the Yoginīs have been represented as the attendants or various manifestations of Durgā engaged in fighting with Śumbha and Niśumbha and the principal Yoginīs are identified with the Mātṛkās. The Orissan village Hirapur contains a temple of sixty-four Yoginīs. In the inner face of the circular wall of the enclosure, there are sixty niches each containing an image of Yoginī. All of them are in standing postures. Orissa has also another temple of sixty-four Yoginīs at Ranipur Jharial in the Bolangir district.[54] In the sixty-four Yoginī temple at Bheraghat near Jubbulpore are found not only the sixty-four Yoginīs but also the eight Śaktis, three rivers, four other goddesses, Śiva and Gaṇeśa, thus making a total of eighty-one figures. The Bheraghat figures are damaged, but most of them fortunately retain their names inscribed in the sixty-five peripheral chapels. The names are not canonical and are evidently adopted from popular cults. The presence of Śrī-Teramvā, a Mahiṣamardinī figure with sixteen hands and of Sarvatomukhī with a lotus underseat containing Tantric emblems in the Bheraghat icons is interesting. At Khajuraho, the sixty-four Yoginīs appear in an oblong temple.

A four-armed standing figure of the goddess of the *saumya* type, found in one of the rock-cut shrines of Ellora, exactly corresponds to the description of Pārvatī. She holds in her hands a rosary, a Śiva-liṅga, a miniature figure of Gaṇapati and a water-vessel. But although in the caves of Ellora and Elephanta separate shrines of Pārvatī are noticed, such a provision was absent in the Pallava and early Cola temples. However, reference to such a shrine is met with in the Ennayiram inscription of Rājendra.[55] A new shrine of Pārvatī was added to the Bṛhadīśvara temple of Tanjore at a later date. Separate images of the Devī of the *āsana* variety are comparatively rare. Several seated images have been discovered in Bengal, and a few of them can be called Aparājitā, Mahālakṣmī, etc. on the basis of various iconographic texts.

With the popularity of Śāktism exaggerated emphasis was laid upon the diverse modes of divine manifestation. One goddess thus began to be conceived as many and came to be known under different names. The Purāṇas enumerate 108 names and holy resorts of the great goddess. Some of these names were mythical but many of them indicate local goddesses later identified with the Supreme Being of the Śāktas. One set of nine names of Durgā—Śailaputrī, Brahmacāriṇī, Caṇḍaghaṇṭā, Kuṣmāṇḍā, Skandamātā, Kātyāyanī, Kālarātri, Mahāgurī and Siddhidātrī—practically sketches her career and functions. Another better known set is composed of Ugracaṇḍā, Pracaṇḍā, Caṇḍogrā, Caṇḍanāyikā, Caṇḍā, Caṇḍāvatī, Caṇḍarūpā, Aticaṇḍikā and Rudracaṇḍā—all signifying the wrathful aspect of the goddess. Pārvatī was differentiated into Durgā, Cāmuṇḍā, Mahiṣāsuramardinī and Mahālakṣmī while Cāmuṇḍā into Karālī and Bhadrakālī, Kalabhadarā and Mahākālī. Sarasvatī and Lakṣmī, though widely worshipped as the respective patrons of learning and riches, practically remained wives of Brahmā and Viṣṇu in Brahmanical religions. In Mahāyāna Buddhism Sarasvatī attained greater independence and evolved many forms. Likewise Lakṣmī enjoyed an independent status in Jainism. Isolated images of Lakṣmī sometimes Aṣṭalakṣmī, including Gajalakṣmī, corresponding to the eight *Śaktis* of Viṣṇu, are found here and there all over India. By the side of the major Śākta deities we have other goddesses like Jyeṣṭhā, the elder sister of Lakṣmī, but associated with misfortune (Alakṣmī), reference to whose temple is made in an eighth century inscription near Madura. The Tamil lexicon *Śendan Divākaram*, a work of the tenth century, mentions eight names of this goddess—Mugaḍi, Tauvai, Kālati, Mudevī, Kakkaikkodiyal, Kaludai, Vāhini, Settai and Keḍalanaṅgu. A few of her images are found in different parts of South India. With the development of the cult of Śakti, there was a conscious attempt to erect her separate shrines near the main sanctum, and this had become a regular feature of the South Indian temple complex. These shrines were known as Tirumurram and the deities associated with them consisted of different varieties of Durgā, as is evident from the Cola inscriptions.[56]

A complete list of the 108 names of the great goddess with the specification of her association with particular holy places is probably to be found for the first time in the *Matsya Purāṇa.*[57] The same text has been quoted in the description of the various manifestations of Bhadrakarṇikā (a form of the goddess) in the *Skanda Purāṇa*[58] as well as in the enumeration of the goddess Sāvitrī in the *Padma Purāṇa.*[59] The same text is also quoted in the *Devībhāgavata*[60] which refers to the holy places, associated with the different manifestation of the goddess, as *pīṭhas.* In the *Kūrma Purāṇa,*[61] the Devī is invoked under more than 1,000 names. Local variations, elaborations and fusions undoubtedly had characterised the evolution of these new names and forms of the goddess. Reinforcement to the Śakti cult also came from the contemporaneous Buddhist revival in which Tārā played a very prominent part, as we have seen above. In the Tantras many of the Buddhist female deities were identified with Śākta goddesses. The most outstanding Śākta upheaval was furnished by the Tantras which necessitated an understanding and an acceptance of the Female Principle in religious worship.

The Barah Copperplate of Bhoja (AD 836) refers to the Gurjara Pratihāra kings as Paramabhagavatībhakta or great devotees of Bhagavatī.[62] The Dhenkanal Copperplate of Jayastambha, the Śulki king of Orissa, refers to the goddess Stambheśvarī as their family deity. The same is said in the Bhimnagarigarh Copperplate of Raṇastambhadeva.[63] The Binka Copperplate of Rāṇaka Raṇabhañjadeva refers to the influence of the goddess Stambheśvarī on the Bhañja rulers.[64] The Tezpur Copperplate of Vanamāla refers to the popularity of Mahāgaurī in the Kāmarūpa region.[65] Hiuen Tsang has referred to the cult of the goddess Bhīmā in the Gandhāra region, to her shapeless image in blue stone and to her pilgrims from different part of India.[66] Bāṇabhaṭṭa in his *Kādambarī*[67] describes Caṇḍikā as a blood-thirsty goddess. In Bhavabhūti's *Mālatīmādhava* Cāmuṇḍā is described in similar terms.[68] In Vakpati's *Gauḍavaho* the goddess Vindhyavāsinī is identified with Śabarī, Kālī and Pārvatī.[69] In Subandhu's *Vāsavadattā* Kātyāyanī is described as Vetālā (*bhagavatī kātyāyanī vetālābhidhāna svayam prativasati*). In Aniruddha's *Āryāstava* the goddess is also called Vetālī.

Perhaps no religious literature has raised so much controversy in evaluation as the Tantras, and hence we should say a few words regarding the practical side of the Tantric cult of the goddess which lays special emphasis upon the *mantras* (prayers and formulae), *bījas* (syllables of esoteric significance), *yantras* (diagrams), *mudrās* (special positions of fingers) and *nyāsas* (feeling the deities in different parts of the body). The aim of the Śākta worshipper is to realise the universe within himself and to become one with the goddess. The successive steps of the spiritual ladder are constituted by three stages *paśu* (animal), *vīra* (heroic) and *divya* (divine). In the first stage, the aspirant can worship any sectarian god, but he must follow all the rules of social morality, and by doing so he would be raised to the second of the heroic level. In this stage the aspirant is able to get himself initiated in *vāmācāra* and *siddhāntācāra*. For the correct understanding of the mystic rites he requires proper training from a *guru* or preceptor. He can not disregard the social convention about sexual purity, defy taboos about food and drink, look up all women as manifestations of Śakti. The rituals of *pañca-makāra*—wine, fish, meat, diagrams and coitus—performed in proper ways under the spiritual guidance of the *guru* elevates the aspirant to the *divya* or divine standard, and in this stage he is free to get himself initiated in the *Kaulācāra*. The *Kaula* worshipper of Śakti is above all moral judgements, free from all worldly attachments. The logic of Tantra is in itself very simple. What appears to be complicated is the technical and esoteric aspects of the rituals. In its social sphere the Tantra is free from all sorts of caste and patriarchal prejudices. All women are regarded as manifestations of Prakṛti or Śakti, and hence they are object of respect and devotion. Whoever offends them incurs the wrath of the great goddess. Every aspirant has to realise the latent Female Principle within himself, and only by becoming female he is entitled to worship the Supreme Being (*vāmā bhūtvā yajet parām*). A woman and even a Śūdra is entitled to function in the role of the preceptor.

References

1. For details see K.R. Venkataraman in *CHI*, IV, 252-59.
2. *HIL*, II, 478.
3. For textual reference see my *IMG*, 109-12.
4. Dasgupta, *HIP*, I, 218.
5. I.1.5; *SB E*, XXXIV, 47.
6. *SBE*, XXXIV, 318-19.
7. See Colebrooke's *SK*, 13.
8. I.6.
9. *IC*, I, 79-80.
10. *ERE*, XI, 189.
11. *ACOPVMCSS*, XX-XXI.
12. Belvalkar and Ranade, *HIP*, II, 414.

13. *SPB,* XI-XII.
14. For references see my *IMG,* 113.
15. See my *HICI,* 66-68.
16. Radhakrishnan, *IP,* II, 427.
17. Altekar, *RT,* 313.
18. Cf. *IA,* VIII.105.
19. *ORC,* 27.
20. Kosambi, *ISIH,* 54; Banerjea, *DHI,* 171; cf. *IHQ,* VII.1-32.
21. *Supra,* see also Chakravarty in *IHQ,* VI, 114 ff.
22. Collected in H.P. Sastri's *Advaya-vajra-saṃgraha,* GOS, XL.
23. GOS, 161.
24. Bagchi, *ST,* 100-101.
25. 508, 647-48.
26. *ST,* 43-44.
27. Getty, *GNB,* 122 ff.
28. Bhattasali, *IBBSDM,* 45-53, XV-XVII.
29. Banerji, *EISMS,* pl. XXXIX.
30. Bhattacharyya, *IBI* (1924), 90-92.
31. Ibid., 97.
32. Majumdar, *IK,* 362 ff.
33. See Goetz in *ABORI,* XXXVI, 133-49.
34. Needham, *SCC,* II, 425 ff.
35. Dikshit, *MG,* 30-36.
36. Seffert, *DCA,* 38 f.
37. Mackenzie, *CPHE,* 237.
38. *S,* 771 ff.
39. *MS,* 2 ff.
40. *SII,* III, no. 205.
41. *SII,* XII, no. 106.
42. Cf. *Skanda,* Aruṇācala, Pūrva, XI; Uttara, XIX; Setu, VI-VII; Nāgara, CXX-CXXI; *Vāmana,* XVII-XX; *Varāha,* XCII-XCV.
43. *Vāmana,* LV-LVI; *Śiva,* Vāyavīya, XXI.
44. *Varāha,* XXVIII, XCVI.
45. Majumdar ed., *HB,* I, 453-54.
46. *Arts Asiatique,* 1964, 44-65; *VIJ,* I.136.
47. XVII.33-37.
48. *Matsya,* CCLXI.24-32; *Agni,* L.19-24; *Vāmana,* LVI; *Varāha,* XCVI; passim.
49. *EI,* XXVIII, 184-85.
50. Majumdar ed., *HB,* I.455.
51. *JMU,* XXXII.154-56.
52. *ARSIE,* 1009, no. 795.
53. *ARSIE,* 1911, no. 316; *SII,* III, no. 191.
54. *OHRJ,* III, 55-75.
55. *ASIAR,* 1917, no. 335.
56. *ARSIE,* 1919, no. 207; *SII,* II, nos. 79, 81.
57. XIII.26-53.
58. Āvantya/Revā, XCVIII, 64-92.
59. Sṛṣṭi, XVII, 184-211.
60. VII.30.55-83.
61. I.12.

62. *EI,* XIX.15; XXIII.242.
63. *JASB,* LXIV.123 ff; *JBORS,* II.168 ff., 395 ff.
64. Bhandarkar, *L,* 204.
65. *KS,* 63.
66. Watters, *YCTI,* I.221.
67. Purva, 216.
68. Act V.
69. VV.285-337.

6

Early Medieval Śāktism (AD 1000-1300)

While the demarcation line between the medieval and the modern periods of Indian history is more or less clear, that between the ancient and medieval is indistinct and problematic. The period between AD 1000 and 1300 which witnessed the invasion and expansion of Turkish power is generally supposed to represent the emergence of the medieval period in India. However, Turkish power was not established in India before AD 1300. Kanauj was ruled by the Gāhaḍavālas, Rajasthan by the Cāhamāna chiefs, the Guhilas of Mewar and the minor branches of the Paramāras, the Bharatpur region by the Yaduvaṃśīs, the Gwalior, Dubkund and Narwar regions by the Kacchapaghātas, Kashmir by the Loharas, Gujarat by the Cālukyas, Bundelkhand region by the Candellas, Malwa by the Paramāras, Tripurī and Ratanpur by the Kalacuris, Bihar by various local dynasties, Bengal by the Pālas and their successors, Assam by the line of Brahmapāla and Orissa by the Eastern Gaṅgas and Somavaṃśīs. In the South, the Western Cālukyas, the Yādavas, the Kākatīyas, the Eastern Cālukyas and later the Pāṇḍyas and Hoysalas ruled over flourishing kingdoms. But the most important of them in extent and power and the most brilliant in cultural achievements was the empire of the Colas of Tanjore.

During this period the kingdoms of Suvarṇadvīpa which comprised the Malay Peninsula, Sumātrā, Jāvā, Bālī, Borneo, kingdom of the Śailendras, Pagan and Kambuja in South-East Asia became greatly Hinduised. They had close contacts with India, especially with South India and Bengal. The kingdom of the Śailendras continued upto the middle of the thirteenth century. The empire of Kambuja (Cambodia, Kampuchia) reached its zenith in the twelfth century when Sūryavarman II built the great temple of Angkor Vat. At the end of the twelfth century the Hinduised kingdom of Campā (Indo-China) under Jayavarman VIII, extended from Bay of Bengal on one side to the Sea of China on the other. Jāvā also continued to be a powerful Hindu kingdom till the fifteenth century. Massive monuments like Barabudur attest to the grandiose art of this period in Jāvā. In AD 1044, the Hindu king Aniruddha, was ruling from Pagan or Arimardanapura in Burma. By the end of the tenth century Hinduism with its vigorous cults inculcating the worship of Śiva, Śakti, Viṣṇu and other deities was firmly established in these countries. The process began much earlier. As early as the fifth century AD king Bhadravarman of Campā was celebrated as a Vedic scholar who constructed a temple of Śiva, called after him Bhadreśvarasvāmī, at Myson. Likewise, towards the close of the fourth or the beginning of the fifth century AD a Brāhmaṇa from India named Kauṇḍinya was elected king by the people of Fu-nan. He probably represented a fresh stream of Indian influence which thoroughly Hinduised Cambodia.

We have already seen that Śāktism as one of the most important streams of Hinduism began to follow its own course from the Gupta period onwards. Its inner strength was observed during AD 700-1000 when the concept of Śakti permeated other main branches of Hinduism including Buddhism and Jainism as well. Its influence transgressed the borders of India and was obviously felt in the Hinduised South-East Asian countries referred to above. In Campā the cult of Śiva and Devī was popular and the goddess was generally known by names such as Bhagavatī, Mahābhagavatī, Gaurī and Mahādevī. From the contents of the inscriptions as well as from the extant images it appears that in Campā the goddess was just the female version of Śiva, both of them having the same postures, same emblems, same vehicle and same type of representation in images. This shows that the conceptual identity of Śiva and Śakti as the static and dynamic aspects of the same reality was already established in Campā. In the Myson inscription of king Bhadravarman (fifth century) Umā is invoked along with Maheśvara. In the Po-Nagar temple inscriptions we find that during the region of Harivarman I (ninth century AD) a stone image of the Bhagavatī of Kothar was reinstalled in her temple, that during the reign of Indravarman III a golden image of the goddess Bhagavatī was installed by the king at a different temple, that liberal donations were made by Jaya-harivarman I and Jayaindravarman IV (twelfth century) to the goddess Kauṭhāreśvarī and that the image of Mātuliṅgeśvarī was installed by the princess Sūryadevī (thirteenth century). The image installed by the princess may have been the one of the Nha Trang temple. This image is seated and contains elevated breast and ten arms, eight of which carry various weapons and two rest on her knees. According to some scholars this image was installed by Indravarman III in AD 965.[1]

Epigraphic and sculptural evidence testifies the popularity of the Devī cult in Kambuja. In the Sanskrit section of the Ponhea Hor inscription (sixth century AD) there is reference to the installation of a Durgā image by a royal official named Pasengagati. In the Snay Pol inscription belonging to the sixth-seventh century AD mention is made of a gift of 80 male and female slaves to the goddess Bhagavatī. In the province of Kandol-Stung there was a celebrated temple of Śiva-Pārvatī known as Vat Vihar Tran. The goddess is represented in the image as seated on the left thigh of Śiva. Epigraphical evidence suggests that the temple was erected in the seventh century. According to the Pra-Ko inscription of AD 879 king Indravarman of Kambuja installed three Śiva and three Devī images. In the Bakong inscription of Indravarman mention is made of the installation of the images of Gaṅgā, Umā, Indrāṇī and Mahiṣamardinī. In the Bhavānī temple inscription at Loley various arrangements made by Śrī Yaśovarma-Narendravarṣa for the service of the goddess Bhavānī have been recorded. One side of the Phnom Sandak stone inscription of AD 895 contains hymns dedicated to the Trinity, Gaurī and Sarasvatī along with a panegyric of the same Yaśovarman and the other side has hymns addressed to the Trinity and the goddess Aparṇā as well as laudatory verses in praise of king Jayavarman. Umā is lauded in the Vat Thipadi inscription (AD 920) of Īśānavarman II. In the Prasat Pram (AD 947), Mebon (AD 952) and Pre Rup (AD 961) inscriptions of Rājendravarman and the Bantay Srei inscription of the time of Jayavarman V (last quarter of the tenth century) mention is made of the installation of several images of Umā-Pārvatī. Likewise the Prasat Khtom inscription of the time of Sūryavarman I (1001-1049), the Sdok Kak Thom inscription of Udayādityavarman (AD 1052) and in the Kuk Trapan inscriptions (AD 1073) record the erection of temples and installation of images of various goddesses.[2]

In Jāvā Śrī or Lakṣmī was worshipped as the Śakti of Viṣṇu while Sarasvatī as that of Brahmā. The former was represented in sculptures as four-armed, each hand containing a lotus, a stalk of corn, a fly-whisk and a rosary respectively. The images of Sarasvatī found in Jāvā are two or four armed, having peacock as her vehicle. Greater variety is, however, observed in the case of the Devī images of Śaiva-Śākta affiliation. The images of Durgā, especially in her Mahiṣāsuramardinī aspect are numerous. The Batavia Museum contains quite a good number of six, eight, ten and twelve armed Mahiṣamardinī images. The temples of Diyeng Plateau of Central Java contained many Durgā images. The cult of Mahākālī or Bhairavī, the terrible form of the goddess, was also popular in Jāvā. Images found in Jāvā show that the goddess Mahākālī is seated on a corpse having garlands of human heads as her necklace and sacred thread. She has two hands, one containing a trident and the other a pot. Among the benign forms, seated Śiva and Umā images are abundant. A good number of such specimens is preserved in the Batavia Museum. The Ardhanārīśvara or Śiva-Devī combined images are also common. At Gedong-Sanga a new type of Durgā image is found. Here the goddess is seated on a bull having caught the neck of the Asura. The site of Candi Kidal has yielded Durgā, Gaṇeśa, Nandīśvara and Mahākāla images which are now in the Leiden Museum. In Bālī also we have evidence of the worship of Pārvatī-Umā, Kālī, Durgā, Lakṣmī and Sarasvatī. Quite a good number of Mahiṣamardinī images have been found in Bālī, the broken one from Kutri being a very interesting specimen. The Pura Dalem type of temples, erected near the cremation grounds, were dedicated to Durgā.[3]

II

The period under review marked the beginning of the dominance of the Turkish tribes over a large part of India. Such dominance of foreign peoples was no new thing in Indian history. The coming of the invaders and their stay in this country did not cause any break in the continuity of Indian history and culture. For they slowly and silently merged themselves into the population of the country and became one with them in all respects without leaving any trace of their separate entity. This was, however, not the case with the Turkish invaders. They not only kept themselves severely aloof and formed a distinct unit—politically, socially and culturally—but drew into its vortex a considerable number of indigenous people to swell their ranks. Before the close of the thirteenth century, the followers of Islam had effected permanent, though scattered, settlements all over northern India.

The term 'Hindu' which we have already used to denote the entirety of the socio-cultural and religio-philosophical complex of India was specially used by the Turkish tribes to designate the conquered peoples of India as a separate unit distinct from them. It was by way of distinction from the Muslims that the term Hindu came into use. This indirectly proves the essential unity of the creeds, beliefs and religious practices of the Indian people in the eyes of the foreigners. As is well known, Hindu, a modified form of Sindhu, was originally a geographical term used by the foreigners to denote, first the region round the Sindhu river, and then the whole of India. The Indians never called themselves by this name before the Turkish conquest. It was reintroduced after the Turkish conquest with the added significance that it denoted the aggregate of peoples in India and their culture and religion, as distinguished from the Muslims.

The aggressive attitude of this new element in the population led to a religious and psychological resistance on the part of the Hindus. They tried to protect their religion, culture and social order, rebuilding on the old foundations wherever they could. The theistic sects like Vaiṣṇavism, Śaivism, Śāktism and so forth were brought on a single platform and attempts were made to mitigate their differences. The Buddhist insistence on faith and devotion, worship of images of different gods and goddesses and the use of Sanskrit in liturgical texts, and the acceptance of the essentials of Buddhism by the non-Buddhists, contributed a great deal to the development of a wide and receptive Hinduism and the identification of the Buddha with Viṣṇu by means of the theory of incarnation completed the process. Jainism was also influenced by this process of assimilation.

In spite of the destruction of some great shrines in North India, the growth of big temples constituted an important feature in the religious development of this period, particularly in South India. Rich endowments made to them by kings, merchants and other men of wealth made them not only centres of religious education, but also those of missionary activity and spiritual inspiration like the Buddhist monasteries. The *maṭhas* which grew up in large numbers, not only supplemented these activities but also took up humanitarian work like feeding the poor and tending the sick. The humanitarian works were initiated by the Jain monasteries which comprised five forms of benevolence—offering of food, water, shelter, medicine and knowledge. These were later taken up by the Śaivas and other theistic sects.

In the preceding period, as we have seen above, the Vaiṣṇava Āḷvars and the Śaiva Nāyanars of the south had invested *bhakti* with the attributes of earthly love. The *Bhāgavata Purāṇa* which was also composed in the South was accepted as the gospel of *bhakti* throughout the country. After AD 1000 Yāmunācārya, who began his apostolic career under the Cola kings, propagated the doctrine of *prapatti* or 'surrendering of the self to the will of God.' His successor Rāmānuja not only developed this doctrine by providing it with a philosophic background, but raised it to the level of a monotheistic religion. When Rādhā came to be associated with Kṛṣṇa in the popular imagination, the *bhakti* movement received a still more powerful impetus. About AD 1150 Nimbārka founded a new school in Andhra emphasising the concept of the Rādhā-Kṛṣṇa combine. Madhva in Karnataka gave a new orientation to the *bhakti* cult from a dualistic philosophical approach.

Śaivism during this period was intextricably blended with Śāktism. Śaivism took a new turn in Kashmir in the preceding age and it continued to flourish in the early medieval period. Of the successors of Abhinavagupta who wrote on the Pratyabhijñā system and whose works are regarded as most authoritative by the Śāktas all over India, mention may be made of Kṣemarāja, the author of the *Pratyabhijñāhṛdaya*, which is an important manual of the Śaivas as well as of the Śāktas. Another school of Śaivism which flourished in South India during the period under review, and which still claims as its followers a large number of Tamils, is Śaiva Siddhānta according to which the supreme reality is Śiva. Its principal theoretical basis has been supplied by Meykaṇḍa's *Śivajñānabodham* and Aruḷnandi's *Śivajñānasiddhiyar*. Śrīkaṇṭha, who was probably a contemporary of Rāmānuja, expounded a system of Śaivism which is called Śivādvaita from a purely monistic point of view.

Among all the Śaiva schools the Vīraśaivas or the Liṅgāyatas were more akin to Śāktism. In fact, the Vīraśaiva philosophy is called Śaktiviśiṣṭādvaitavāda which means the non-duality of Śiva as qualified by Śakti. Śakti is the power which eternally resides in Śiva as his inseparable attribute. It is the ultimate creative principles, *mūlaprakṛti* or *Māyā*, which evolves itself into the phenomenal universe. As heat is to fire and light to sun, Śakti is to Śiva, inseparably united with him as his attribute. It is through his Śakti that Śiva becomes the cause of the universe. Śiva lends his own nature to Śakti; and in its discriminative or differentiating aspect (*vimarśākhyā*), it becomes the agent of world-manifestation. Out of Śakti come all beings that constitute the universe. And in *pralaya*, all return to Śakti and remain therein in a seedal form. It is also interesting to note that the

Vīraśaivas were also socially conscious. They believed in the spiritual merit of social works. Manual and professional labour was highly extolled as meritorious act. The establishment of charitable institutions was encouraged by them and education for all was their top priority. Women were held in high esteem. The *dīkṣā* ceremony which took the place of *upanayana* was performed in the case of the girls also, and the women, too, had to wear the *linga*, like men. The widows were allowed to marry and women were not considered to be polluted during their monthly periods. The Kāpāla and Kālāmukha sects were also pro-Śākta.

III

Tantric ideals associated with the cult of Śakti changed Buddhism to such a great extent that it ceased to be Buddhism at all. Belief in the efficacy of *mantra*, *maṇḍala* and other elements of esoteric practices was firmly established while the conception of ultimate reality as a duality of Male and Female Principles—Upāya and Prajñā in Buddhism, Śiva and Śakti in Śaivism and Kṛṣṇa and Rādhā in Vaiṣṇavism—became a common basis of philosophical understanding. The conceptions of Śūnyatā and Karuṇā of Mayāyāna Buddhism later developed into those of Prajñā and Upāya of Tantric Buddhism symbolizing the Female and Male Principles respectively. Prajñā is viewed as a goddess (Bhagavatī). The term is also used to denote *mudrā*, technically a woman to be adopted for the purpose of ritual. In some Buddhist Tantras, a beautiful girl of sixteen to be adopted for the *sādhanā* is styled Prajñā. Again in some places Prajñā is the word for female organ which is the seat of all pleasure (*mahāsukha*). Upāya and Prajñā are also called the thunder (*vajra*) and the lotus (*padma*) respectively, the former symbolizing the male organ (*maṇi*, *linga*) and the latter, the female (*yoni*).

According to the original Mahāyāna conception, Śūnyatā or perfect wisdom, and Karuṇā, or universal compassion, generate in one's mind the *bodhi-citta*, a state in which one is free from all worldliness. The *bodhi-citta* next proceeds on an upward march, through ten different stages (*bhūmis*), and when the last stage is reached one becomes a perfect Bodhisattva. Tantric Buddhism interprets the whole thing in a different way. Hence Śūnyatā is identified with Prajñā, the Female Principle, and Karuṇā with Upāya, the Male, and it is held that the inner union of the two produces supreme bliss. Since the human body is the abode of the Buddha, and also the epitome of the universe, liberation must come through the actions of the body alone (*kāyā-sādhanā*) and thus sex even can lead one to the realisation of the ultimate reality.

With the identification of Prajñā and Upāya with the Female and Male Principles respectively, the idea of Śakti and Śiva was established in the Buddhist Tantras. From a metaphysical point of view Prajñā is the passive spectator, while Upāya or Karuṇā is the active agent that stirs up 'waves of mentation' in Prajñā. This idea seems to be closely akin to the popular Sāṅkhya view, and thus the metaphysical significance of Prajñā and Upāya has a close bearing on the conception of Śakti and Śiva. The only difference is that in Śāktism, the male spirit (Śiva or Puruṣa) is the passive spectator whose existence is necessary to stir up energy in Prakṛti (Śakti or the Female Principle), and it is Prakṛti or Śakti that is the only active world force. But notwithstanding this difference in notion, Prajñā and Upāya have throughout been drawn in the image of Śiva and Śakti.

In the first state of its transformation, as we have already pointed out, Mahāyāna Buddhism was subdivided into two district schools, the Mantrayāna (*nāya*) and Pāramitāyāna. The former seems to be the introductory stage from which other offshoots like Vajrayāna, Kālacakrayānā, Sahajayāna, etc. arose in later times.

The justification of the name Vajrayāna is probably due to the term Vajra in place of Śūnyatā, i.e. the void nature of the self and all entities. According to this school, the ultimate reality is Vajrasattva who as the Primal Enlightened one is Ādi-Buddha, possessed of five kinds of knowledge as attributes that give rise to five Dhyānī-Buddhas, viz. Vairocana, Ratnasambhava, Amitābha, Amoghasiddhi and Akṣobhya, each associated with a Female Principle (Śakti) of his own viz. Vajradhātvīśvarī, Locanā, Māmakā, Pāṇḍarā and Ārya-Tārā respectively. The consort of Vajrasattva himself is variously called as Vajra-Sattvātmikā, Vajra-Vārāhī, Prajñā-Pāramitā, etc. Each god is to be meditated on as in union with his Śakti or Prajñā. In sculpture we have reflection of this. About the tenth century AD, the Kālacakrayāna school developed within the fold of Vajrayāna, the supreme deity of which is Śrī Kālacakra. Kāla represents Prajñā and Cakra Upāya, and thus Kālacakra implies the absolute union of the Female and Male principles. Essentially there is little difference between Vajrayāna and Kālacakrayāna. Sahajayāna on the other hand was a revolutionary form which denied all conventionalism, ceremonialism, muttering of *mantras*, etc. of Vajrayāna. The Sahajiyā Buddhists adopted human nature itself as the best appliance for realising the truth, and hence they called their path the easiest and the most natural (*sahaja*).[4] To explain their viewpoints, we think, something more should be stated. The real origin of the Buddhist Sahajiyā cult, observes S.B. Dasgupta,

> is not to be sought exclusively or even mainly in any of the theories and practices of Buddhism proper either in its Hīnayāna or Mahāyāna aspect. The real origin of the cult lies more outside Buddhism than inside it. The Buddhist Sahajiyā cult, notwithstanding the Buddhist tone and colour which it assumes, is essentially an esoteric yogic cult. Side by side with the commonly known theological speculations and religious practices, there has been flowing in India an important religious undercurrent of esoteric yogic practices from a pretty old times; these esoteric practices, when associated with the theological speculations of the Śaivas and the Śāktas, have given rise to the Śaiva and Śākta Tantrism, when associated with Buddhist speculations these esoteric practices have given rise to the composite religious system of Buddhist Tantrism, and, again, when associated with the speculations of Bengal Vaiṣṇavism the same esoteric practices have been responsible for the growth of the esoteric Vaiṣṇavite cult, known as the Vaiṣṇava Sahajiyā movement.[5]

The Sahajiyās never prescribe any unnatural strain on human nature. Great importance is laid in Sahajiyā literature on human body which is believed to be the abode of truth and also the medium of realising the truth. The bliss produced through the union of the male and the female, symbolising Prajñā and Upāya, i.e. the Bodhicitta, is conceived as Sahaja or the innate nature of the self and the world around. Prajñā or the goddess manifests herself in every woman, and every man is the embodiment of Upāya, the Male Principle, and their union alone can produce supreme bliss. In the Caryā songs we find mention of this Female Principle variously called as Ḍombī, Śabarī, Yoginī, Nairāmaṇi, Sahaja-sundarī, etc. and there is also frequent mention of the union of the aspirant with this personified female deity.

The conception of the four plexuses or lotuses located in different parts of the body along the spinal cord is a prominent aspect of Buddhist Kāya-sādhana. The first situated in the navel region represents the Nirmāṇa-kāya of the Buddha, the second in the cardiac region represents the Dharma-kāya; the third near the neck represents the Sambhoga-kāya; and the fourth in the *uṣṇīṣakamala* or head represents the Vajra-kayā or Sahaja-kāya. The Female Principle remaining in the Nirmāṇa-kāya is symbolized as Caṇḍālī, and in her upward march she is often described as Ḍombī, and when raised in the highest stage, she is Sahaja-sundarī. The aspirants, both male and female, must realise their true self as Upāya and Prajñā respectively and with this realisation they are to perform sexual intercourse and act in such a way as the downward motion of the seed may be checked and an upward motion given to it till it reaches the *uṣṇīṣakamala* and remains there motionless. The Buddhist conception was influenced by the Śākta Tantras according to which six nerve-plexuses of lotuses (*ṣaṭ-cakra*)—Mūlādhāra, Svādhiṣṭhāna, Maṇipura, Anāhata, Viśuddha and Ājñā—can be located in the human body.[6]

Tantric Buddhism was very popular in eastern India and also in parts of Kashmir and Nepal. In Eastern India Nālandā, Odantapurī and Vikramaśīlā were important monasteries. The monastery of Somapurī, the site of which is represented by Paharpur in north Bengal, was in a flourishing condition till the eleventh century. Another was at Jagaddala in north Bengal which was established by Rāmapāla. In Kashmir, as in Bengal, Vajrayāna and Kālacakrayāna found a fertile soil. The Tangyur furnishes us with the names of a fairly large number of Vajrācāryas and Kālacakrācāryas of Kashmir of this period.

IV

While Buddhism was passing through a process of metamorphosis during this period. Jainism was a very active force in Gujarat and Rajasthan. Its followers contributed much to the causes of architecture and literature during the period under review. Many temples of Rajasthan, Gujarat and Kathiawar bear evidence of the Jain contribution to architecture. Medieval sculptures hailing from diverse sites of Rajasthan are associated with Jain cults. Special mention should be mentioned in this connection of the ceiling reliefs of the Neminātha temple of Mount Abu, built by Tejaḥpāla in AD 1230. In the field of literature the Jain authors did much for the progress of Prakrit and Apabhraṃśa. Jainism, due to its innate rigidity and conservative character was not swayed by the Tantric wave, but the concept of the Female Principle and some rituals of Tantric character crept into its fold. Under the patronage of the later Cālukyas and Hoysalas, it was able to maintain itself in the Deccan and South India. But the Hoysala rulers were later converted to Vaiṣṇavism, while the Colas and the Pāṇḍyas, who were bigoted Śaivas, did not favour the Jains. The Jain Kalacuri ruler Vijjala was dethroned by a revolution led by the Vīraśaivas. Still Jainism survived, and survives even today, mainly due to three reasons. First of all, Jainism had its maximum followers among the wealthy merchant communities. Secondly, the strongholds of Jainism suffered less from the iconoclastic fury of the early Turkish invaders. And lastly, the influence of Tantrism upon Jainism was not so vigorous as to change its basic character.

V

A section of the Vaiṣṇavas of Bengal developed a typical Sahajiyā cult of their own.

> A close study of the literature of the Vaiṣṇava Sahajiyās will leave no room for doubting the clear fact that it records nothing but the spirit and practices of the earlier Buddhist and Hindu Tantric cults, of course in a distinctly transformed form wrought through the evolution of centuries in different religious and cultural environments.[7]

The Mainmati Plate (13th century) speaks of the existence of the Sahajiyā cult in Tripura. Caṇḍidāsa (14th century) was probably a Vaiṣṇava Sahajiyā and in his *Śrī Kṛṣṇakīrtana* we can trace some of the fundamental doctrines of this sect. In Sahajiyā Vaiṣṇavism, Kṛṣṇa and Rādhā, like Śiva and Śakti, or Upāya and Prajñā, symbolise the Male and Female principles. The Vaiṣṇava Sahajiyā, ideal holding men and women to be nothing but physical manifestation of Kṛṣna and Rādhā should therefore be taken into account in its proper historical perspective.

The conception of Rādhā was not developed even in the *Bhāgavata Purāṇa* which was composed about the tenth century AD. But in the *Gītagovinda* of Jayadeva, composed about the twelfth century, and in the *Brahmavaivarta Purāṇa* (thirteenth century) we find that Rādhā has become a driving force of Vaiṣṇavism. This gradual increase of her influence was probably the religious consequence of the dualistic interpretation of the Vedānta by the Vaiṣṇava philosophers. According to Rāmānuja (1016-1137), Māyā or Prakṛti, the Śakti of Brahman, is subject to transformation or *pariṇāma* and hence the instrumental cause of creation. This energy of Brahman is deified in the form of Śrī or Lakṣmī, the consort of Nārāyaṇa. This idea was advanced by Nimbārka (twelfth century AD) who gave exclusive prominence to the conception of Kṛṣṇa attended by the cowherdesses headed by Rādhā. Madhva (thirteenth century), founder of the Dvaita school, however, did not favour the conception of Kṛṣṇa attended by Rādhā. Following Rāmānuja, he conceived on Brahman and his Śakti in the forms of Viṣṇu (Nārāyaṇa) and Lakṣmī (Śrī) residing in heaven, and this conception emphasises their greatness and majesty (*aiśvarya*). But the conception of Rādhā, which distinguishes the followers of Nimbārka, and later Vallabha and Caitanya, reveals a taste of God's companionship in the Vṛndāvana-līlā, the most intimate human social relationship in which he appears along with his consort as human being among other humans without transcending the limitations of manhood.[8]

In Bengal and Orissa specially Śākta-Tantric ideas exerted a tremendous influence on Vaiṣṇava ideas and practices. The Śākta goddess Ekānaṃśā was able to find her way into the Vaiṣṇava religion as the consort of Kṛṣṇa. Her image between Kṛṣṇa and Balarāma can be seen in the sanctum of the Ananta-Vāsudeva temple at Bhuvaneshwara. In the Jagannātha temple at Purī she is placed between Jagannātha and Balarāma as their sister Subhadrā. Jagannātha was a tribal god worshipped with primitive Tantric rites. Subsequently he was taken into the fold of Vaiṣṇavism, but the Tantric rites associated with his cult continue to exist even today. According to the Śākta-Tantric tradition, the presiding deity of the Śrīkṣetra is the goddess Vimalā and Jagannātha is her consort or Bhairava.[9]

In the *Lakṣmītantra*, a Pāñcarātra text composed between the ninth and twelfth centuries AD the doctrine of Śakti is accorded such a high place that later Śākta philosophers and commentators like Bhāskara Rāya, Nāgeśa Bhaṭṭa, Appaya Dīkṣita and others have not only mentioned it but also cited it as an authoritative work for the understanding of Śāktism. The text has two objective in view—to establish the supremacy of Lakṣmī as a cosmic principle, ranking if not higher than Viṣṇu then at least equal to him, and to set down a full record of exclusive Śākta *upāsanā* within the framework of the Pāñcarātra system. Here the Vyūha doctrine is explained in terms of Lakṣmī as the Supreme Being. Pure creation is traced to Lakṣmī, the embodiment of six ideal attributes. In this work emanations of Mahāśrī, Mahāvidyā and Mahāmāyā from Mahālakṣmī are dealt with. Evolution of the material world from *prakṛti* has been traced in terms of the Sāṅkhya categories. The six *kośas* of Śakti have been described. Other topics include the *tattvas* and *jīva* as the object and subject of knowledge; the *avatāras* of Lakṣmī in the six sheaths; the exclusive incarnations of Śakti; the true nature of Śakti or Lakṣmī; the course of *mantras* and their characteristics; the origin of letters; explanation of the *mātṛkās*; description of Lakṣmī's *mantra* form; Tārā and Anutārā *mantras*; elucidation of seven *vidyās*; different aspects of Śakti; Tārikā in the three stages of existence; purification, images, external sacrifice and worship, initiation, *puraścaraṇa* and so forth; Lakṣmī's various manifestations; etc. Moreover, it alludes to the peculiar *sādhanā* of the left-handed Tantras that requires a female partner.[10]

VI

Śaivism during the period under review had theoretically merged into Śāktism and also the latter into the former. As we have stated above, in spite of all criticisms of Śaṅkara against the Śākta religion, two authoritative Śākta texts—*Prapañcasāra Tantra* and *Saundarya-laharī*—are ascribed to him. A section of the followers of Kashmir Śaivism developed a peculiar monistic form of Śāktism known as Śāktyadvayavāda according to which Śakti is not different from Śiva and as such the material world is the *pariṇāma* or consequence of Śakti. Somānanda criticised this Śāktyādvayavāda for its emphasis on Śakti as the only substance. Although he was a Śaiva in conviction, his analysis of Vāk is a valuable contribution to Śākta thought. Śāktism has also been thoroughly dealt with in Abhinavagupta's *Tantrāloka, Mālinīvijayavārttika, Parātriṃśikavivaraṇa, Pratyabhijñā-vivṛttivimarśiṇī,* etc. In Kṣemarāja's *Pratyabhijñahṛdaya*, Gorakṣa's *Mahārthamañjarī* and others, the mystic, theological, epistemic, psychological and metaphysical aspects of the Śaiva-Śākta Āgamas have been discussed. According to the *Śivardṛṣṭi,*[11] *Iśvarapratyabhijñā*[12] and *Pratyabhi-jñāhṛdaya*[13] the important modes of Śakti are *cit* (intelligence), *ānanda* (bliss), *icchā* (wish), *jñāna* (knowledge) and *kriyā* (action). With the opening out of Śakti the world appears, and with her closing it disappears. There is an equilibrium between Śiva and Śakti, and the latter is conceived of as the essence of the former. Śakti is called

Prakāśa-Vimaraśamaya. Of the numerous meanings of *vimarśa* one is vibration, and the term is used expressly in the case of Śakti while Śiva is *prakāśa*. If the example of a man is used, *prakāśa* is his mental and intellectual faculties and the awareness of those faculties is *vimarśa*. According to Kashmir Śaivism the Supreme Being is at the same time static and dynamic, changeless and changing. The dynamic aspect is Śakti, that power which manifests itself in the world, as a banian tree manifests itself from a seed (*vatadhānikāvat*).

Vīraśaivism or Liṅgāyatism, which resorts to the primitive aspects of the Śiva-Śakti cult, envisages an integral association between Śiva and Śakti, known as Śaktiviśiṣṭādvaitavāda. Here the potential and material moment of the Absolute is called Śiva while the actual and formal moment is called Śakti. It holds that creation is the result of the *vimarśa-śakti*. According to the *Siddhāntaśikhāmaṇi*[14] the real nature of Śiva is like the luminescence of a gem which the gem itself can not realise. This realisation is possible only by Śakti. That is why the relation between Śiva and Śakti is that of identify, *tādātmya* or *sāmarasya*, as that between heat and fire, light and sun. Here an objection may be raised by saying that there may be a subtle difference between Śakti and its container. The Vīraśaiva answer to this point is that in the case of the heat and fire or the light and the sun, there is no difference of quality with the nature of substance. Here quality and substance can not be differentiated because of their identity. That is why Śakti is called Brahmaniṣṭhā Sanātanī.

Another school of Śaivism which flourished in south India during the period under review was Śaiva Siddhānta. This school conceives of Śiva as the operative cause of the world and not as the material cause. Śakti (*māyā*) is existent and material cause of the world. The followers of this school think, of the basis of the Satkāryavāda of the Sāṅkhya, that the material world, which is an effect, must have a material cause, and the constituents of the cause cannot be qualitatively different from those of the effect. The world is material, devoid of consciousness, and therefore the immaterial Brahman cannot be regarded as its cause. Māyā is the primordial stuff of which the world is made. Being non-intelligent, Māyā cannot evolve of itself. It requires the guidance of Śiva who acts on it through his *cit-śakti*. Thus guided Māyā projects from itself the *tattvas* which constitute the universe.

Śrīkaṇṭha, a contemporary of Rāmānuja, expounded a system of Śaivism which is called Śivādvaita. According to this school Śiva or

Brahman is the material as well as the operative cause of the world. He is both immanent and transcendent, but effects the manifestation of the world through his Śakti or power which is divided into three aspects—*icchā* (will), *jñāna* (knowledge) and *kriyā* (action).

While the different schools of Śaivism were thus setting up their cosmological ideas in terms of the relation between Śiva and Śakti, there were others who were still following the older tribal rituals. Mention should be made in this connection of the Kāpālikas and Kālāmukhas who were mentioned by their opponents as representing the horrid and repulsive forms of Śaivism. In the absence of any literature of their own, any conclusion drawn from the writings of the opponents must be one-sided and unhistorical. According to tradition, Śaṅkara had a philosophical contest with them. Their beliefs and practices are mentioned, evidently in a distorted way, in the *Śiva Purāṇa* and other Śaiva texts. According to Rāmānuja, the Kāpālikas maintained that an individual could attain the highest bliss by concentrating his mind on the soul seated on the female organ. They worshipped Śiva as Bhairava with his wife Caṇḍikā.[15]

In the literary products of this age, the male and female principles in their personified forms were given much prominence. The anthologies compiled between AD 1000 and 1300—e.g. the *Subhāṣitāvalī* of Vallabhadeva, the *Saduktikarṇāmṛta* of Śrīdhardeva, the *Śuktimuktāvalī* of Jalhaṇa, etc.—give a nice picture of the domestic life of Śiva and Devī, their love-plays and quarrels and other aspects collected from different sources. The *stotrakāvyas* of this age, e.g. the *Caṇḍīkucapañcāśikā* of Lakṣmaṇa Ācārya describe the physical charms of the goddess. In regional literatures also Śiva and Pārvatī began to figure as hero and heroine. The popular theme of Śiva's marriage with Pārvatī found expression in Harihara's Kannada work *Girijākalyāṇa* which was composed about the twelfth century AD. Nannecoda's Telugu *Kumārasambhavam* should also be mentioned in this connection. The Tamil Śaiva Siddhānta scriptures reveal much of the philosophical aspects of Śiva and Śakti, and this also holds good in the case of Marathi Nātha literature. The Caryāpadas, generally regarded as the specimens of Old Bengali, although they deal with Buddhist esoterism, are really the precursors of later Śiva-Śakti-oriented literature of which we shall refer to in the next chapter.

VII

The *Hevajra Tantra* of the Buddhists, which was composed about the middle of the eighth century AD, enumerates the following four holy regions as *pīṭhas* or resorts of the goddess: (1) Jālandhara, (2) Oḍiyāna, (3) Pūrṇagiri, and (4) Kāmarūpa.[16] Other Buddhist works, such as the *Sādhanamālā*,[17] give the four names as Oḍiyāna or Uḍḍiyāna, Pūrṇagiri, Kāmarūpa or Kāmākyā and Śrīhaṭṭa or Sirihaṭṭa. Jālandhara in the Punjab region seems to have been recognised as one of the four *pīṭhas* even down to the late medieval period. Oḍiyāna or Uḍḍiyāna is located in the Swat valley, although some scholars have wrongly identified it with Oḍra or Orissa in eastern India. Hiuen Tsang not only noticed the prevalence of Śakti worship in Gāndhāra, but has also left an account of the Tantric practices among the peoples of Uḍḍiyāna. Its eminence in the Tantric world is indicated by the recognised association of its name with the worship of the Buddhist deities Mārīcī, Kurukullā, etc. The identification of Pūrṇagiri is uncertain. Later sources locate it in Maharashtra. The name may not be unconnected with that of the Pūrṇā (modern Paira), a branch of the Godavari.[18] It is interesting to note that the Chinese pilgrim Hiuen Tsang who lived for some time at the court of the Kāmarūpa king Bhāskaravarman in the seventh century was silent about the goddess Kāmākhyā. It is therefore not improbable that the presiding deity of Kāmarūpa did not quite attain her pre-eminence in the days of Hiuen Tsang. The goddess seems to be called Mahāgaurī in the records of Vanamāla (10th century) and Indrapāla (12th century), kings of Kāmarūpa.[19]

The *Rudrayāmala*, which was composed about the tenth century AD, mentions ten holy places associated with Śākta-Tantric practices. These ten *pīṭhas*, which include the celebrated four mentioned above are: (5) Vārāṇasī (Benaras), (6) Jvalantī (Jvālāmukhī of later texts), (7) Māyāvatī (near Haridwar), (8) Madhupurī (Mathurā), (9) Ayodhyā (near Faizabad, U.P.), and (10) Kāñcī (Conjeeveram in the Chingleput district). The *Kubjikātantra* enumerates 42 centres of Śakti cult: Māyāvatī, Madhupurī, Kāśī, Gorakṣakāriṇī, Hiṅgulā, Jalāndhara, Jvālāmukhī, Nāgarasambhava, Rāmagiri, Godāvarī, Nepāla, Karṇasūtra, Mahākaraṇa, Ayodhyā, Kurukṣetra, Siṃhala, Maṇipura, Hṛṣikeśa, Prayāga, Badari, Ambikā, Vardhamāna or Ardhanālaka, Triveṇī, Gaṅgāsāgara-saṅgama, Nārikela, Virajā, Uḍḍiyāna, Kamalā, Vimalā, Māhiṣmatī, Vārāhī, Tripurā, Vāgmatī,

Nīlavāhinī, Govardhana, Vindhyagiri, Kāmarūpa, Ghaṇṭākarṇa, Hayagrīva-Madhava, Kṣīragrāma and Vaidyanātha.[20]

About AD 1030, Alberuni wrote: "In inner Kashmir, about two or three days' journey from the capital in the direction towards the mountains of Bolor, there is a wooden idol called Śāradā, which is much venerated and frequented by pilgrims"[21] The Śaradā *maṭha* on the borders of Kashmir is mentioned in such other works as the *Śaktisaṅgama Tantra.*[22] The temple of Śāradā is also mentioned in Kalhaṇa's *Rājataraṅgiṇī.*[23] The ruins of Sardi, where it stood, lie at the confluence of the Kishenganga and Kankatori rivers. The old shrine is substituted by the late Śāradā temple at Gusha which is now visited by pilgrims.[24] It should be pointed out in this connection that very few independent Śakti temples existed in north India during the period with which we are concerned in the present chapter. In South India also Śakti shrines could only raise their heads within the compounds of the great Śiva temples. We had already occasion to refer to the Cola inscriptions speaking of two different varieties of temples, *Srikoyil* and *Tirumuṟṟam,* respectively denoting the shrines for male gods and female deities.

In Rajasthan, the shrines of Saciyā Mātā and Piplā Devī, belonging to the later series of the Osian group of temples, should be mentioned in this connection. The principal back niche of the former preserves an image of Mahisaṃardinī addressed as Saccīkā or Saciyā in the inscriptions of vs 1234 and 1236.[25] At Bikaner, there is a temple of the eight-armed Durgā, popularly known as Nāgenekji and another of this kind is at Bhainsolgarh in the Udaipur district. Shrines dedicated to the goddess Kālikā are found at Achalgarh (Mt. Abu), Chitor, Nasirabad and Dholpur and those to the goddess Cāmuṇḍā at Jodhpur, Jaswantpur, Bhinmal, Ajmer and other places. An image of Ambā was installed at Amba by the Kacchwaha king Kankal Rao in AD 1037, who built a temple over it. The Mātṛkā cult was popular at Mandor. Besides the forms mentioned above, Śakti was worshipped under different local names in Rajasthan, e.g. Karṇimātā (Deshnokh), Mokalmātā (Bālī), Khokrimātā (Tivri), Śākambharī, Āśāpurī (Sambhar), Kaivasamātā (Parvatsar), Khimalmātā (Vasantgarh), Kailādevī (Karauli), Sakraimātā (Khandela), Jinamātā (Raivasa), Susānimātā (Morkhana), etc. Of the Śakti temples of Gujarat of this age mention may be made of the shrine of Raṇik Devī at Wadhwan in Kathiawar and that of Limboji Mātā at Dhelmal.

In Central India, a few of the Amarkantak and Khajuraho group of temples were dedicated to Śakti. An image of Sarasvatī was installed at Dhara by Bhoja (AD 1000-1055) which reveals Paramāra sculpture at the best. Other specimens of the goddess is found at Mandu, on the walls of the Nīlakaṇṭha temple at Udaipur, within the enclosures of the Mahākāla temple at Ujjayinī, and other places. The temple of Devī Jagadambā at Khajuraho is marked by exuberance of sculptures and rich ornamentation. The Caunsaṭh Yoginī temple at Khajuraho[26] should specially be mentioned for its architectural traits. Temples dedicated to sixty-four Yoginīs are scattered all over Central India. We have already referred to the temple at Bheraghat which is 116 feet in internal diameter with 81 peripheral chapels together with a shrine containing an image of Umā-Maheśvara. The sixty-four Yoginī temples at Mitauli near Padhauli (eleventh century) is marked by 65 principal chapels and a circular central shrine with *maṇḍapa* in front.[27] Circular Yoginī temples are also found at Ranipur Jharial in the old Patna State,[28] Dudhai in the Lalitpur district[29] and in the Old Kalahandi state.[30]

The temples of Mohinī, Kapālinī and Gaurī at Bhuvaneswara, Vimalā at Purī, Kicakeśvarī at Khiching, Virajā at Jaipur, Maṅgalā at Katakpur, Curcikā at Banki, Ugratārā at Bhusandapur, Vārāhī at Chaurāsī, Śāralā at Jhankad, Solapuamā and Caṇḍī at Cuttack, Saptamātṛkā at Belkhandi, Dharamśālā and the neighbouring areas of Jaipur, Yoginīs at Hirapur, Śamaleśvarī at Sambalpur, etc. show the wide distribution of Śakti cult in Orissa. A few of these temples however belong to a later date. The Gaurī temple at Bhuvaneswara contains a Śakti image as its presiding deity and in the Anantavāsudeva temple of the thirteenth century AD. Ekānaṃśā is worshipped along with Balarāma and Vāsudeva. Images of Mahiṣamardinī are found on the walls of the Vaitāla, Śiśireśvara and Mārkaṇḍeśvara temples. A large number of Tantric Buddhist deities like different kinds of Tārā, Heruka, Kurukullā, Aparājitā, etc. are found from Udayagiri, Ratnagiri and Lalitagiri.[31]

From different sites of Bengal numerous Śakti images, belonging to the period under review, are found, many of which are identified with the Tantric deities. Special mention should be made in this connection of the famous Caṇḍī image from Dalbazar, Dacca (3rd year of Lakṣmaṇasena) which is often identified with Bhuvaneśvarī. A four-armed image of Śarvāṇī, found at Maṅgalbari, Dinajpur, has been assigned to the Pāla period. Another image of the same age, that of a two-handed Durgā, hails from South Mohammadpur in the

Tippera district. Of other four-armed goddesses, reference should be made to the images of the Devī from Mandoil (Rajshahi) and Maheswarpara (Khulna), and seated images from Bogra, Nowgong (with Kārttikeya and Gaṇeśa; identified with Sarvamaṅgalā) and Niamatpur (sandstone image identified with Aparājitā). From Kagajipara, Vikrampur, is found a four-armed goddess rising from a *liṅga.* This image has been identified with Mahāmāyā or Tripurabhairavī. A six-armed seated goddess, identified with Bhuvaneśvarī, is found at Shekati in Jessore district, while another, a twenty-armed goddess identified with Mahālakṣmī, belonging to the tenth century, is found at Simla in the Rajshahi district. Ten-armed Mahiṣamardinī forms are found from Dulmi (Manbhum) and Sakta (Dacca), both belonging to the twelfth century. From Porsha in Dinajpur is found a relief of Navadurgā. The central figure is eight-armed while the others are sixteen-armed. At Betna in the same district is found an image of a thirty-two-armed goddess fighting with the demons. Of the Mātṛkā images reference should be made to those of Cāmuṇḍā from Betna, the ruins of Rampal and Attahasa. A Brahmāṇī image is found at Devagram in Nadia. Images of the Buddhist goddess Tārā are found at Ujani (Faridpur), Sompara (Dacca) and Majvadi (Faridpur) and that of Ugratārā at Sikarpur (Bakarganj). Of other images of Buddhist goddesses reference should be made to those of Prajñāpāramitā (Maldah), Sitatapatrā (Tippera), Cundā (Niyamatpur, Rajshahi) and Parṇaśabarī (Vikrampur). A Jain image of the goddess Ambikā with children is found at Nalgora in 24 Parganas. Umā-Maheśvara and Ardhanārīśvara images of this age are rare in Bengal.[32]

VIII

The *Yāmalas* give us for the first time a well-developed Tantric pantheon. The existence of the principal *Yāmalas,* excepting the *Brahma Yāmala* and fragments of the *Rudra Yāmala,* is not known to us. The former is preserved in Nepal in a manuscript of AD 1052. It has two supplements, known as the *Jayadratha Yāmala* and the *Piṅgalāmata.* The *Jayadratha Yāmala* also exists in a manuscript of about the same period. It is divided into four sections called *ṣaṭka,* each containing six thousand *ślokas.* The text gives detailed information on the various modes of Tantric *sādhanā,* together with a description of the various branches of the Tantric literature and also of divinities, mostly Śaktis, such as Kālikā, Saṅkarṣaṇī Kālasaṅkarṣaṇī, Carcikā, Ḍāmbarakālī, Gahaneśvarī, Ekatārā, Śavaśabarī, Vajravatī, Rakṣākālī, Indīvarakālikā, Dhanadakālikā, Ramaṇīkālikā, Īśānakālikā, Mantramātā, Jīvakālī, Saptākṣarā, Ṛṣakkarṇī, Bhairavaḍākinī, Kālāntakī, Vīryakālī, Prajñākālī, Saptārṇakālī and Siddhilakṣmī. The supplementary literature of the *Yāmala* group thus indicates a Śākta orientation of the Tantric culture. This character of the Tantras became firmly established by the thirteenth century.[33]

The *Sammoha Tantra,* another descriptive work of this period, deals with various traditions and *mantras* of the Kālikāmata, the geographical classification of the Tantras and a detailed account of the *vidyās* or cults belonging to different schools. So far as the geographical classification is concerned, it distributes the Tantras into four areas—Kerala, Kāśmīra, Gauḍa and Vilāsa. Then it gives a detailed description of the Vidyās or goddesses, nearly hundred in number, all representing various aspects of Śakti, showing that the Tantras by this time had assumed a complete Śākta character and that they had assimilated a very large number of cults of various origins, regional, tribal and sectarian. This state of things must have been attained by the fourteenth century, when the *Sammoha Tantra* seems to have assumed its final form.[34]

According to the *Kaulajñānanirṇaya,* a work of the eleventh century, the Kaula class of Tantras was introduced by Matsyendra Nātha, who was probably the founder of the Yoginī-kaula of Kāmarūpa. The term *kula,* as we have seen above, stands for Śakti. There were a good number of Kaula-schools, e.g., Vṛṣaṇottha, Vahini, Sadbhāva, Padottiṣṭha, Mahā, Siddha, Jñānanirṇīti, Siddhāmṛta, Sṛṣṭi, Candra, Śaktibheda, Ūrmi, Jñāna and so on. According to Bagchi[35] the Yoginī-kaula of Matsyendra Nātha had something in common with the Buddhist Tantras of the Sahajiyā class. This syncretism probably led to the growth of the Nātha sect and the Vaiṣṇava Sahajiyās of the succeeding centuries.

The aspirants of all these groups believed in the use of psychic energy in bringing about the union of the two principles. The body was recognised as the abode of all truth, and the best medium for realising the truth. Reference has already been made to the Buddhist form in which we have the conception of four plexuses or lotuses within the body. Among the innumerable nerves of the body, three are the most important, two by the two sides of the spinal cord and one in the middle. With these two side-nerves are identified the Buddhist principles of Prajñā and Upāya. In the Śākta Tantras the nerve in the right, Upāya of the Buddhist, is known as *piṅgalā,* and that of the left, Prajñā of the Buddhists, as *iḍā.* These two represent the principle of duality, and the middle one, variously known as *suṣumnā, avadhūtikā* or *sahaja* represents absolute unity. The Śakti which resides in man, and the development of which is one of the aims of Tantrism, is called *kuṇḍalinī.* It resides in the *mūlādhāra,* the lowest extremity of the spinal cord, where it remains latent and sleeps quietly. When roused up by successful manipulation, this *kuṇḍalinī* ascends to the next higher stage, viz. *svādhiṣṭhāna* which is situated near the root of the generative organ. Hence it moves on to the centres, *maṇipura* (the navel region), *anāhata* (heart region) and *viśuddha* (junction of the spinal cord and the medulla oblongata) and finally to the *ājñā* (between the eyebrows) where the Śakti becomes manifest in the form of a flash of light. At *sahasrāra* or the highest cerebral region, the Śakti meets its source.

The goddess Śākinī resides in the *mulādhāra,* Lākinī in *maṇipura,* Rākinī in *anāhata,* Ḍākinī in *viśuddha,* Kāminī in *svādhiṣṭhāna* and Hākinī in the *ājñā,* according to the later Tantric manuals. The Kuṇḍalinī Śakti is the original Female Principle, the Devī, whom the aspirant has to send from the lowest extremity of the spinal cord to the highest cerebral point where she meets Śiva, and their union produces the liquor of immortality. Wine is the nectar which flows from the union of the Kuṇḍalinī Śakti with Śiva at the *sahasrāra* in the head. *Maithuna,* one of the five *tattvas,* symbolized by the concept of unity behind all duality, is also brought in harmony with the concept of the union of Śiva and Śakti which takes place in the *sahasrāra.*

Most of the available Tantric texts belong to the late medieval period, and hence it appears that from about the fourteenth century onwards, the Śākta-Tantric cults had gained a qualitatively changed character and become woven into the texture of all the religious practices current in India. It was due to the fact that the Śākta-Tantric cults offered a sharp criticism and rejection of all external formalities in regard to religious practices and spiritual quests, revived the mystical, obscure and esoteric, but protestant and heterodox elements of the existing religious systems and upheld a new philosophy of life which consisted of the recognition of the *guru* as essential for any spiritual exercise and quest, of the human body as the seat and habitat of all religious and spiritual experience, and of the experience of the ultimate reality on one of inexpressible happiness and absolute non-duality.

References

1. Majumdar, *AICFE*, I, 5, 62-64, 138-39, 189-95.
2. Majumdar, *IK*, 8, 13, 50, 61, 66-67, 143, 151, 161, 180, 193-94, 234, 281-82, 366 ff.
3. Sarkar, *DB*, 158 ff; Majumdar, *AICFE*, II.101 ff.
4. Dasgupta, *ITB*, 83 ff; *ORC*, 39 ff; Bagchi, *BDS*, 71 ff.
5. *ORC*, XXXIV.
6. *Infra*.
7. Dasgupta, *ORC*, 134-35.
8. For the antiquity of the Radha cult see *ABORI*, XXXVI, 231-57, also Dasgupta.
9. See my *HTR*, 253.
10. Ed. with Eng. trans. by Sanjukta Gupta, Leiden, 1972.
11. III.7.
12. I.5.14.
13. IV with com.
14. V.39.
15. For details see Lorenzen.
16. Bagchi, *ST*, 38.
17. 453, 455.
18. Sircar, *SP*, 94.
19. Bhattacharya, *KS*, intro.
20. Sircar, *SP*, 17-19.
21. Sachau, *AI*, I.117.
22. *IC*, VIII, 38, 49.
23. VIII, 2556, 2706.
24. Stein, *RT*, II, 279-89.
25. *JBRS*, XLI (I), 1-12.
26. Coomaraswamy, *HIIA*, 110.
27. *ASIAR*, 1915-16, 18.
28. Fergusson, *HIEA*, II, 151.
29. Mukherji, *RARLD*, Pl. 39.
30. Cunningham, *ASR*, XIII, 132 ff.
31. Sahu, *BO*, 181 ff.
32. Banerjea in *HB*, 450 ff.
33. Bagchi, *ST*, 109 ff.
34. Ibid., 96 ff.
35. *KMT*, intro., 33.

7

Late Medieval Śāktism (AD 1300-1700)

It has been shown in the preceding chapter that the major part of India remained free from the Turkish domination till almost the very end of the thirteenth century. But the political situation changed gradually in favour of the Muslim rulers, and the evolution of the political process was complete when the Mughals established a stable empire in the second half of the sixteenth century. The beginning of the Turkish rule was characterised by a almost wholesale destruction of temples and monasteries. The invasions, fired with the fanatic zeal for demolishing idols and temples, born of the crusading spirit of Islam, were let loose on the plains and cities of Hindustan. The pictures depicted by the victors themselves enables us to get a faint echo of how the Muslims consolidated their political authority by inflicting crushing defeats on the disunited Indian states and established their religious system by destroying the temples and idols and converting some Hindus either by persuasion or by force.

There can be no denial of the fact that although a large number of Hindu temples were destroyed and plundered by the Turkish rulers and a good number of persons were converted into Islam. India could not be Islamised. The majority of the Indians preferred to remain as Hindus. There were certain reasons behind it. Despite some major military defeats, the political importance of the Hindu rulers was not diminished. To a great extent they were able to maintain their power and position by offering allegience to the Turkish sultans and by acting as their vassals. The Muslim rulers fought not only against the Hindus, but also amongst themselves, and in many such cases they had to depend on the political and economic support of the Hindu chiefs and landlords, and also on the bankers who were mostly Jains. Very few of the Muslim rulers could reign in peace, and challenge to their authority came, not from the conquered Hindus, but from men of their own religion, even from their kinsmen. The Muslim powers in India did not belong to the same level of material culture. Alauddin Khalji fought against the

Mongols who were also Muslims and did not hesitate to put countless Muslim prisoners to death. The relation between the Muslims who had already settled in India and those who were still outsiders was bitter. The Hindus who were converted into Islam were looked down upon by other groups. This inner conflict of the Muslim interest in India was one of the causes for the survival of Hinduism under the Muslim rule.

Most historians have been guided by the over-simplified idea that the success of the Muslims in India was due to the degradation of Hinduism during the medieval period. They argue that the overall picture was one of decadence in every respect as compared to the high standard of older times. The degraded religious and social life sapped the vitality of the people and destroyed its manhood. Buddhism came down from its high pedestal and was vulgarised. This held good to other systems as well. Erotic and sensual practices undermined the sense of moral values. Whatever views may be entertained regarding the ideas and practices of Tantra in their essence and origin, there can be no denying of the fact that they led to gross debauchery and perversion of morals and ethics. The sculptural extravagance of Khajuraho, and other temples was reflection of social perversion. The sexual depictions on temples accord with the Kāmaśāstra descriptions of sexual acrobatics. The great fabric of culture and civilization, reared up in course of centuries, was tottering, and it was no longer a question of whether but when it would fall. Foreign invasions merely accelerated the process of decay and hastened the downfall which was inevitable in any case. The caste-structure of Indian society, the distinction between high and low, untouchability and social injustice were the forces contributing to the break up of the Hindu states. The Muslims drew into their vortex a considerable number of indigenous peoples, mainly from the lower castes.

Historians having a Hindu bias who believe that the medieval period is a negative period of Indian history, a great tragedy which befell India since the eleventh century, put forward such arguments as self-criticism emphasising the humiliating and degrading aspects of Hindu religion and society, while those with a Muslim bias regard this period as representing the glorious aspects of Islamic culture and its superiority. But from a strictly historical point of view it may be said that every age has its own aberrations and also its progressive aspects. A succeeding century must be more progressive than its preceding century as well as more aberrant—this is the historical process. True, there were some aberrations in Hindu society and life as there were aberrations also among the Muslims. But one thing which is generally ignored by most historians is that Indian society was always a 'civil society' and not a 'political society' in the Western sense, and that is why the appearance of a Muslim ruling class had little to do with the entirety of the Hindu way of life, especially when the Muslim rulers shared power with their subordinate Hindu chiefs and officials. The inequalities arising out of the hierarchical caste system, class division and social stratification among the Hindus also prevailed among the Muslims. It cannot also be proved that the peoples belonging to the lower ranks of the caste-hierarchy embraced Islam for the sake of social justice because the rate of conversion was indeed very low in those places of northern India which were the strongholds of the Muslim power. In the South it was minimal. But in Bengal, especially in its inaccessible eastern portion, it was very high.

In fact, Hinduism did not suffer owing to the advent of Islam in India. The intrusion of an absolutely monotheistic creed like Islam was responsible for the establishment of closer relation among the diverse religious communities of India. It is interesting to note that during the age of the Delhi Sultanate all the Vaiṣṇava and Śaiva sects sharpened their monotheistic tendencies to the extreme. One of the reasons of this monotheistic development must have been to counter Islam from a theoretical point of view. Numerous commentaries on the ancient texts were composed during the early and late medieval period which also saw the emergence of great religious and philosophical personalities such as Nāthamuni, Yāmunācārya, Rāmānuja, Nimbārka, Śrīnivāsa, Kesáva Kāśmīrī, Madhva, Jayatīrtha, Vidyādhirāja, Vallabha, Śrī Caitanya and others among the Vaiṣṇavas, Meykaṇḍa, Aruṇandi, Marayajñānasambandha, Umāpati, Aghora Sivācārya, Śrīkaṇṭha, Vasava, Abhinavagupta, Kṣemarāja, Yogarāja, Jayaratha, Bhāskarakaṇṭha, etc. among the Śaivas, Maheśvarānanda, Puṇyānanda, Nayanānanda, Amṛtānanda Svatantrānanda, Brahmānanda, Rāghavabhaṭṭa, Lakṣmaṇa Deśikendra, Bhāskararāya, Parivrājakācārya, Pūrṇānanda, Kṛṣṇānanda Āgamavāgīśa, Nīlakaṇṭha, Navamiśra, Śrīnivāsa Bhaṭṭa, Jagannivāsa, Kāśīnātha Bhaṭṭa etc. among the Śāktas. The dwindling condition of Hinduism during the Muslim rule is thus an overstatement.

II

There is a popular view that the so-called decline and downfall of Buddhism was due to its Śākta-Tantric association.[1] But it should be pointed out in this connection that the Tantric elements which are supposed to have vulgarised the pristine purity of Buddhism were not a sudden development at a given point of time; these elements were associated with all forms of Indian spiritual systems since time immemorial, and if they did not vulgarise other systems surviving in the fold of Hinduism, there is no reason why should they vulgarise Buddhism. Alex Wayman seems right when he says that "the Buddhist Tantras do not appear to have fostered Buddhism's success in India, not really in any observably significant degree to have caused Buddhism's decline."[2] Apart from its association with Tantrism, Buddhism since its inception had admixture with various heterogeneous ideas and elements as a result of which at every stage of its development it acquired new form and content. Like its own basic doctrine, the history of Buddhism was also in a perpetual flux, nothing but that of metamorphosis of ideas, each stage of its transformation being marked by a qualitative change. And at each turning point of its historical development Buddhism had acquired new dimensions and new suggestivities, no matter whether in this process the name of the Buddha became redundant or not.

Overlooking this basic feature of transformation by which the history of Buddhism has been characterised through the ages, the question of its decline and extinction at a given period of its multifarious channelization becomes irrelevant. Various causes have been attributed by scholars to its so-called decline such as just old age and sheer exhaustion,[3] internal corruption and moral decadence,[4] departure of the Buddhist scholars *en masse* to China causing a brain-drain,[5] social failure,[6] sectarianism, withdrawal of royal patronage, Muslim invasion and so forth.[7] None of these views should be taken seriously. Moreover, scholars are not at all unanimous in regard to the time of the so-called decline of Buddhism. Some think that it was in the thirteenth century; some want to go back to the seventh century; some still earlier.[8] What is the harm in accepting U. Mishra's contention that "both the rise and decline of Buddhism began almost simultaneously?"[9] It should also be pointed out in this connection that it was in the supposed declining period that Buddhism went in a renovated vigour in south-east Asia; it was in the eleventh century that Atīśa went to Tibet. Was he a product of decadence?

Some scholars hold that the most important factor of the so-called decline of Buddhism in India was really a gradual assimilation of Buddhism to Hinduism[10] in the process of which people found no difference between the worship of Viṣṇu and Buddha, Śiva and Avalokiteśvara, of Pārvatī and Tārā. The acceptance of the Buddha as an incarnation of Viṣṇu, the disapproval of animal sacrifice, organisation of monastic communities on the line of the Buddhist Saṅgha, emphasis on image worship, prayers and incantations pompous ceremonies and rituals, incorporation of many folk-beliefs, etc. were responsible for this assimilation.

> In the post-Gupta period the Tantra practices harmonized the two systems so completely that Buddhism's independent existence might have appeared needless or even impossible. In spite of their being 'proclaimed by the Buddha' the Buddhist Tantras are almost identical with the Śaiva and Śākta Tantras. A large number of gods and goddesses became common to the pantheon of Hinduism and Buddhism. The Śākta *pīṭhas* became equally important and holy for Hindu and Buddhist Tantrikists.[11]

The flaw of this line of reasoning is not in the conclusion, but in the major premise itself. Most scholars, though understood the identity of Hinduism and Buddhism, imagined a difference between the two and counted the latter as a different form of religon. T.W. Rhys Davids frankly admitted that 'Gotama was born, brought up and lived and died as a Hindu' and that 'Buddhism grew and flourished within the fold of orthodox belief.'[12] Mrs. C.A.F. Rhys Davids held that the Tripiṭaka did not show any rupture with the Brāhmaṇas and the preaching of the Buddha agreed those of Brahmanism.[13] The same was the view of R.G. Basak,[14] Radhakrishnan[15] and Upadhyaya.[16] According to Coomaraswamy, "the more profound is one's study of Hinduism and Buddhism, more difficult it becomes for him to distinguish between the two."[17]

But while dealing with Buddhism scholars use a different standard. A distinction is generally made between Hinduism and Buddhism. This artificial distinction was due to the early European contact with the Buddhist countries, the Christian missionaries and traders being responsible for popularising the idea that in the Eastern countries people practised a cult of the Buddha. Thus the term Buddhism was coined at a period when its intimate relation with Hinduism was not known. Subsequently when this relation was discovered, the Western scholars who made pioneering researches on Buddhism admitted it without any hesitation, but they preferred to maintain a distinction between the two. Because Buddhism went to many countries outside India and acquired a functional significance of religious character, its separate identity was stressed. There also might have been some political motivation for introducing this separation. Although the relation between Hinduism and Buddhism was thought of in terms of identity-in-difference, this principle was not boldly used to explain the Indian situation of Buddhism. Had it been done the question of the so-called decline and extinction of Buddhism could never have arisen.

And a basic point which is generally missed is that Buddhism has always been a thought-complex and not a religion in the real sense. It acted as a crucible which generated numerous ideas and practices. Its role as a thought-complex was similar, if not the same, to that of the Vedānta in generating the growth of multifarious spiritual systems, and as such its decline and extinction became meaningless since there is a difference between generated objects and the generating principle. The period which has been stigmatised by most historians as that of the decline and disappearance of Buddhism was in reality the only period in which it was able to come out of its dry academic shell and renovate all the existing traditional and popular spiritual disciplines by its own spirit.[18]

III

During the period of the Delhi Sultanate there were three powerful Hindu kingdoms in India—Vijayanagara, Orissa and Mewar—and also a number of independent Hindu states like Kāmarūpa, Nepāl, Mithilā, etc. The early kings of Vijayanagara were ardent Śaivas. To their credit goes the construction of a good number of temples each of which contained an Amman shrine, representing a subsidiary temple for the enshrinement of the consort of the installed deity. The temples also contained Kalyāṇa-maṇḍapa, an open pillared pavilion with an elevated platform in the centre for the exhibition of the image of the deity and his consort on ceremonial occasions. Among the Kalyāṇa-maṇḍapas that may be assigned to the Vijayanagara epoch mention may be made of those in the Pārvatī temple at Chidambaram, in the temples of Varadarājasvāmin and Ekāmbaranātha at Kāñcipuram, in the Jambukeśvara temples near

Trichinopoly and in the Mārgaśākheśvara temple at Virinjipuram.[19] Vīraśaivism continued to spread in the Kannada country and even beyond its borders.

Later kings of Vijayanagara developed a partiality for Vaiṣṇavism, and under the Tuluva rulers it gained further strength. In South India, Rāmānuja's school of Vaiṣṇavism was divided into a number of sub-sects, like the Vaḍakalai, Tenkalai, etc. Another school of Southern Vaiṣṇavism was set up by Viṣṇusvāmin, which was developed by Vallabha, (born in 1479) the propounder of Śuddhādvaitavāda. The Vallabha group insisted upon the concept of Rādhā as the consort of Kṛṣṇa, and its adherents sometimes dressed and acted like women, a parallel of which is found in Bengal Vaiṣṇavism also. Their aim was the realization of the Rādhā-bhāva, the emotions of Rādhā. Bengal Vaiṣṇavism received a great inspiration from Caitanya (1486-1533) who believed that Kṛṣṇa took his birth as a human being in order to experience the ardour of Rādhā's passion for him. No other saint carried to such an extent the emotional approach to God as a lover to his beloved.

Of other mystic saints Rāmānanda (fourteenth century) occupied a unique place in the history of religion in Medieval India. He was also a follower of Vaiṣṇavism and probably belonged to the school of Rāmānuja. He made no caste-distinction; rather he made it a fundamental tenet of his doctrine. In the place of the worship of Kṛṣṇa and Rādhā, Rāmānanda introduced the cult of Rāma and Sītā. Among the disciples of Rāmānanda, Kabīr (died in 1518) made no distinction between Hinduism and Islam. He refused to acknowledge caste-distinctions and like all other mystic saints insisted upon regional languages. He held that religion without *bhakti* was no religion at all. He had a large following both among Hindus and Muslims.[20] The same attitude was shared by Nānak (1469-1538) the founder of the Sikh religion, to whose credit goes the successful attempt to bring together the Hindus and Muslims in a common fold of spiritual and social brotherhood. According to him, "at God's gate there dwell thousands of Brahmās, of Viṣṇus, of Śivas; thousands upon thousands of exalted Rāmas; there is one Lord over all spiritual lords, the creator whose name is true."[21]

Of the esoteric cults of Medieval India Nāthism is important. It is heterodox in character and its followers are still found in different parts of northern and north-eastern India. Once it was also popular in some parts of Maharashtra. Modern Nāthism of Punjab, Uttar

Pradesh, Nepal and Bihar has been mixed up with the principal existing religions of the said regions, while in Bengal and Assam, the Nātha-yogīs want to preserve their separate identity. They often proclaim themselves as Rudraja-Brāhmaṇas and trace the essentials of their creed to the Vedas. The origin of Nāthism is covered with mystery. Fragments of medieval Nātha literature are preserved in Bengali language, a critical examination of which must show that Nāthism was originally a primitive Mother Goddess cult that came into Bengal from outside.

However, judging by the North Indian regional literatures on the Nātha-yogīs and the variety of myths and legends connected with them, it would seem that the Nātha movement in its developed form was a North Indian one and that it had amalgamated itself with the Śakti cult. Their religious discipline was that of Haṭhayoga which was an article of faith with them. Their objective was to attain the state of Jīvanmukti or immortality in the span of life. Through the process of Ultā-sādhanā, that is, by making the semen flow upwards instead of flowing downwards and the Kāya-sādhanā, that is, by the disciplining of physical body, they believed that the imperfect body could be transformed into perfect and then into divine, which was the only way to overcome decay and death. The right and left nerve channels were designated as the sun and the moon, the former standing for fire or heat and the latter for *somarasa,* the nectar essence. The sun was identified with Śakti or the female and the moon with Śiva or the male. The latter being the source of creation it was supposed to hold in its bosom the nectar which the former was always after to consume.[22] In Jayaratha's commentary on Abhinavagupta's *Tantrāloka* it is stated that the Kulācāra section of the Tantras were introduced by Matsyendranātha or Mīnanātha. According to the *Gorakṣasiddhānta-saṃgraha* also *Tantrarājatantra,* the Tantras were introduced on earth by the nine Nāthas.

IV

Now we shall deal with Śāktism in its manifold forms. During the period under review three important Śākta Purāṇas were produced, viz. the *Devī Purāṇa,* the *Kālikā Purāṇa* and the *Devībhāgavata.*

In the *Devībhāgavata,* the Śākta goddess is conceived as the Ādyā Śakti or primordial energy that resides in Brahmā as the creating principle, in Viṣṇu as the sustaining principle and in Śiva as the destructive principle. This Ādyā Śakti pervades all space and animates everything of this phenomenal world.[23] The goddess who is unmanifested, takes three forms of Mahālakṣmī, Mahākālī and Mahāsarasvatī representing the *rājasa, sāttvika* and *tāmasa* attributes or *guṇas* of Prakṛti. Mahālakṣmī produces Brahmā and Śrī, Mahākālī produces Rudra and Trayī and Mahāsarasvatī produces Viṣṇu and Umā. The union of Brahmā and Trayī produces the world, that of Viṣṇu and Śrī maintains it and that of Rudra and Umā destroys its.[24] In the *Devīgītā,* which forms a part of the *Devībhāgavata,* the following is put in the mouth of the Devī:

> O king of the mountains, it was I who existed before the days of creation, and there was nothing beyond me. Wise men think me in terms of *cit, saṃvit, parabrahman* etc. My original form is beyond inference, beyond end, beyond illustration and even beyond the concepts of life and death. I am identical with my energy called *Māyā.* This *Māyā* is neither *sat* (existent) neither *asat* (non-existent), nor a combination of both; it is beyond all these which exists until the final end. This *Māyā* which is my inherent perpetual energy is like the heat of the fire, rays of the sun and light of the moon....
>
> This *Māyā* of mine is variously called *tapas, tamas, jaḍa, jñāna, pradhāna, prakṛti, śakti, aja,* etc. The Śaivas call it *vimarśa* while those well-versed in the Vedas call it *avidyā.*[25]

The conception of the Devī as the Supreme Being is further developed in the *Kālikā Purāṇa* in which she is described as the supramental Prakṛti, the material cause of the phenomenal world, and the embodiment of all energy, consciousness and bliss. The world owes its origin to her, while she does not owe her origin to anything.[26] Similar ideas are met with in the *Devī Purāṇa,*[27] which also explains the significance of the various names of the goddess by which she is invoked by the gods in the Devīmāhātmya.[28]

The Śākta Purāṇas also elaborate the exploits of the Devī mentioned in the earlier Purāṇas. In the *Devī Purāṇa* the goddess is conceived as the goddess of victory and is known by such names as Jayā, Vijayā, Aparājitā, Jayantī, etc.[29] Here she is associated with the slaying of the demons like Ghora, Subala, Ruru and others.[30] Though the *Kālikā Purāṇa* does not narrate any description of war, it occasionally refers to the slaying of Mahiṣa and others.[31] The *Devībhāgavata*[32] records the Devī's fight with Mahiṣāsura, Śumbha-Niśumbha, Durgama and Aruṇa.

The aforesaid Purāṇas also give a realistic picture of the local goddess later identified with the Supreme Being of the Śāktas. The *Kālikā Purāṇa* thus refers to the temple of the Tantric goddess Siddheśvarī near Nandikuṇḍa, to the north-west of Kāmarūpa, that of another Siddheśvarī on the river Vahurokā issuing from the Surasa mountain, that of Tripurā to the south-east of Kāmarūpa and that of the celebrated goddess Kāmākhyā.[33] It also mentions seven *pīṭhas* associated with the limbs of Satī: Pūrṇagiri (neck and shoulder), Devīkūṭa (feet), Uḍḍīyāna (thighs), Kāmagiri (genitalia), the eastern point of Kāmarūpa (navel), the western point of Kāmarūpa (head) and Jālandhara (breast).[34] According to the *Devīpurāṇa,* in the tract between the Vindhya and Malaya, the goddess was worshipped as Maṅgalā, in the south of the Himalaya as Nandā, on the Kiṣkindhyā hills as Bhairavī, at Kurukṣetra as Jayantī, at Kuśasthalī as Rudrāṇī, at Jālandhara as Bhadrakālī, at Kola as Mahālakṣmī, on the Sahyādri as Kālarātri, on the Gandhamādana as Ambikā, at Ujjayinī as Ujjanī, at Jambumārga as Mahākālī, in Videha as Bhadrakālikā, at Muṇḍi-pīṭha as Khaṇḍa-muṇḍā, on the Malayādri as Aghorā, on the Laṅkādri as Kālikā, in Śākadvīpa as Vijayā, in Kuśadvīpa as Caṇḍā, on the Krauñca mountain as Yoginī, in Śālmaladvīpa as Varāṅgaṇā, on the Mandāra hills as Dhūtimā, and in the Puṣkara as Nārāyaṇī.[35] The *Devībhāgavata* also gives an important list of the Śākta *tīrthas.*[36]

In the *Devībhāgavata,*[37] we come across the process through which inumerable local goddesses are identified with the Supreme Goddess of the Śāktas. In every creation of the universe, it is said, the *mūlaprakṛti* assumes the different gradations of *aṃśarūpiṇī, kalārūpiṇī* and *kalāṃśarūpiṇī,* or manifests herself in parts, smaller parts and further subdivisions. In the first grade she is represented by Durgā, Lakṣmī, Sarasvatī, Sāvitrī and Rādhā, in the second by Gaṅgā, Tulasī, Manasā, Ṣaṣṭhī, Maṅgalacaṇḍikā and Kālī; and in the third by the *grāmadevatās* or village mothers and by womenfolk in general. This indicates that with the development of the conception of an all-embracing Female Principle when need was felt for regarding the local goddesses as the manifestation of the Śākta Devī, they were primarily given recognition to represent the fragments of Prakṛti, while the more important and popular goddesses were given relatively higher positions.

The presiding deities of the *pīṭhas* were also originally local goddesses, and the story of Satī's death, the falling of her limbs in different *pīṭhas,* etc. were obviously invented to bring all these goddesses in relation to the Śākta Devī. The *Mahābhārata* and the earlier Purāṇas, as we have seen above, make no mention of Satī's death. According to the versions of the *Devībhāgavata*[38] and the *Kālikā Purāṇa,*[39] Dakṣa did not invite Śiva at his sacrifice, and this humiliation led Satī, the wife of Śiva, to destroy her body. Other sources relate that Śiva became so inconsolable at the death of his wife that he took her dead-body on his shoulder and travelled aimlessly. In order to save Śiva from this madness the gods planned to cut the dead body piece by piece. Parts of Satī's body thus fell at different places, and these places came to be known as the *pīṭhas.* Later accounts, especially those found in the late-medieval Bengali literature, had elaborated this episode while dealing with the holy resorts of the goddess.

V

The well known story of Rāma's Durgā worship before his final encounter with Rāvaṇa is absent in the *Rāmāyaṇa* of Vālmīki. The Bengali version of the *Rāmāyaṇa,* attributed to Kṛttivāsa (fifteenth century) however, narrates the story. According to the *Devībhāgavata,*[40] Rāma worshipped the Devī by performing the Navarātra rite and by the grace of the goddess, he was able to rescue Sītā. According to the *Kālikā Purāṇa,*[41] Brahmā worshipped the Devī in Laṅkā from the first to the ninth full-moon day of Āśvina. For this, the goddess favoured Rāma and graced the battlefield with her presence. The earlier *Bhāgavata Purāṇa*[42] says that it was Rāma who worshipped the goddess on the sea-shore in Laṅkā, and Brahmā was the priest. The *bodhana* of the Devī commenced on the ninth new-moon day of the autumn. She was worshipped in a general way up to the sixth full-moon day, and from the seventh to the ninth she was specially worshipped. On the tenth day the image of the Devī was immersed and a victory festival (*vijayā*) was held because on the previous day Rāvaṇa was killed by the grace of the goddess. The same account is also found in the *Bṛhaddharma Purāṇa.*[43]

It is not definitely known as to when the Durgā worship, in the present form, came into vogue. Vidyāpati (fourteenth-fifteenth century) in his *Durgābhaktitaraṅgiṇī* refers to the worship of the clay-image of the goddess, and detailed informations are found in Śūlapāṇi's *Durgotsavaviveka, Vāsantiviveka* and *Durgotsavaprayoga* (fifteenth-sixteenth century) Jīmūtavāhana's *Kālaviveka* (fifteenth century) and in the writings of Śrīnātha, Govindacandra, Raghunandana and others (sixteenth century). On the basis of the works mentioned above it may be suggested that the worship of Durgā, as we have it today, flourished between the fourteenth and the sixteenth centuries.

The *Māyātantra* speaks of the Kulācāra in connection with the Durgā worship. The Devīcarita and Navadurgāpūjārahasya sections attributed to the *Rudrayāmala* give the story of Durgā's advent, the details of her worship in connection with the Navarātra festival in autumn and those of what are called the nine forms of the goddess, viz., Śailaputrī, Skandamātā, Kuṣmāṇḍī, Kātyāyanī, Brahmacāriṇī, Caṇḍaghaṇṭā, Kālarātri, Mahāgaurī and Devadūtī. The Matsyasūkta, quoted in the *Prāṇatoṣaṇītantra,* gives details of the autumnal festival and refers to the worship of different forms of the deity in different parts of the country, e.g., eight-handed form in Oḍra, Kaliṅga and Madhyadeśa; eighteen-handed in Ayodhyā, Surāṣṭra, Śrīhaṭṭa and Kośala; twelve-handed in Mahendra, Himalaya, Kuru, Mathurā and Kedāra; ten-handed in Makaranda, Virāṭa, Kaumāra, Gauḍa and Pāripātra; four-handed in Marahaṭṭa, Nepāla, Kaccha and Kaṅkaṇa; two-handed near the sea.[44] The *Tantrasāra* describes Durgā, the mode of her worship as well as a list of her hundred names. Some of her forms are also described in the *Śāradātilaka.*[45] Besides, there are quite a good number of *stotras* and *kavacas,* related to Durgā, in various Tantras of the late-medieval period.

In the Durgā worship of the late-medieval and also of recent times primitive elements are found, and we may refer to Śābarotsava in this connection. In the *Kālaviveka* of Jīmūtavāhana it is stated that this festival included topics and songs about sex organs and also about sexual intercourse with requisite movements of the body. Śūlapāṇi in his *Durgotsavaviveka* quotes an account of Śābarotsava from the *Kālikā Purāṇa*[46] according to which maidens and prostitutes must accompany the image on the day of its immersion, and people must exchange words relating to sexual organ and coitus in default of which they would be cursed by the goddess. The same is also stated by Raghunandana. The *Bṛhaddharma Purāṇa,* composed about the seventeenth century, introduces some modifications in regard to the words expressive of sexual organs and acts. It says that one should not pronounce such words before one's mother and daughter and also before the uninitiated.

Some of the authors, cited above, provide for a spring festival called Vāsantī-pūjā, just in the manner of the autumnal one. Govindānanda recommends the worship of Durgā on the eighth day of the bright half of Caitra while Śrīnātha and Bṛhaspati recommend the worship of Mahiṣamardinī on the ninth day. It appears that these recommendations were responsible for the present day worship of Annapūrṇā which falls on the above mentioned days. One form of Durgā is known as Jagaddhātrī whose special worship is prescribed by Śrīnātha and Bṛhaspati of the fifteenth century.

Many of the Tantric texts known to us are quoted in the digests which occupy a very important place in the literature of the Tantras. Of the earlier digests may be mentioned the *Prapañcasāra* attributed to the great Śaṅkara and the *Śāradātilaka* of Lakṣmaṇa Deśika. There are about half a dozen commentaries on the former including one attributed to Padmapādācārya, the well known disciple of Śaṅkara, while the latter had been commented upon by Mādhavabhaṭṭa, Rāghavabhaṭṭa and others. Rāghava's commentary was composed in AD 1484. Of the later digests Kṛṣṇānanda's *Tantrasāra* stands unique, and it has a nice agreement with the *Śāradātilaka* regarding the descriptions of the deities. The Tantras describe numerous forms of Śaktis, a number of them being classed as the Mahāvidyās or Vidyās and the Nilyās. The *Tantrasāra* quotes two lists of Mahāvidyās from the *Mālinīvijaya* and the *Muṇḍamālā,* of which the first one refer to Kālī, Tārā, Mahādurgā, Tvaritā, Chinnamastā, Vāgvadinī, Annapūrṇā, Pratyaṅgirā, Kāmākhyavāsinī, Bālā, Mātaṅgī and Śailavāsinī, while the second one mentions Kālī, Tārā, Bhuvaneśvarī, Bhairavī, Chinnamastā, Dhūmāvatī, Vagalā, Mātaṅgī and Kamalā as names of the ten Mahāvidyās. The *Bṛhaddharma Purāṇa*[47] substitutes Sundarī for Kamalā and Vagalāmukhī for Vagalā. Some later Tantras correlate the ten Mahāvidyās with the ten *avatāras* of Viṣṇu.[48]

In both the lists Kālī or Mahākālī is the first name whose cult must have become popular by this time. Even in the preceding age Abhinavagupta in his *Tantrāloka* referred to her thirteen forms: Sṛṣṭikālī, Saṃhārakālī, Sthitikālī, Raktakālī, Sukālī, Yamakālī, Mṛtyukālī, Rudrakālī or Bhadrakālī, Paramārakakālī, Mārtaṇḍakālī, Kālāgnirudrakālī, Mahākālī and Mahābhairavaghoracaṇḍakālī. In the *Tantrasāra* and the *Āgamatattvavilāsa* of Raghunātha, we have the following forms: Dakṣiṇakālī, Mahākālī, Smasānakālī, Guhyakālī, Bhadrakālī, Cāmuṇḍakālī, Siddhakālī, Haṃsakālī and Kāmakalākālī. The worship of Kālī had been widely prescribed for the *raṭantīcaturdaśī* day (fourteenth day of the dark fortnight of the month of

Māgha) by Govindānanda, Śrīnātha, Vācaspati and others. Her worship on the Diwali day is not mentioned in the earlier works. The oldest reference to it is found in the *Śyāmāsaparyāvidhi* of Kāśīnātha composed in the Śaka year 1669. A work called *Tārātantra* is dedicated to Tārā, also known as Nīlā. Eight forms of Tārā are described in the *Māyātantra,* quoted in the *Tantrasāra,* viz. Tārā, Ugrā, Mahogrā, Vajrā, Nīlā, Sarasvatī, Kāmeśvarī and Bhadrakālī. The names of seven and eight Mātṛkās are found in the Tantric lists of Nāyikās or Yoginīs. Such a list is also given in the *Kālikā Purāṇa.*[49] In some of the texts quoted in the *Tantrasāra,* the eight Mātṛkās are brought in relation to the eight Bhairavas. The *Prāṇatoṣaṇī* quotes a text which gives a list of sixteen Mothers.

VI

In the third quarter of the fourteenth century Shams-i-Siraj 'Afif mentioned the idol of Jvālāmukhī, which was situated on the road to Nagarkot, and wrote:

> Some of the infidels have reported that Sultan Firuz went specially to see this idol and held a golden umbrella over its head.... Other infidels said that Sultan Muhammad Shah held an umbrella over this same idol; but this also is a lie.[50]

Abul Fazl's *Ain-i-Akbari,* composed about the end of the sixteenth century, contains an interesting description of the *pīṭha* near Nagarkot together with the legend about the origin of the four *pīṭhas* as was known to him. His account is reproduced below:

> Nagarkot is a city situated on a hill: its fort is called Kangarh. Near the town is the shrine of Mahāmāyā (a name of the Indian Mother Goddess indicating 'the goddess having great magical power') which is considered as the manifestation of the divinity. Pilgrims from distant parts visit it and obtain their desires. Strange it is that in order that their prayers may be favourably heard, they cut out their tongues: with some it grows again on the spot, with others after one or two days. Although the medical faculty allow the possibility of growth in the tongue, yet in so short space of time it is sufficiently amazing. In the Hindu mythology Mahāmāyā is said to be the wife of Mahādeva, and the learned of this creed represent by this name the energizing power of the deity. It is said that on beholding the disrespect (shown to herself and her husband Śiva) she cut herself to pieces and her body fell in four

> places: her head and some of her limbs in the northern mountains of Kashmir near Kamraj and these relics are called Śāradā: other parts fell near Bijapur in the Deccan and are known as Tuljā (Turjā Bhavānī). Such portions as reached the eastern quarter near Kāmarūpa are called Kāmākhyā and the remnant that kept its place is celebrated as Jālandharī which is this particular spot. In the vicinity torch-like flames issue from the ground in some places and other resemble the blaze of lamps. There is a concourse of pilgrims and various things are cast into the flames with the expectation of obtaining temporal blessings. Over them a domed temple has been erected and an astonishing crowd assembles therein. The vulgar impute to miraculous agency what is simply a mine of brimstone.[51]

Abul Fazl thus knew four holy places attributed to the goddess. The first one was Śāradā at modern Sardi in northern Kashmir of which we had occasion to refer from Alberūnī's *Kitabul Hind* and Kalhaṇa's *Rājataraṅgiṇī.* Abul Fazl has substituted Kashmir for Uḍḍīyāna. The second was Jālandharī near Nagarkot in the Punjab by which he had referred to Jvālāmukhī and not the neighbouring Jālandhara *pīṭha.* The third was the Bijapur region, which may be same as Pūrṇagiri mentioned in the Tantras and the *Kālikā Purāṇa.* The shrine of Bhavānī stands at Tuljāpur to the south of Osmanabad. Such was the celebrity of this goddess that when Śivajī built the fort of Pratagaḍh, he set up there an image of Bhavānī as the Bhavānī of Tuljāpur was beyond his easy reach.[52] The fourth was Kāmarūpa, the seat of the goddess Kāmākhyā. This goddess was originally of tribal origin, whose name may be traced to the Austric words Kamoi (demon), Kamoit (devil), Komin (grave), Kamet (corpse in Khasi), Kamru (a god of the Santals) etc.[53] Worship of the Mother Goddess was widely prevalent among the tribes of Assam. The Chutiyas, for example,

> worshipped various forms of Kālī with the aid, not of Brāhmaṇas, but of their tribal priests or Deoris. The favourite form in which they worshipped this deity was that of Kecāi Khāti, 'the eater of raw flesh' to whom human sacrifices were offered. After their subjugation by the Ahoms, the Deoris were permitted to continue their ghastly rites; but they were usually given, for the purpose, criminals who had been sentenced to capital punishment. Failing them, victims were taken from a particular clan, which in return accorded certain privileges. The person selected was fed sumptuously, until he was in sufficiently plump condition to suit the

supposed taste of the goddess, and he was then decapitated at the Copper Temple at Sadiya, or at some other shrine of the tribe. Human sacrifices were also formerly offered by the Tipperas, Kacharis, Koches, Jaintias and other Assam tribes.[54]

When the new temple of Kāmākhyā was opened, the occasion was celebrated by the immolation of no less than a hundred and forty men, whose heads were offered to the goddess on salvers made of copper. Similar sacrifices were offered to various aboriginal deities. According to the *Haft Iqlim,* there was in Kāmarūpa a class of persons called Bhogīs, who were voluntary victims of a goddess named Āi who dwelt in a cave; from the time when they announced that the goddess had called them, they were treated as privileged persons; they were allowed to do whatever they liked, and every woman was at their command; but when the annual festival came round they were killed.[55]

We have already seen that the *Kālikā Purāṇa* mentions seven *pīṭhas* or holy resorts of the goddess, while the *Rudrayāmala* mentions ten, the *Kulārṇava Tantra* eighteen and the *Kubijikātantra* forty-two. The *Jñānārṇava Tantra* has two lists of *pīṭhas*; one containing eight names and other fifty. The second list was taken into account in the *Tantrasāra* which was composed about the seventeenth century. The Śākta *pīṭhas* had become a popular theme of the medieval writers, many of whom took the greatest liberty in fabricating the place names, the goddesses and their Bhairavas. The association of a holy place with one of Satī's limbs was determined usually by their individual imagination. This is clearly demonstrated by the sixteenth century Bengali poet Mukundarāma in the Dakṣa-yajña-bhaṅga section of his *Caṇḍīmaṅgala.* A list of fifty-one *pīṭhas* is found in the Pīṭhanirṇaya or Mahāpīṭhanirūpaṇa section of the *Tantracūḍāmaṇi* composed about the closing years of the seventeenth century. It has been quoted in such modern works as the *Prāṇatoṣaṇī Tantra* (1820), the *Śabdakalpadruma* (1822-52) and others and appears to have been used by Bhāratacandra in his *Annadāmaṅgala* (1752) and modified by the author of the *Śivacarita.*

Various texts of the *Pīṭhanirṇaya* have cited by D.C. Sircar in his *Śākta Pīṭhas* in which the names of the *pīṭhas,* the *pīṭha-devatās* (forms of the goddess), the *kṣetrādhīśas* (Bhairavas) and the Devī's *aṅga-pratyaṅga* (limbs including ornaments etc.) have been arranged in tabular forms, and the discrepancies that concern them are also indicated. Here we shall not reproduce the dull lists. We shall only touch upon the important ones. It fact, in this vast country, holy resorts of the goddess are innumerable and the popularity of her cult is proved even the place-names of India. Referring to the Panjab region Niharranjan Ray observed:

> Very few people pause to consider this social phenomenon, or to consider the significance of such toponyms in these regions as, for instance, Ambala which is derived from Ambā, one of the many names of Durgā, Chandigarh which is named after Caṇḍī, Panchkula (a growing town between Kalka and Chandigarh), a technical term of unmistakable Tantric significance, Kalka which is vulgarisation of Kālikā, Simla which is Śyāmalā Devī in its anglicised version. A careful and close look at the postal directories of the Punjab, Haryana and Himachal would yield a long list of such toponyms from which one may draw one's own conclusion. Besides, throughout these regions one still finds a countless number of small, lowly shrines with all but shapeless or crude form placed on their altars, which worshippers, lowly village folks, describe as Manasā, Caṇḍī, Kālī, Nayanā, Durgā, etc.[56]

The important feature of the *Pīṭhanirṇaya,* cited above is that its list of the *pīṭhas* together with the names of the Devī and the Bhairava, includes a number of places in the rural areas of Bengal. Thus, the *pīṭha* of Sugandhā, where the presiding goddess is Sunandā, is located at Shikarpur near Barisal; that of Vaidyanātha, where the goddess is Jayadurgā, at the Deoghar-Vaidyanāthdhām in the Santal Parganas district; that of Bahulā where the goddess is also of the same name, at Ketugrāma near Katwa in the Burdwan district; that of Ujjayinī, where the goddess is Maṅgalā or Maṅgalacaṇḍī, at Ujani or Kogram in the Burdwan district; that of Caṭṭala, where the goddess is Bhavānī, at the Sītākuṇḍa on the Chandranath hill in the Chittagong district; that of Tripurā, where the goddess is Tripurā, or Tripurasundarī, at Radhakishorepur in the Tripura state; that of Trisrotā where the goddess is Bhrāmarī or Amarī, at Salbari in the Jalpaiguri district; that of Yugādyā, where the goddess is of the same name, at Khirgram near Katwa in the Burdwan district; that of Kālīpīṭha, where the goddess is Kālī, at Kalighat in the southern suburb of Calcutta; that of Kīriṭa or Kīriṭakoṇā, where the goddess is Bhuvaneśī or Vimalā, at Vatanagar near Lalbag in the Murshidabad district; that of Karatoyā, where the goddess is Aparṇā, at Bhavānīpur in the Bogra district; that of Vibhāsa, where the goddess is Bhīmarūpā, near Tamluk in the Midnapur district; that of Nalahāṛi, where the goddess is Kālikā, at Nalhati in the Birbhum district; that of Vakreśvara, where the goddess is Mahiṣamardinī, at Bakreswar in the Birbhum district; that of Yaśora, where the goddess is Yasoreśvarī, at Iswaripur in the Khulna district; that of Aṭṭahāsa, where the goddess is Phullarā, near Labhpur in the Birbhum district; and that of Nandīpura, where the goddess is Nandinī, near Sainthia in the Birbhum district.

The history of the literature on the *pīṭhas* no doubt points unmistakably to the great contribution Bengal must have made to the Tantric culture in the medieval period. But the greatest centre of Tantrism seems to have originally been in north-western India, although in the late medieval age its importance had been diminished. Both Jvālāmukhī and Jālandhara, where the goddesses are Siddhidā or Ambikā and Tripuramālinī respectively, are mentioned in the list of the *pīṭhas*, the former lying in the Kangra district of Panjab. The latter, although it is the chief city of the Jullundhur district, is located near the former, the *pīṭha* of Hiṅgulā, where the goddess is known as Koṭṭari, Koṭṭavi or Kottarīśa (meaning a naked woman) is modern Hinglaj in Baluchistan. The goddess is locally known as Bībī Nānī, probably the same and Nanā of the Kuṣāṇa coins. The *pīṭha* of Śarkarāra, where the goddess is Mahiṣamardinī, may stand for modern Sukkur, the chief city of the district of that name is Sind. According to the *Pīṭhanirṇaya*, the goddess is known as Mahāmāyā in Kashmir but, strangely enough, as there is no reference to the celebrated Śaradā (Sardi) and Amaranātha *tīrthas* of Kashmir, there seems to be a fantastic element in the description of this *pīṭha*. Likewise, the non-mention of Paśupatinātha, the most celebrated deity of Nepal, in this context seems to explore the imaginary character of the description, despite the mention of Nepāla as a *pīṭha* and Mahāmāyā as its presiding goddess. The *pīṭha* of Mānasa, where the goddess is Dākṣāyaṇī, may be located near the source of the Sutlej while that of Pañcasāgara, where the goddess is Vārāhī, to the five Kuṇḍas near Hardwar.

Of other *pīṭhas*, the aforesaid text mentions Ujjayinī and Mālava, but it should be noted that the celebrated god Mahākāla is not referred to as Bhairava in connection either with the former or with the latter. Rāmagiri (modern Ramtek near Nagpur) is mentioned with Śivānī as its presiding deity. Lalitā and Viśālākṣī, the presiding goddess of the the *pīṭhas* of Prayāga and Vārāṇasī, seem to be adaptations from the earlier Purāṇic lists. The same holds good in the case of the goddess Sāvitrī of Kurukṣetra. At Utkala, the goddess is Vimalā and her Bhairava is Jagannātha. It is interesting to note that the cult of the latter, who is evidently a Vaiṣṇava deity, is marked by some important Śākta-Tantric rites. The Śākta claim on the Vaiṣṇava *tīrthas* is also proved by the fact that Vṛndāvana, the celebrated Vaiṣṇava *tīrtha*, is described as the original resort of the goddess Umā. The *pīṭha* of Gaṇḍakī, where the goddess is Gaṇḍakī-Caṇḍī is located at Sālagrāma at the source of the Gandak, and that of Mithilā, where she is Umā, at Janakpur in the Nepalese Tarai.

The *pīṭha* of Kāmagiri, where the goddess is Kāmākhyā, is Kāmarūpa to which reference has already been made. According to the *Kāmākhyātantra,* the goddess is worshipped in five different forms—Kāmākhyā, Tripurā, Kāmeśvarī, Śāradā and Mahāmāyā. There is no image in her temple; only a *yoni*-shaped stone, smeared with vermilion, is set up to represent the goddess. The worship of this goddess is said to have been introduced by the Asura Naraka, the king of Kāmarūpa. However, in the first quarter of the sixteenth century when Kāmarūpa was occupied by the Koch king Viśvasiṃha, an attempt was made to revive the ancient Kāmākhyā cult. The present temple was built in 1565 during the reign of his son Naranārāyaṇa alias Malladeva. A century later the Ahom kings who conquered the eastern zones of Kāmarūpa took the charge of her worship. According to the popular tradition, king Naranārāyaṇa employed a Brāhmaṇa named Kendukalai as her priest and the goddess was so pleased with his worship that she used to dance before him assuming the form of a beautiful damsel. The king bribed Kendukalai and saw her dance. At this the goddess punished the king and cut off the head of Kendukalai. There is an Assamese proverb: *Kendukalair murchigār dare mur chingim.* A similar legend centering round the goddess Artemis is found in Greek mythology.

Of other seats of the goddess in eastern India, reference must be made to the *pīṭha* of Jayantī where the goddess is also of the same name. The *pīṭha* is located at Kalajor-Baurbhog in the Sylhet district.

> There is a spot in the Faljur Pargana where part of Satī's left leg is to have fallen and where human victims were immolated yearly on the ninth day (*mahānavamī*) of the Durgā-pūjā. Similar sacrifices were also offered on special occasions, such as birth of a son in the royal family, or the fulfilment of some request made to the gods. Frequently the victims were self-chosen, in which case, for some time previous to the sacrifice, they enjoyed the privilege of doing whatever they pleased without let or hindrance.[57]

The *pīṭha* of Kayanāśrama, where the goddess is Śarvaṇī, is located at Kumārīkuṇḍa in the Chittagong district and that of Maṇivedaka where she is Gāyatrī, somewhere in Maṇipura.

Of the *pīṭhas* of the Deccan and South India, the *Pīṭhanirṇaya* refers to Janasthāna and Godāvarītīra with Bhrāmarī and Viśveśī as the presiding goddesses. Śrīśaila and Śrīparvata (in the Nallamalur range to the south of the Krishna) are separately mentioned, but the non-mention of Mallikārjuna (Śiva) and of Devī Bhramarāmbā on the Śrīśaila shows that the description is imaginary. That the writer of the *Pīṭhanirṇaya* had absolutely no idea of South India is also proved by the non-mention of the celebrated Kāmākṣī of Kāñcī, although Kāñcī is mentioned as a *pīṭha* with its presiding goddess Devagarbhā.

Here we like to say a few words about the goddess Kāmākṣī of Kāñcī. The Malabar legends as found in the *Kāḷikarpam* and the *Bhadrotpatti* associate her with the slaying of an Asura called Dāruka.[58] In the Lalitopākhyāna of the *Brahmāṇḍa Purāṇa* she is identified with Mahālakṣmī, and according to the Tamil tradition, Pārvatī, having committed a sin by covering the eyes of Śiva, an act by which the universe was going to the perished, made a penance for six months on the bank of the Kampā at Kāñcīpura, and since then the people of that region began to worship her as Kāmākṣī. According to another tradition this goddess was very blood-thirsty, but she changed her habit thanks to the efforts of Śaṅkarācārya. A dumb (*mūka*) poet was said to have been gifted with the power of speech and poetic imagination by the grace of the goddess. He composed a poetical work, known as *Mūka Pañcaśatī* or *Devī Pañcaśatī,* in praise of the goddess.

The most popular goddess of South India in the late-medieval period was Mīnākṣī. Her original temple was built in the early medieval age which was destroyed by Malik Kafur, the general of Alauddin Khalji. It was rebuilt by Tirumala Naik (1623-59). The city of Madura is, in fact, the city of this goddess. The immense precincts of the present Mīnakṣī temple are dominated by nine exquisitely carved *gopurams,* the tallest of which is 152 ft. high. There are many popular legends about Mīnākṣī, one of which has a close bearing on the *Śilappadikāram* story.[59]

VII

In view of what we have stated above, we get a fair idea about late-medieval Śāktism. The picture will become more clear if side by side the Śākta-Tantric authors and their works are taken into account. It is, however, not possible to give anything like a comprehensive account of the extensive literature produced by writers hailing from all parts of the country at different times over a long period. Of the earlier Tantric works, we have already occasion to refer to those attributed to Śaṅkarācārya, the *Tantrāloka* of the Kashmirian scholar Abhinavagupta and the *Śāradātilaka* of Lakṣmaṇa Deśika. A house of Tantric saints and authors flourished in Bengal during the late-medieval age. Mahamahopadhyaya Parivrājakācārya, whose first name is still unknown, was one of the earliest Bengali writers on the Tantras whose *Kāmyayantroddhāra* was probably composed about the fourteenth century AD. Lakṣmīdhara, one of the court poets of Pratāparudra Gajapati of Orissa (1497-1539), commented on the *Saundaryalaharī,* attributed to Śaṅkara, and his commentary contain valuable information on the manifestations of Śakti. Brahmānanda-giri's *Śāktānandataraṅgiṇī,* dealing with various rites to be performed in connection with the worship of Śakti and *Tārārahasya,* dealing with the worship of Tārā in her various forms, were composed in the sixteenth century. His disciple Pūrṇānanda was the celebrated author of such Śākta-Tantric works as *the Śāktakarma, Śrītattvacintāmaṇi, Śyāmārahasya, Tattvānandataraṅgiṇī, Ṣaṭkarmollāsa,* etc. Mahīdhara's *Mantramahodadhi* was composed in AD 1589. Mahīdhara was an inhabitant of Ahicchatra (modern Ramnagar in Bareilly district) who later settled at Vārāṇasī. The *Puraścaraṇadīpikā* and *Kulapūjanacandrikā* of Candraśekhara were also composed about the sixteenth century. Śaṅkara of Gauḍa, whose full name seems to have been Śaṅkara Āgamācārya, composed his *Tārārahasya-Vṛttikā* about the beginning of the seventeenth century. To the same period belonged the great *Tantrasāra* of Kṛṣṇānanda Āgamavāgīśa which is the most comprehensive and popular of the numerous digests that are known in Bengal. A few manuscripts of this work are found in non-Bengali scripts, and outside Bengal, indicating thereby the extent of its popularity. Towards the end of the seventeenth century Raghunātha Tarkavāgīsá of Andul near Calcutta composed his *Āgamatantravilāsa* which was abridged by his son Rāmakṛṣṇa. Śrīnivāsa Bhaṭṭa Gosvāmin of this period, who was originally a South Indian, was the celebrated author of the *Śivārcaṇasaṃhitā, Caṇḍisaparyākramakalpavallī* and other works. Of the seventeenth century writers, reference should also be made to Navasiṃha alias Ādyānandana of

Nepal who was the famous author of the *Tantracintāmaṇi, Kulamuktikallolinī, Puṣparatnākaratantra* and other works.[60]

More important in this respect is the evidence furnished by the regional literatures. We have seen that during the late medieval period Śāktism had become a social outlook. Its spirit was not confined within the limit of a single religion. Those who did not call themselves Śāktas, peoples belonging to different religious sects, did not hesitate even to propagate the spirit of Śāktism which they adopted ideologically as a means to serve some social purpose. As for example, Guru Govind Singh, the tenth guru of the Sikhs, composed the *Caṇḍi-di-var* which shows that the spirit of Śāktism animated his imagination, although his religious theories and practices were different from those of Śāktism. In the next chapter we shall discuss more about Guru Govind Singh's inclination towards Śakti. His compositions of more than a couple of pieces on Caṇḍī and Durgā can be explained by the fact that the need of the community in his time was indeed Śakti or power and energy against the imperial persecution of the Mughuls.[61] The same was probably the inspiration of the poets and *cāraṇas* of Rajasthan who composed verses and songs in praise of Mahiṣāsuramardinī, Kālī, Cāmuṇḍā, Mātājī, Karṇimātā, Naganekji and others. A very large number of Rajasthani manuscripts, now in the Anup Sanskrit Library, Bikaner, mostly illustrated, give us sufficient proof of this. Folk songs written by Moonkhan Mev of Alwar and Jaichand Yati show that even Muslims and Jains worshipped Śakti or composed verses in her praise.[62] It is interesting to note that in some parts of India, among the Muslim community, the cult of Alī and Fātimā, as the male and female principles, is in vogue. In some areas of Uttar Pradesh Amīnā Satī, the deified mother of the Prophet, is worshipped, while among some matriarchal tribes of Baluchistan it is believed that the mother of Muhammad was really the Prophet. Village Mothers, like the smallpox goddess, the serpent goddess, etc. are worshipped by the Muslim peasants as well. In Lower Bengal, the Muslims still worship Banabībī, the presiding goddess of the Sundarban region, whose exploits are dealt with in a poetical work called *Banabibir Jahurānāmā* written by Munshi Bayanuddin.

In the *Pṛthvīrāj Rāso* of Chand Bardai, one of the most popular works of Hindi literature, the goddess is invoked in many places in the forms of Caṇḍī, Cāmuṇḍā and Kālī. Here she is described as the saviour of the world whenever it is oppressed by the demons. Even a

Śākta background we can trace in the *Rāmacaritmānasa* of Tulasīdāsa in which the speaker is Śiva and the hearer is Devī. Many of the Devī legends are incorporated in the *Rāmacaritmānasa.* Tulasīdāsa's Sītā was a worshipper of Gaurī by whose grace she had Rāma as her husband. Tulasīdāsa also composed a separate work entitled *Pārvatī-maṅgala* which was inspired on the one hand by the *Kumārasambhava* of Kālidāsa and on the other by the *Maṅgala Kāvyas* of Bengal. His *Vinaya Patrikā* contains two hymns dedicated to the goddess. Although Kabīr did not favour Śāktism, a few of his verses reflect the concept of *Māyā* as the material cause of the universe. The same is also found in the verses of Dādū. The goddess Vindhyavāsinī of Mirzapur is an interesting figure in popular Hindi literature to whom is dedicated a type of poems called *cālīsā,* each consisting of forty verses. Apart from this *Vindhyeśvarī-cālīsā* other folk songs in praise of the goddess are found, a good number of which have been collected by Ahlad Misra. Subsequently *Durgā-cālīsās* and *Śakti-cālīsās* came into vogue, and these were recited during the worship of the goddess. In modern Hindi literature, however, as we shall see in the next chapter, the role of Śāktism has become more significant.[63]

Mithila was a prominent centre of Śāktism, as is proved by the existence of a number of Śākta holy places like Uccaitha, Caṇḍikāsthāna, Ugratārāsthāna, Cāmuṇḍāsthāna, Janakpur, etc. In Maithili literature numerous poems were composed in praise of Śiva and Devī and these were mainly concerned with the marriage of Śiva and Pārvatī, their married life and family life. The celebrated poet, Vidyāpati was also included among the writers of such poems. Locana's *Rāgataraṅgiṇī* contains a number of devotional songs dedicated to the goddess Kālī. In Nepal, Bhūpatīndra Malla composed more than fifty Śākta songs in Maithili which form the subject matter of his *Bhāṣāsaṅgīta.* A good number of dramas, centering round the Śiva-Śakti theme, were composed in Maithili. Of such works reference should be made to Jagajyotirmalla's *Hara-Gaurī Vivāha* (AD 1629), Jitamitramalla's *Bhāratanāṭakam,* Vaṃśamaṇi Jha's *Gītadigambara* (AD 1655), Lāla Kavi's *Gaurī-Svayamvara,* Śivadatta's *Gaurī-pariṇaya,* Kānhārām Dāsa's *Gaurī-svayamvara,* etc. all of which deal with the theme of Śiva's marriage with the Devī. The aforesaid works were evidently inspired by Kālidāsa's *Kumārasambhava.* Lāla Dāsa's *Sāṅga Durgā Prakāśikā* is a Maithili translation of the Devīmāhātmya section of the *Mārkaṇḍeya Purāṇa.* Guṇavantalāl Dāsa composed his *Gaurī-pariṇaya-prabandha* on the basis of the *Brahmavaivarta Purāṇa.*

Riddhinātha Jha's *Satī Bhibhūti* and Gaṇeśvara Jha's *Devī Gītā* are also important Maithili contribution to the Śakti cult.

The temple chronicle of Orissa, the *Mādalā Pāñjī*, gives some important information regarding the functioning of Śakti cult in that region. It gives details of the cult of the Seven Mothers whose images were installed by Bhīmakeśara (Bhīmaratha of the Somavaṃśī dynasty) who was a great worshipper of the Devī. The *Pāñjī* also mentions the construction of the Sāmālāi temple of Sambalpur by one Yadukeśarī. In Oriya literature Sārala Dāsa's *Caṇḍī Purāṇa* is a remarkable production which deals with the exploits of the Devī. It is a nice admixture of the Purāṇic and popular legends, and what is more, it gives a very useful account of the local goddesses of Orissa, who were regarded as the manifestations of the great Devī. In his *Bilaṅkā Rāmāyaṇa*, the same poet identifies Sītā with the great goddess who killed the hundred-thousand headed Rāvaṇa. His *Mahābhārata* has also a Śākti background, in the preface of which he says that he had undertaken the task of its composition by the command and grace of Sāralā Devī. Besides his chosen deity Sāralā, his *Mahābhārata* deals with such goddesses as Ugratārā, Cāceśvarī, Bāseli, Māheśvarī, Kālikā, Kaṅkālī, Ahimmukhī, Jambukī, etc. Jagannātha Dāsa, the sixteenth century poet, famous for his translation of the *Bhāgavata*, also composed a work on Śaiva-Śākta doctrine. This work came to be known as *Tulabhina*. In the *Bāta Abauāṣa* of Balarāma Dāsa (sixteenth century), Lord Jagannātha is described as being attended upon by sixty-four Yoginīs, Kātyāyanīs, Sapta Mātṛkā, Vimalā and Virajā. The work also mentions seventy-six local goddesses identified with different aspects of Śakti. The *Prācīmāhātmya* of Dvija Trilocana mentions deities like Caṇḍaghaṇṭā, Rāma-Caṇḍī, Bhagavatī, etc. The Orissa State Museum contains several Tantric manuscripts, and in this context reference may be made to Jagannātha Ācārya's *Durgāyajñadīpikā*, Keśava Ratha's *Tāriṇīkulasudhātaraṅgiṇī*, Godāvara Misra's *Śāradārcanā-paddhati* and Raghunātha Dāsa's *Vanadurgāpūjā*.

The post-Caitanya revival of Vaiṣṇavism in Orissa was not very favourable for the growth of Śākta literature. In Assam also a similar phenomenon came into existence owing to the advent of Śaṅkaradeva (1449-1568), the great Vaiṣṇava saint and the founder of Assamese literature. Although Assam was a stronghold of Śāktism, the neo-Vaiṣṇava movement, launched by Śaṅkaradeva, could restrict the scope of Śāktism in the field of literature. Of the literary works dealing with the domestic life of Śiva and Pārvatī, reference must be made to Rāmasarasvatī's *Bhīmacarita* (fifteenth-sixteenth century) in which Bhīma of the Great Epic is brought in relation to the domestic life of Śiva and Pārvatī. The cult of Manasā was popular in Assam and we know of three *Manasāmaṅgalas* (poems in praise of the goddess Manasā) composed respectively by Manakara, Durgāvara and Sukanāni between the fifteenth and the seventeenth centuries. Towards the close of the seventeenth century Rucinātha and Raṅganātha translated the *Devīmāhātmya* section of the *Mārkaṇḍeya Purāṇa* in Assamese. Ananta Ācārya's *Ānandalaharī*, composed about the same period, was an adaptation of the famous *Ānandalaharī* or *Saundaryalaharī* attributed to Śaṅkara.[64]

In Bengali literature, the *Rāmāyaṇa* of Kṛttivāsa (fifteenth century AD) contains the story of Rāma's Durgā worship before his final encounter with Rāvaṇa. Its purpose was simply to give an emotional satisfaction to the peoples of the goddess cult. In regional literatures numerous such stories are found in which the success of the hero was dependent upon the grace of the goddess. It is interesting to note that in the *Adbhuta Rāmāyaṇa*,[65] a late work highly favoured by the Kashmirian Śāktas, Sītā is stated to have killed Rāvaṇa assuming the form of Kālī. The said work identifies Sītā with the Supreme Being of Śāktas. The attempt of associating Śāktism with Rāma-Sītā legends may be traced even to the Sanskrit *Rāmacarita* of Abhinanda which is a work of the tenth century. This tradition was later adopted by the later *Rāmāyaṇa* writers. In Sārala Dāsa's Oriya *Rāmāyaṇa*, which has been mentioned in the preceding section, the tradition of the *Adbhuta Rāmāyaṇa* is followed in which Sītā herself killed Rāvaṇa in the form of Bhadrakālī. The story of the slaying of Rāvaṇa by Sītā is also found in the *Jaiminībhārata* and other later Bengali *Rāmāyaṇas*. According to the popular Rāma legends of the Mathurā region it was Sītā who killed Rāvaṇa, and having accomplished the task went straight to Calcutta instead of Ayodhyā and settled there permanently as Kālī Māī.

The story of Behulā and Lakhindar, the adventures of Lausena, the story of the merchant Dhanapati and his son Śrīmanta, and of Kālaketu and Phullarā were current in popular narrative poems, and these formed the nucleus of the great *Maṅgala Kāvyas* which became established in Bengal by 1600. The purpose of these *Maṅgala Kāvyas* was to popularise the cults of the lower goddesses among the higher section of the peoples and to identify them with different manifestations of the Śākta Devī. Thus, the *Manasā-maṅgalas* (composed at different times by Kānā Haridatta, Vijaya Gupta, Vipradāsa Piplai, Ketakādāsa Kṣemānanda, etc.) were attempts to popularise the cult of the snake-goddess Manasā. Chānd Sadagar, a rich merchant and an influential person in society, who was a devotee of Śiva, was unwilling to worship Manasā as a goddess, and hence Manasā was not getting social recognition. The goddess thereafter, following the most unscrupulous and unfair methods, compelled the Sadāgar to worship her and to regard her as the manifestation of the great Śakti, the consort of Śiva. Likewise Kṛṣṇarāma's *Ṣaṣṭhīmaṅgala, Śītalāmaṅgala* and *Kamalāmaṅgala* show that even such minor goddesses as Ṣaṣṭhī, Śītalā and Kamalā also came to be identified with the Supreme Being of the Śāktas.

More important in this respect are the *Caṇḍīmaṅgalas*. The goddess whom we meet in these poems is Maṅgalacaṇḍī. Here two goddesses are merged in one, the Caṇḍī of the Purāṇas and the local goddess Maṅgalā who was worshipped by the females on every Tuesday. In the *Caṇḍīmaṅgalas* the demon-slayer form of the goddess is absent (although in a later work called *Abhayāmaṅgala* of Dvija Rāmadeva we have the story of her killing a demon called Maṅgala). She is usually depicted as a goddess who bestows wealth and happiness upon her worshippers, but if anyone offends her she takes terrible revenge. Of the writers of the *Caṇḍīmaṅgalas*, Dvija Mādhava and Mukundarāma Cakravartī are most important, both of whom flourished in the sixteenth century. The latter was really a great poet in whose work we come across a touch of realism and a critical description of the social life of sixteenth century Bengal. The *Caṇḍīmaṅgalas* contain two legends one of which describes how Kālaketu, a hunter by profession who belonged to the lowest stratum of society, became king of Gujarat by the grace of the goddess Caṇḍī. The other legend deals with the fate of a merchant called Dhanapati who was going to be ruined for his disregard to the goddess. But he regained his fortune for one of his wives who was a devotee of Maṅgalacaṇḍī. A third legend describes her Kamalekāminī form, the goddess swallowing an elephant and taking it out once again from her mouth, which was seen by Dhanapati and his son Śrīmanta. In Mukundarāma's *Caṇḍīmaṅgala* we come across details of Satī's death, the conception of ten Mahāvidyās, the tradition of the *pīṭhas* and other allied subjects, and side by side, in such works is depicted the human form of the Devī, the sorrows and joys of her domestic life with her poor old husband Śiva, who does not know how to earn, and a lot of children always crying for food. The goddess is conceived of as a young lady who, according to the custom of the land, has been married at an early age and taken away from her parents to the house of her husband, whence she visits her paternal home only occasionally. This human conception of the Devī and her impoverished household has further been elaborated in works like Rāmeśvara's *Śivāyana* and in the later Śākta lyrics.

References

1. Joshi, *SBCI*, 391-94; Eliot, *HB*, II.6.
2. *SHB*, 360-61.
3. Conze, *SHB*, 86.
4. Morgan, *PB*, 48
5. Edkins, *CB*, 99.
6. Pande, *BDVI*, 491-92.
7. See Mitra, *DB*.
8. Ibid., 2; Bagchi in *AMSJV*, III, 4-20; Joshi, *SBCI*, 302.
9. *JGNJRI*, IX (1), 111-12.
10. Smith, *EHI*, 368; Radhakrishnan, *IP*, I.609; Barua, *PHBP*; Kane, *HD*, V(2) 1004-05; Levi, *N*, II.317; Majumdar in *CHI*, IV, 47-48; Mitra, *DB*, 150-55.
11. Goyal, *HIB*, 397-98.
12. Rhys Davids, *B*, 83-85.
13. *IHQ*, X.276-84.
14. *BRKMIC*, XIV.333-34.
15. Foreword to Bapat's *2500 YB*, IX.
16. Upadhyaya, *EBB*, 105.
17. Coomaraswamy, *HB*, 452.
18. For details see my *BHIA*.
19. Fergusson, *HIEA*, I.360 ff.
20. Westcott, *KK*, 18-19.
21. Macauliffe, *SR*, 41.
22. Ray, *SGSS*, 129.
23. I.8.
24. Ibid.
25. VII.32.
26. V.14 ff.
27. XVI.14.
28. XXXVII.
29. II-XX.
30. XXXIX; LXXXIII-LXXXVI.
31. LX
32. V.2-18, 21-31; VII-28; X.13.
33. LXXVII ff.
34. XVIII.42-51.
35. XXXVIII.3-9; XXXIX.1-5, 16-21; XLIII.64.

36. VII.38.5-30.
37. IX.1.
38. VII.30.
39. XVI.18.
40. III.30.
41. LX.
42. XXXVI-XLVIII.
43. I.21-22.
44. Chakravarty, *TSTRL*, 94-95.
45. XI.25, 37, 46.
46. LXI.17-21.
47. II.6.126.
48. Sircar, *SP*, 48.
49. LXI.84.
50. Elliot, *HI*, III, 318.
51. Jerrett's tr. II, 312-14; cf. Sircar, *SP*, 14.
52. Sarkar, *HA*, IV, 32.
53. Sircar, *SP*, 15.
54. Gait, *HA*, 56.
55. Ibid., 58.
56. *SGSS*, 27.
57. Gait, *HA*, 268.
58. Menon in *SKACV*, 234-39.
59. Whitehead, *VGSI*, 112 ff.
60. Chakravarty, *TSTRL*, 66-79.
61. Ray, *SGSS*, 28-30.
62. Majumdar in *SCT*, 99-100.
63. Dasgupta, *BSSSS*, 383 ff.
64. For the Śākta cult and literature in Assam see Nīrmalprabhā Bardoloi, *Devī*, Guwahati, 1986.
65. XXV.29-31.

8

Modern Śāktism (from AD 1700)

The disintegration and downfall of the Mughal empire and the rise of new social forces once again brought some fundamental changes in the religious outlook of the people. During the Mughal rule the Hindu and Muslim inhabitants of India came in close touch with each other, and a spirit of tolerance prevailed. The Grand Mughals, excepting Akbar, were devout Sunni Muslims, but their attitude towards the Hindus was to a certain extent liberal. As a result of this the Hindus felt themselves more or less safe in the Mughal regime.

But the situation changed, all on a sudden, with the accession of Aurangzeb on the Mughal throne. The fanatic Islamism of this monarch which was revealed in his religious policy, contributed a lot to the downfall of the Mughal empire as is known to all students of Indian history. Aurangzeb was greatly influenced by the orthodox reform movement in Indian Islam launched by Mujaddid Alf-i-Sani Shaikh Ahmad Sirhindi (1563-1624), the aims of which were regeneration and rejuvenation of Islam in strict accord with the *Shariyat* and "the establishment of a true Islamic state conforming to Islamic ideas and practices in all its activities."[1] In 1664 he forbade old temples to be repaired and in 1669 issued order to the governors of the provinces "to demolish the schools and temples of the infidels and put down their teaching and religious practices strongly."[2] Besides numerous temples throughout the empire, even the famous Hindu temples of Viśvanātha at Vārāṇasī, Keśava Deva at Mathurā, and Somanātha at Patan were destroyed. Sixty-six temples were razed to the ground at Amber. In 1668 all Hindu religious fairs were prohibited. In 1679 he imposed the *jizya* tax on the Hindus "with the object of spreading Islam and overthrowing infidel practices."[3]

But a side-issue of this religious policy was equally important and that was Hindu revivalism. And in this revivalism the role of the Śakti cult was very important. The concept of the goddess as the embodiment of all power and the revival of her demon-killing form became symbol of the Hindu resistance. This spirit was shared by Sivaji whose favourite goddess Bhavānī symbolised that power which the Marathas needed for their struggle against the Mughals. The popular name of the great goddess is Bhavānī in Maharashtra and the Marathas believe that their success against the Mughals was due to the grace of Bhavānī who was responsible for infusing power and strength among them. The temple of Bhavānī, the chosen goddess of Guru Rāmdās and Sivaji is situated at Tuljapur near Osmanabad. Hence the goddess is known as Tulja-Bhavānī. She is eight-armed, seated on a tiger, and engaged in slaying Mahiṣāsura.[4] Another Bhavānī temple associated with the name of Sivaji is at Pratapgarh in Pune.

We have seen that Guru Govind Singh's insistence on the doctrine of Śakti was not due to his inclination towards Śāktism as a religion, but to his understanding of the spirit of Śāktism in terms of the cult of power which the Sikh society needed for its consolidation. In the *Caṇḍī-caritra* the Guru says that in the past God had deputed Durgā to destroy the evil doers, and this duty had now been assigned to him. He sang

> the praises of Caṇḍī so that they might be chanted for warlike purposes, and that even cowards on hearing her story might obtain courage and the hearts of the brave beat with fourfold enthusiasm. Such being the achievements of a woman, what ought not a brave man to accomplish?[5]

Guru Govinda Singh invited Pandit Kesho from Varanasi to conduct the *homa* ceremony of the goddess on the hill of Nainadevi, close to Anandpur. The ceremony began on the Durgā-aṣṭamī day, two days before the Dusehra festival in October 1698, and lasted for full six months. At the close of this period the sacred days (*navarātras*) began on 21 March 1699.

> When all the *ghee* and incense had been burnt, and the Pandit had tired himself out by mumbling *mantras* without being able to produce the goddess, the Guru came forward with a naked sword and, flashing it before the assembly declared: 'This is the goddess of power!'[6]

The power aspect of the goddess attracted popular imagination during the period of turmoil that followed from the disintegration of the Mughal empire to the consolidation of the British rule in India. Devisiṃha of Bundel who was the disciple of the Śākta-Tantric teacher Jagannivāsa, son of the celebrated Tantric author Śrīnivāsa Bhaṭṭa Gosvāmin, was also a preacher of the doctrine of power.

Jaitrasiṃha of the Veghela dynasty also belonged to the same line of thinking. He was the author of a work relating to the method of worshipping Bhairava. It is said that Mahārāja Krishna Chandra of Nadia (eighteenth century) ordered all his subjects to perform the worship of Kālī. We are also told that during the period of his imprisonment he failed to perform the annual Durgā worship and the goddess advised him in dream to perform after his release her worship in the four-armed Jagaddhātri-on-the-lion form. Many of the local rebellions like the Sannyāsī rebellion, the Chuar rebellion, etc. were inspired by the name of Kālī. Even the robbers and dacoits worshipped the goddess Kālī for power and success; and among her devotees there were Muslims as well. It is also interesting to note that the Kuki rebellion of 1919 was inspired by the name of the goddess and its leaders like Nongmaijing Vaiṣṇavi and Chingakham Sanajaoba were reputed Śākta *sādhakas.* The period which marked the transition from late-medieval to modern was characterised, especially in Bengal, by the installation of numerous Śakti temples mainly dedicated to the goddess Kālī.

II

In the preceding chapter we have seen that in the Mughal age a good number of Śākta-Tāntric works were composed by eminent scholars who were well known for their saintly character and spiritual widsom. These works attempted to make the Tantric ideas popular among the masses. They did not make much discrimination between the Brāhmaṇas and the non-Brāhmaṇas in the spiritual sphere. They admitted the right of all classes to the Tantric *gāyatrī,* and *sandhyā.* All were entitled to read the Tantras and recite the Tantric *mantras.* According to these works average persons belong to the *paśu* category who are slaves to the six passions, namely, lust, greed, anger, pride, illusion and envy. It should be the aim of every individual to transgress the slavery of six passions and attain the *vīra* stage in which he is fearless, self-confident and enterprising. Men with the highest or *divya* disposition are contented, fearless, truthful, attentive to all and loved by all. The doctrine of *pañca-makāra* should not be taken in its ordinary sense. The nector which flows from the union of the *kuṇḍalinī-śakti* with Śiva at the *sahasrāra* in the head is true wine. He who kills by the sword of knowledge or *jñāna* the animals of demerit and devotes his mind on the supreme Śakti is the true eater of flesh.

He who controls all his senses and places them in his self truly takes fish. He who is permeated by the bliss which arises out of the union of the supreme Śakti and the self enjoys the true sexual union. Muhsin Fani, the acute Muslim observer of the seventeenth century, has referred to the high morals of the Śāktas.[7] A special modernism in outlook is found in the *Mahānirvāṇa Tantra* which is said to have been composed by Hariharānanda, the teacher of Raja Rammohan Roy. The latter was deeply influenced by its liberal outlook, especially towards women. Even the Vaiṣṇavas believed in the authority of the Tantric texts. Sanātana Gosvāmin in his commentary on the tenth book of the *Bhāgavata Purāṇa* has cited the authority of the *Trailokyasammohana Tantra* and *Rudrayāmala Tantra.*[8] Gopāla Bhaṭṭa has quoted the authority of many of the Tantras like the *Gautamīya, Trailokyasammohana, Nārada Sammohana* and *Sanatkumāra* Tantras.[9]

The philosophical consequence of this new social role of Śāktism was the emergence of some outstanding contributors to Śākta philosophy like Bhāskararāya or Nīḷakaṇṭha of Deccan. Bhāskararāya's *Setubandha* is a significant commentary on the Nityaṣoḍaśikārṇava section of the *Vāmakeśvara Tantra.* Of his other works dealing with the Tantra topics, the outstanding ones are the *Saubhāgyabhāskara,* which is a commentary on the Lalitāsahasranāma section of the *Brahmāṇḍa Purāṇa* and the *Guptavati* which is a commentary on the *Devīmāhātmya* section of the *Mārkaṇḍeya Purāṇa.* His *Varivasyārahasya* is an independent work which explains different aspects of the Tantric worship of Śakti. Bhāskara flourished in the first half of the eighteenth century. Among his distinguished disciples, Nityānandanātha is also famous for his important work *Nityotsava.* Nīlakaṇṭha of Maharashtra, who flourished about the middle of the eighteenth century, commented upon the *Devībhāgavata* and the *Kātyāyanī Tantra* and also composed two independent works. *Śaktitattvavimarśinī* and *Kāmakalārahasya.* Of other Tantric works of the eighteenth century mention may be made of Rāmagopāla Śarman's *Tantradīpanī,* Kāśīnātha Tarkālaṅkāra's *Śyāmāsaparyāvidhi,* Keśava Viśvarūpa's *Āgamatattvasaṃgraha* and Premanidhi Pantha's *Mallādarśa, Dīpaprakāśa, Pṛthivīpremodaya, Jagatpremodaya, Prayogaratnākara,* etc.

The traditional seventy-seven Āgamas belonging to the Śakti cult are divided into five *śubhāgamas* which teach practices leading to knowledge and liberation, sixty-four *Kaulāgamas* which teach practices intended to develop magical powers and eight *miśrāgamas* which aim at both. Śiva and Śakti stand in the Tantras in relation of *prakāśa* and *vimarśa* respectively, the former being the nature of pure consciousness, impersonality and inactivity. Bhāskararāya in his commentary on the *Lalitāsahasranāma* defines *vimarśa* as the spontaneous vibration of the *prakāśa,* the power which gives rise to the world of distinctions but which remains latent in the absolute. The potentiality of the whole object-world exists as the *vimarśa* or Śakti. Prakṛti or *Māyā* is looked upon as the substance of Śakti under whose direction it evolves into the several material elements and the physical portions of all sentient beings. Instead of the twenty-five *tattvas* of the Sāṅkhya we have thirty-six, classed into Śivatattva or the absolute, Vidyātattva or the subtle manifestations of Śakti and Ātmatattva or the material universe from *Māyā* down to the earth. The individual under the influence of *Māyā,* looks upon himself as a free agent and enjoyer, and it is only the knowledge of Śakti that leads him to the way of liberation. *Jīvanmukti* or liberation in this life is admitted by Bhāskararāya which depends on self-culture and on the awakening of forces within the organism. The theories of *karma,* rebirth, gross and subtle bodies, etc., are also accepted by the Śākta thinkers of the eighteenth century.

III

The concept of the Supreme Goddess as the embodiment of power which in the material sense can destroy the forces of evil and also as that which in the philosophical sense is responsible for the creation of the world must have been inspired from the primitive concepts in the wonder-working power of the Mother Goddess worshipped in various names and forms in numerous villages and tribal settlements and regarded as a living entity determining the fate of her votaries. Though this primitive Mother Goddess was endowed with quite a good number of motherly and benevolent qualities she was more an object of fear and reverence, of appeasement and propitiation, than an object of simple love and devotion. The very idea that the goddess is to be dreaded was responsible for the subsequent emergence of her terrible, warlike and blood-thirsty forms. The association of the goddess with strength, vigour and violence contributed a great deal to her conception as the personification of primordial energy, not passive but active which in its divine form manifests in the demon-slaying goddess whose exploits are narrated in the *Devīmāhātmya* and in other Devī-oriented Purāṇas. In the cosmic level, this primordial energy becomes the *vimarśa* or the vibrating or dynamic energy of the Absolute with the movement of which the universe appears into existence.

The Purāṇic mythology pertaining to various divine forms of the Female Principle eventually culminated into three main streams. The first stream was represented by Umā-Pārvatī, the second by Durgā and the third by Kālī. The first stream represents benign characters. We have the stories of the resurrection on Satī, the first wife of Śiva, as Umā or Pārvatī, her austerities to win her husband again, the marriage of Śiva and Pārvatī, their domestic life and so on. These were and have been extremely popular and served as the most effective link in the process of bringing the other two streams in close relation to each other which eventually resulted in the identification of Umā-Pārvatī, Durgā and Kālī with one another. Durgā was originally the goddess of war identified with Caṇḍikā and other warlike goddess in the Purāṇas, but in the present form of her worship, despite her demon-slaying mould, the Umā-Pārvatī influence on her personality has added as new dimension. She is the wife of Śiva, mother of children and apart from the task of demon-slaying, she is the Corn Mother worshipped in *navapatrikā,* nine forms of plants by which she is symbolised. On the evidence of the *Devībhāgavata, Kālikā Purāṇa, Bhāgavata Purāṇa, Bṛhaddharma Purāṇa,* Kṛttivāsa's Bengali *Rāmāyaṇa,* Vidyāpati's *Durgābhaktitaraṅgiṇī,* Śūlapāṇi's *Durgotsava-viveka, Vāsantīviveka* and *Durgotsavaprayoga,* Jīmūtavāhana's *Kālaviveka* and the writings of Śrīnātha, Govindacandra, Raghunandana and others it may be suggested that the worhip of Durgā, as we have it today, flourished between the fourteenth and the sixteenth centuries.

The induction of Kālī into the Pārvatī-Umā-Durgā complex was also attempted by the Purāṇic writers. Originally regarded as one of the seven tongues of Agni, the deified form of Kālī is met with in the Purāṇas which offer various legends as to her origin. In the *Devīmāhātmya* she is a secondary warlike godling created from the Devī's wrath, but in the other Purāṇas she has been described as emanating from the black muscles of Pārvatī which eventually led her identification with the former and also with Durgā. But she had an independent and distinct development against the backdrop of the corresponding development of the Śākta-Tantric cults. Her conception came from a variety of sources—Purāṇic, Tantric, Buddhist and even Jain. Local variations, elaborations and fusions undoubtedly had characterised the evolution of her new names and forms as we find in the lists of the Mahāvidyās or Vidyās, Nityās, Mātṛkās, Nāyikās and Yoginīs. Reinforcement to the cult and conception of Kālī also came from the contemporaneous Buddhist metamorphosis in which Tārā, later identified with Kālī, played a very important part. Eight forms of Tārā are identified with Kālī. They are Tārā, Ugrā, Mahogrā, Vajrā, Nīlā, Sarasvatī, Kāmeśvarī and Bhadrakālī. In the Tantras many of the Buddhist female deities were identified with the Śākta goddesses, each of which in her turn was identified with Kālī.

Tantric goddesses belong mostly to the Kālī group. Unlike Purāṇic goddesses, they have no mythology. They are all mind-born, intended solely for the purpose of contemplation and meditation. Her Mahāvidyā forms comprise Kālī, Tārā, Mahādurgā, Tvaritā, Chinnamastā, Vāgvādinī, Annapūrṇā, Pratyaṅgirā, Kāmākhyāvāsinī, Bālā, Mātaṅgī, Śailavāsinī, Bhuvaneśvarī, Bhairavī, Dhūmāvatī, Vagalā, Kamalā and Sundarī. Names and forms of Kālī have been multiplied and the number is almost endless. The worship of Kālī was popularised in Bengal by Kṛṣṇānanda Āgamavāgīśa, the well-known author of the *Tantrasāra.* It is said that the image in which she is worshipped at present was also conceived by him. It should be specially noted in this connection that the concept of Kālī which was established by Āgamavāgīśa and which received wide acceptance especially among the Bengalis had nothing to do with the Purāṇic descriptions of her fearful exploits. It was basically Tantric and the goddess represented all forms of cosmological abstractions. Every aspect of her image—her nakedness, her standing on Śiva, her dishevelled hair, her cloud colour, her garland of skulls, her weapons, her stretched tongue pressed by the teeth—evoked popular curiosity and the exponents of her cult were never tired of supplying suitable consistent and attractive interpretations of all these features, in consequence of which, despite her apparently horrible iconic form, she was able to touch the most sensitive cords of the Indian, especially of the Bengali, psyche.

IV

The three streams outlined above were eventually amalgamated into one and the identity of Pārvatī-Umā, Durgā and Kālī was finally established. In the eighteenth century Bengal, although a good number of Tantric works were composed and numerous Śakti temples were constructed, it was the human and domestic form of the goddess that took the lead. The tradition of the homely and benign conception of Śakti was continued in the *Annadāmaṅgala* of Bhāratacandra Ray which was composed about 1752-53 under the patronage of Mahārāja Krishna Chandra of Nadia. The *Annadāmaṅgala* comprises three independent parts. The first part is the Maṅgala Kāvya proper, dealing with the episodes of Śiva and Pārvatī, the problems of their domestic life, their love-quarrels. It contains the legend how Annadā (giver of food) or Pārvatī in the guise of an old woman deceived Vyāsa when the latter had established a Kāśī of his own to bestow salvation to anyone dying there. Pārvatī's description of her own life in verse of *double entendre* conveying two diametrically opposite ideas is very interesting. The gods and goddesses are endowed with human sentiments. The second, the best of the three parts, is romantic story of secret love of Vidyā and Sundara. It relates how by the grace of the goddess Kālī Sundara was saved from death and married to Vidyā. The third part deals with an historical theme.

Following the same tradition Rāmaprasād Sen (born 1720-21) composed, the *Kālikāmaṅgala*, but it was especially his songs, the real Śākta lyrics, that opened not only a new horizon of the Śakti cult but made it acceptable to all, irrespective of caste and creed. Whether Rāmaprasād was the first to write the Śākta lyrics is difficult to say. He composed more than three hundred songs on Kālī. His lyrics can be broadly classified into two categories—Līlā Saṅgīta and Sādhana Saṅgīta. The former deals with the home coming of Umā from her husband's place only for three days in a year and her going back. In these songs the Supreme Being in the homely form of Umā-Gaurī predominates. The latter deals with the conceptual and meditational aspect of the Supreme Being. In this sphere the all-embracing form of Kālī received greater attention of the Śākta lyricists. But in the process of becoming associated with Śiva and identified with particular goddesses like Umā, Pārvatī, Ambikā, Gaurī, etc., Kālī inherited their maternal forms. Unlike the Vaiṣṇava lyrics, the Śākta lyrics were based on harder realities of life. In the lyrics of Rāmaprasād, instead of any sectarian affiliation, we come across a typical scepticism which questions about the efficacy of the wonder-working power of the Supreme Mother. The poet who happened to live in the anarchical condition of the eighteenth-century Bengal, amongst numerous sorrows and sufferings—not spiritual but dry material—repeatedly wanted to know, although admitting the supreme authority of the goddess, the Eternal Mother, whether she is at all capable of bestowing any real grace on her devotees.

The political anarchy of the age and the economic disorder were reflected in the social life which is testified by the *āgamanī* and *vijayā* songs. The impact of Kulinism and polygamy on the one hand and the custom of child-marriage on the other acted very adversely on the social life of Bengal. The Umā or Gaurī of Rāmaprasād is the typical child-wife of the eighteenth century Bengal who was wedded to an elderly and impoverished fellow, incapable of earning and maintaining his family. The girl goes to her husband's household. It is no better than a cremation ground; it is full of poverty; the family members are quarrelsome; the husband is indifferent, disbalanced and addicted to narcotics; moreover, there are co-wives. The golden complexion of Umā becomes black, but she gradually accustoms herself with this precarious way of life. The news of her predicament soon reaches in her father's house. The father comes to know of everything. But what can he do? He becomes a *pāṣāṇa*, motionless as a mountain. But how can the mother bear all this? Her mind is not consoled. She weeps, giving up eating and sleeping. She urges her stone-like husband to bring the daughter back. Eventually Umā comes back her father's home only for three days. The lights are illumined. The joy of the mother knows no bounds. But the three stipulated days pass like dream. Umā returns to her husband's place leaving all in double darkness.

More than eighty Śākta poets appeared in Bengal after Rāmaprasād and a good deal of their composition have been collected in various anthologies. Prominent among them were Kamalakānta Bhattacharya (1771-1821), Dāsarathi Ray (1804-57), Rasik Chandra Ray (1820-83), Nīlakaṇṭha Mukhopadhyaya (1830-90), Iswar Chandra Gupta, Girish Chandra Ghosh, Ramakrishna Ray, Ramlal Das Datta, Mahatab Chand, Ram Basu, Raghunath Ray, etc. By 1900, the number of Śākta lyrics exceeded 4000. And the tradition still survives. But none of them went outside the guideline in regard to contents and expressions as set forth by Rāmaprasād. Even those celebrated poets of the nineteenth century such as Michael Madhusudan Dutt, Nabin Chandra Sen or Girish Chandra Ghosh or Sir Asutosh Mukherjee, the legendary Vice-Chancellor of the Calcutta University, or Kazi Nazrul Islam who had nothing to do with Śākta *sādhanā* and who occasionally resorted to the *āgamanī-vijayā* or devotional theme from a purely literary inspiration, followed the style and sentiment of Rāmaprasād.

The credit of Rāmaprasād lies in the fact that he was able to give the Śākta ideas a new orientation and to raise them above all forms of sectarianism. In many of his songs he equated Kālī with Kṛṣṇa.

Whatever Kālī or Kṛṣṇa seems to be,
They are none but the same to me.

He was able to impress the idea of cult-syncretism upon the subsequent generation of the Śākta poets. The same spirit is found in the songs of Kamalakānta Bhattacharya who sang:

Don't you know, O mind,
Kālī, the cause eternal,
Is not always of female kind.
Often assuming a cloudy form,
Into a male she does transform.

From a theoretical point of view Rāmaprasād, Kamalakānta and their poetic successors believed that the Male and Female Principles of creation are complementary to each other, being expressions of the stream of consciousness which is the cause eternal. When this stream of consciousness in the form of primeval energy is viewed in its static aspect it is conceived in terms of the Male Principle symbolised by Brahmā, Viṣṇu or Śiva and when it is viewed in its vibrating or dynamic aspect, it is conceived in terms of the Female Principle symbolised by Kālī, Durgā, Lakṣmī, Rādhā, etc. That is why Rāmaprasād says, it is the same Mother who holds horn in the form of Śiva, plays on flute in the form of Kṛṣṇa, takes up the bow in the form of Rāma and wields the sword in the form of Kālī. The same is echoed by Kamalakānta:

The one with dishevelled hair and scabbard bare,
Makes the demons shake in fear.
The same one as the chanting flute player,
Hearts of the Vraja maids does conquer.

The lyrics of Kamalakānta are well known and are often confused with those of Rāmaprasād because of the close proximity of ideas and expressions existing between the two poets. Like Rāmaprasād, the devotional attitude of Kamalakānta is characterised by the apparently sceptic and pessimistic tone which complains of the heartlessness of the Mother. But side by side he believes that the Mother tests her devotees through trials. His *āgamanī* and *vijayā* songs closely follow Rāmaprasād. Many of his lyrics, however, aims at elucidating in a very popular way the intricate teachings of the Tantras. Besides stray songs, he composed a work called *Sādhakarañjana* in which the basic principles of Tantra and Yoga have been interpreted in simple Bengali verse. It is also interesting to note that, although he was a Śākta saint-poet, Kamalakānta's basic initiation was in Vaiṣṇavism under Prabhupāda Candraśekhar Goswami of the Śrīpāṭha of Govinda *maṭha* in Burdwan. He used Vaiṣṇava imagery to describe Kālī. In his *Sādhakarañjana* he has described the upward march of *kuṇḍalinī* to meet its source in Vaiṣṇava terms as the meeting of Rādhā and Kṛṣṇa in the forest.

The spirit of the Śākta lyrics is to a great extent different from that of the Purāṇas and the Maṅgala Kāvyas. The Śākta poets of Bengal had little interest in the Purāṇic legends of the exploits of the Devī. In the Purāṇas the legends of Dakṣa-*yajña* and Satī's death appear as a prelude to the story of Pārvatī-Umā. But these are not found in the Śākta lyrics. The great Caṇḍikā of the Devīmāhātmya fails to attract the imagination of the Śākta poets. They take the identification of Pārvati-Umā with Durgā and Kālī as granted while the Purāṇas relate many stories, regarding the emergence of Durgā, Kālī, Caṇḍikā, Kauśikī, etc., from various sources. The character of Śiva has also been somewhat changed. The composers of the Śākta lyrics projected their favourite goddess emphasising on her universal qualities, her benevolence and majesty. There is scepticism, wit, satire and also the spirit of absolute surrender and devotion to the universal mother in the Śākta lyrics. Unlike the Vaiṣṇava lyrics, these are absolutely free from erotic elements. The goddesses of the Maṅgala Kāvyas who are also humanised have some rustic characteristics. They are easily flattered and instantly angered, helping but at the same time punitive. The Śākta poets insisted on the unity of Umā, Durgā and Kālī, the humanisation and personalisation of the goddess in these three forms and the motherhood of Kālī, her transformation from the awe-inspiring demon-slaying goddess to an all embracing merciful mother. As we have stated above the dread-inducing characteristics of Kālī has numerous suggestivity. Each of her emblems are open to various symbolic interpretations. Although in the songs Umā or Gaurī is mentioned as the Supreme Being, her absolute humanisation has made her an agent under bondage and not a free agent. The conception of the Supreme Being as a daughter under the parent and a wife under the husband, however appealing it may be from the view point of sentiment, cannot fulfil the clause of omniscience and omnipotence. That is why the identification of Umā with Kālī, the goddess who tramples Mahākāla under her feet, was essential.[10]

V

In other parts of India although stray poems were composed extolling the greatness of the Devī, there was no special development of the Śākta poetic literature as we find in the eighteenth and nineteenth century Bengal. In the regional literature, though there is no dearth of eulogistic compositions pertaining to the greatness of the local goddesses and their shrines during the period under review, the Female Principle was not universalised or given a new dimension, as was done in the Bengal Śākta lyrics, until the first quarter of the twentieth century when the concept of Śakti became a driving force in the freedom movement of India. In Gujarat, however, the Śakti cult received a great impetus from the writings of Vallabha Bhaṭṭa (1680-1751), Nāth Bhawan (1681-1769) and Mitnu Bhagat (1738-96). Vallabha Bhaṭṭa's *Garbas* are sung in Gujarat even today during the Navarātri festival. They are full of tender sentiments, humility and the spirit of self-surrender to the goddess.

In the Maithili literature the doctrine of Śakti is visibly present, though not in the form of the Bengali Śākta Padāvalī. But it is interesting to note that Vidyāpati, widely celebrated as the pioneering writer of the Vaiṣṇava lyrics of the finest type, was personally a Śākta and he composed some Śākta lyrics as well which were known as *nācāḍi*. Purāṇic legends pertaining to the goddess have been translated into Maithili by Achyutanand Dutt, Ramchandra Jha, Ramlochan Saran, Gauri Sankar Jha and others. E.T. Predux has compiled and published the Maithili folklore dealing with various aspects of the goddess under the title *Kamala Maik Gīt*. These have three distinctive features, namely, invocation (*dhyāna*), praise of power and miracle (*guṇakathana*) and prayer (*nivedana* or *minati*). The works of Rajeshwar Jha, Brajkishore Verma, Radha Krishna Chaudhuri, Prafulla Kumar, Anima Rani Singh, Joganand Jha etc., of modern times have unearthed many treasures of the Śākta folklore in Maithili. In the works of Chandra Jha, Lal Das, Sitaram Jha, Kavisekhar Badarinath Jha, Munshi Raghunandan Das, Jibnath Jha and a host of others various aspects of Śakti have been given novel interpretation. For example, the goddess Chinnamastā denotes the elimination of ego from the self. While Kālī is the main stream of Śāktism in Mithila, Durgā, Lakṣmī, Sītā and other Purāṇic goddesses are also identified with the Supreme Śakti. These goddesses have their invocatory songs in Maithili. Village goddesses are also extolled.

In Assamese also there was no development of Śākta lyrics. We have already had the occasion to refer to *Maṅgala Kāvya* type of poetical works in medieval Assamese like those of Durgāvara and Nārāyaṇadeva, the Śākta cosmogony described in Śaṅkaradeva's *Anādi Pātana,* the Assamese translation of the Devīmāhātmya by Pītāmbara of the sixteenth century and by Rucinātha and Raṅganātha of the seventeenth century, the poetical works of Rāmasarasvatī and so forth. Ananta Ácārya's *Ānandalaharī,* as we have seen above, was a special work on Śāktism composed in the eighteenth century during the reign of the Ahom king Svargadeva Śivasiṃha. It was modelled after Śaṅkarācārya's *Saundaryalaharī.* Regarding the purpose of this work Ananta Ācārya says that there are many Tantras dealing with *dharma, artha* and *kāma.* Likewise the *mokṣaśāstras* (science of liberation) are many and subject to various interpretations. In the Kali age people are bound to be confused with this variety of scriptures and they are likely to misinterpret the words of the Śāstras. That is why Śiva wished this text to be composed by going through which people should find the right way of spiritual exercise. The *Ānandalaharī* is a metrical amplification of the teachings of the Tantra. It deals with the Tantric concepts of Śiva and Śakti, *kuṇḍalinī* or serpent power, *nāda* and *bindu,* creation, individual and universal self, disciple, teacher, *mantra, siddhi,* the penetration of the six nerve plexuses, the methods of making *śrīcakra,* erotic techniques and so forth.

In Manipur, the tribal goddesses of the Meiteis were identified with the Śākta goddesses. Brahmanical migrations from Bengal and Assam were responsible for the Hinduisation of the Meitei community. It should be remembered in this connection that a copperplate of the eighth century found at Phayeng includes the worship of Devī along with other Purāṇic gods.[11] The Manipuri lore contains a number of hymns addressed to various female deities regarded as manifestations of Mother Earth. Goddess Pānthoibi is the counterpart of Durgā in Manipuri mythology. Among the Meiteis seven Lairemas or goddesses were regarded as the ancestresses of the seven *salais* or clans, later identified with seven Brahmanical *gotras* with the expansion of Hinduisation. According to Manipuri legends Śiva and Umā came to Manipur to perform *rāsa* dance at the imitation of Kṛṣṇa and the *gopīs*. In the ballad of *Numit Kāppa* (shooting the sun) the exploits of this goddess are narrated. In the *Pānthoibi Khongun* (foot-prints of the goddess Pānthoibi) composed in the medieval period in five chapters by an unnamed author the goddess Pānthoibi is regarded as a war goddess who like Durgā combined energy of all the gods. The work describes the story of her love, her unsuccessful marriage and her gradual elevation in the hierarchy of deities. The *Leithank Leikhārol* composed about AD 1606 describes how the goddess Pānthoibi kills demon after the pattern of Mārkaṇḍeya Caṇḍī. In the royal diary, *Chithārol Kumbābā*, we find mention of the first recorded Kyong (temple) of the goddess erected in 1686 and her first recorded idol in 1699. King Charāirongbā built two Kālī temples of brick in 1706-07. A Burmese architect was incharge of constructing them. It should be noted in this connection that Mahārāja Candrakīrti introduced the festival of Durgā-pūjā in a pompous way consisting of *lāirema dhumel* (drum movement), offering of milk of 108 cows. He dedicated one temple to the Devī in Ziri in 1868.[12]

By the seventeenth century the Manipuris were aware of the Śākta Purāṇas and Tantras and the Devī legends. A good number of Tantric manuscripts have been found in Manipur, some of which have been edited and published. Mention may also made in this connection to noted Manipuri Śākta *sādhakas* or aspirants such as Mahārāṇi Induprabhā, Nongmaijing Vaiṣṇavī, Paona Brajavasi and a few other saints who were instrumental in mixing up Bengal Vaiṣṇavism with Śāktism in the nineteenth century. The Asheibās (lyricist/poet-singers) were apt to treat every talented woman (such as princess Thoibi of the *Moirang* epics) as an incarnation of the Devī. Kings like Chaurajit (1806-13), Candrakīrti (1850-84) were patrons of Śāktism. Manipuri physicians were well-versed in Tantric practices and tried to cure diseases with the seed *mantra* of the Kāmākhyā-yantra. Devī icons are well known as also the cult of *yoni* or female organ. Durgā-pūjā became a state festival in Manipur since the time of Mahārāja Garib Niwas (1709-49). She is worshipped for ten days commencing from *chaorel houba* or the Devī's starting from her home. The first day is called *lairemba mayum chanba* (entering the father's home). The third day is celebrated as *hiyangthang-bora* which is a matter of interest to the ladies. The goddess Kāmākhyā (identified with Hiyangthang Lairembi) is invoked on a slab of a black stone.

Besides the goddess Durgā, Kālī, is also worshipped.[13]

VI

A remarkable feature of the religious life in the eighteenth century was the emergence of liberal sects among the Hindus which insisted on a simpler approach to spiritual experience and a spirit of social reformism. The founders of such sects belonged to different social and cultural levels. Some of these sects were in favour of Hindu-Muslim harmony. Prāṇanāth of Bundelkhand who recruited his followers both from the Hindus and the Muslims tried to prove that there was no essential difference between the teachings of the Vedas and the Holy *Quran*. Jagjivan Das of Awadh, an exponent of the Satnāmīs was also a promoter of Hindu-Muslim unity. So was Śiva-Nārāyan, a Rajput from Uttar Pradesh, who founded a sect in the first half of the eighteenth century with the object of bringing the Hindus and Muslims closer. Garibdas of Rohtak also attempted to build up a synthesis between the Hindu and Muslim faiths.

The greatest of the reforming sects in Gujarat was founded by Sahajānanda Swāmī who became famous as Swāmī Nārāyaṇa (1781-1830). Charandās of Alwar (born AD 1703) denounced the prevailing tendency to moral laxity and laid great emphasis on the purity of character. Towards the close of the eighteenth century a liberal sect was founded by Paltudās, the adherents of which are to be found in Awadh and Nepal. The Rāma cult received a new orientation in the poetic compositions of Rāmasakheji. His works are considered as authoritative texts by the Rasika subsect of the Rāma cult. Vrindāvana and its surrounding areas became centres of propagation of the Bengal school of Vaiṣṇavism. A new sub-sect of the Vaiṣṇavas, known as the Kartābhajās arose in the district of Nadia. They were far in advance of the orthodox communities in matters relating to social reform. There also arose a number of saintly reformers amongst peoples belonging to the lower ranks of the caste-hierarchy. Following the wake of Ravidās, the sweepers organised a sect called the Hariścandris. Balarāma Hāḍi of Nadia founded the Balarāmī sect. Dapā Muci of Santipur founded the Darpanārāyaṇī sect. These movements had a general liberalising influence on society.

With the establishment of British rule in India, the English educated persons, bewildered by the achievements of the British, lost faith in the potency of the age-old traditions of India. They came under the sway of an exotic civilization, of the European ideas and of Christianity. This came as a challenge to those who believed in the traditional values, customs and institutions. This cultural conflict led to a synthesis which was accelerated by the reform movements, the earliest of which was the Brahmo Samāj founded in 1828 by Raja Rammohan Roy, who based his religious doctrines upon the Upaniṣads and built up a lofty monotheistic creed that could easily vie with the Christian faith. The Brahmo Samāj worked for the emancipation of women and for the abolition of the caste system, and also by introducing a Church-system it could stop the wild craze of the young intelligentsia for changing their religion. The Prārthanā Samāj of Maharashtra, founded in the sixties of the nineteenth century, put in substantial service in the same direction through the efforts of R.G. Bhandarkar and M.G. Ranade. In the seventies of the nineteenth century, the Ārya Samāj movement was launched by Svāmī Dayānanda who stood for the revival of the ancient Vedic religion. In different parts of northern India, especially in the Punjab, the Ārya Samāj movement found a good following. Another religious movement which came from abroad could also check, to a certain extent, the influence of Christianity. This was the Theosophical movement.

But since all these reform movements were confined only among the English-educated intelligentsia, they had very little access among the greater section of the people. The pride of modern education among the followers of these new creeds created a gulf of difference between them and the ordinary people who were still living in the midst of poverty and superstitions and did adhere strictly to their old creeds, remaining suspicious of the highbrows coming to convert them. Existing Hinduism became debased for the lack of proper leadership and for the apathy of the intelligentsia towards it. The orthodox section, rightly or wrongly, chose to stand or fall with the entirety of Hindu traditions and refused to accept any type of sectional Hinduism from the reformers. The Dharma Sabhā, established in 1830 by Raja Radhakanta Deb insisted on maintaining of the orthodox form of the Hindu way of life. It also gathered a few supporters from the intelligentsia. Indological researches revealed an apparently 'glorious' picture of Ancient India. The 'Indian Culture' was immensely praised by some European Indologists. This roused a tendency of glorifying everything regarded as the Hindu heritage among a section of the English educated Indians.

VII

The followers of the reformist sects in their pride of superiority kept themselves aloof from the masses while the orthodox section lived in the world of exaggerated notions. But the common people needed an ideology in their struggle for existence, an ideology which would serve the practical purposes of life and at the same time would overcome the intellectual and spiritual crisis of the age. Such an ideology was supplied by Rāmakṛṣṇa Paramahaṃsa, the Śākta saint, who offered a remarkably broad and synthetic vision of Hinduism and an extraordinarily simple and illuminating exposition of all the ideas of Hindu theology.

Before dealing with Rāmakṛṣṇa's contribution to the cause of society and religion we should say a few words about the Śākta saint heritage of which he was a lineal. We have seen that what is called the Śākta outlook was theoretically established by the Tantric authors. The Śākta lyricists like Rāmaprasād, Kamalakānta and others elucidated in a very popular way the intricate teachings of the Tantras. There were another group of the spiritual aspirants who preferred to be occupied with religious practices themselves, rather than with the interpretation of the Tantric texts. Many of them were even illiterate. Among saints of this class mention may be made of Sarvānanda who flourished in the sixteenth century at Mehar in the district of Tippera. It is stated that all forms of the Divine Mother were revealed to him. The Kālī temple which he established at Mehar is a place of pilgrimage to the peoples of Bengal. His descendants have to this day a large number of disciples all over Bengal. Ratnagarbha or Gosāin Bhaṭṭācāryya who flourished towards the close of the sixteenth century, attained liberation in the temple of Digambarī at Mayaisar in the Dacca district. Jayadurgā or Ardhakālī, the female Śākta saint who flourished about the seventeenth centuiy in the Mymensingh district, is believed to have been an incarnation of the Divine Mother. Of similar saints of Mithila reference may be made to Gaṅgeśa Upādhyāya, Devāditya, Vardhamāna and others.

Rāmakṛṣṇa was a spiritual descendant of these Śākta saints of Bengal. We have seen that long before Rāmakṛṣṇa the saintly poet Rāmaprasād had discovered the universal appeal of the Mother cult, and his conception of the relation between the supreme being and the worshipper as that between the mother and her child was further developed by the Śākta saints and lyricists. This shows that from the eighteenth century onwards Śāktism was evolving as a liberal universal religion and this evolution achieved a completeness in Rāmakṛṣṇa who held from his Śākta experience that the aim of all religions was the same and that the difference between the personal and the impersonal god was no more than that between ice and water. The conflict between concrete and abstract, between form and formless, between personal and impersonal, he solved in his own unique synthetic way. Theoretically he believed in the existence of the formless all-pervading Mother, but he did not find any offence in the worship of the image of Kālī, his own personal goddess, since he regarded all forms as mediums leading to the understanding of the formless. He solved the distinction between the so-called deism and theism, between the concrete and abstract conceptions of the Supreme Being, by postulating the theory of *adhikārībheda* or the individual capability. To him the Brahman and his personal deity Kālī were forms of one reality, the former standing for passivity and inaction and latter for just the reverse. To his disciples he could impress the idea that the quarrels between different religions arose from over-emphasis on secondary details and that it was owing to this mistaken attitude towards the externals of religion that different sects and communities fought with one another. It was this liberal attitude of Rāmakṛṣṇa, which evolved out of his Śākta experience, helped his disciples, especially the Vivekānanda group, to bring another qualitative change in the interpretation of religion.

Rāmakṛṣṇa could attract around himself a number of noteworthy intellectuals of his day who carried his ideas far and wide. He was introduced to the educated middle class of Calcutta from which section came most of his disciples. But there were other Śākta saints living in distant villages. Mention may be made in this connection of Vāmācaraṇa, popularly known as Vāmā Kṣepā whose centre of spiritual activity was Tārāpīṭha in the Birbhum district where he practised meditation from his young age. He was a devotee of Tārā but seldom did he offer any formal worship. To a great extent his views were in agreement with those of Rāmakṛṣṇa. In fact the latter voiced the spiritual demand of his age, and the same voice was also heard from other corners.

A symbolic interpretation of the Devīmāhātmya section of the *Mārkaṇḍeya Purāṇa* was offered by Śrī Satya Deva in his *Sādhanasamara* in which he held that the purpose of the Devīmāhātmya was to identify the individual soul with the universal soul. The goddess who is Mahāmāyā in the Devīmāhātmya is no other than the universal soul, the absolute Brahman. What the Devīsūkta of the *Ṛgveda* says with reservation is explained in the Devīmāhātmya in the forms of legends. His disciple Vijayakṛṣṇa made an attempt to rationalise the Tantric conceptions of the ten Mahāvidyās in terms of the doctrine of evolution. It is interesting to note that a similar attempt was made by the poet Hem Chandra Bandyopadhyay in his famous poetry entitled *Daśamahāvidyā.* Since the nineteenth century was the age of reason, there was a tendency of connecting the religious concepts and the Purāṇic legends with history and science. Nabin Chandra Sen's trilogy *Raivataka-Kurukṣetra-Prabhāsa* likewise connects the ten *avatāras* of Viṣṇu with the ten stages of biological evolution.

In the twentieth century Aurobindo Ghosh has interpreted the doctrine of Śakti in a new light. The Tantric conception of transforming the mortal and material body into pure and then into divine has been echoed, with greater intellectual comprehension, in Aurobindo's conception of the Life Divine. According to Aurobindo, spiritual quest is the quest of complete existence, and that is not possible by the denial of the existence of the outer world. The higher levels of spiritual attainment cannot be perfect unless the spirit and experience of the higher levels are infused into those of the lower. In his own words:

> If in passing from one domain to another we renounce what has already been given us from eagerness for our new attainment, if in reaching the mental life we cast away or belittle the physical life which is our basis, or if we reject the mental and physical in our attraction to the spiritual, we do not fulfil God integrally nor satisfy the conditions of His self-manifestation. We do not become perfect, but only shift the field of our imperfection or at most attain a limited attitude. However high we may climb, even though it be to the non-Being itself, we climb ill if we forget our base. Not to abandon the lower to itself, but to transfigure it in the light of the higher to which we have attained, is true divinity of nature.

So long the Divine does not descend upon each level of our entity, we live in the midst of and are guided by the laws of the impure nature. But when that happens, we are guided by the divine laws. The human being then is transformed into a perfect instrument of God.

> He would feel the presence of the Divine in every centre of his consciousness, in every vibration of his life-force, in every cell of

> his body. In all the workings of his force of Nature he would be aware of the working of the supreme World Mother, the Supernature; he would see his natural being as the becoming and manifestation of the power of the World Mother.

According to Aurobindo, there are two things that come out from all evolution. One is a transformation and the other is a consequence of that transformation. The Śakti or Mother is the driving force of all evolutions and hence human entity should be revealed to her so that she may work therein, and this should be done through complete and unconditional surrender to the will of the Mother.

> In proportion as the surrender and self-consecration progress the *sādhaka* becomes conscious of the Divine Śakti doing the *sādhanā* pouring into him more and more of herself, founding in him the freedom and perfection of the Divine Nature.... And afterwards you will realise that the divine Śakti not only inspires and guides, but initiates and carries out your works; all your movements are originated by her, all your powers are hers, mind, life and body are conscious and joyful instruments of her action, means of her play, moulds for her manifestation in the physical universe.... The last stage of this perfection will come when you are completely identified with the Divine Mother and feel yourself to be no longer another and separate being, instrument, servant or worker but truly a child and eternal portion of her consciousness and force. Always she will be in you and you in her; it will be your constant, simple and natural experience that all your thought and seeing and action, your very breathing or moving come from her and hers. You will know and see and feel that you are a person and power formed by her out of herself, put out from her for play and yet always safe in her, being of her being, consciousness of her being, consciousness of her consciousness, force of her force, *ānanda* for her *ānanda.*[14]

VIII

From the middle of the nineteenth century the cult of Śakti began to contribute to the growth of Indian nationalism. The conception of the country in the form of Divine Mother became a strong basis of Indian freedom movement, and this conception was given shape and colour by eminent writers and thinkers. Not all of them were religiously Śāktas, because Śāktism had by this time ceased to be a sectarian religion, and there was no difficulty for anyone to accept its essence. The feeling which they cherished finds a very nice expression in the following words of Sri Aurobindo: "Mother India is not a piece of earth; she is power, a godhead, for all nations have such a Devī, supporting their separate existence and keeping it in being." Iswar Chandra Gupta, the first nationalist poet of modern Bengali literature, composed a number of poems, popularising the aforesaid idea, and he was followed by a number of poets like Michael Madhusudan Dutt, Hem Chandra Bandyopadhyay, Nabin Chandra Sen, Rangalal Bandyopadhyay and others. The real initiator of mother-consciousness in national life, however, was Bankim Chandra Chattopadhyay whose 'Vandemātaram' anthem, in which the country is identified with the *daśapraharṇadhāriṇī* Durgā, is still a source of inspiration to the people of India. This celebrated song occurs in his famous novel *Ānandamaṭha* which is based upon the Sannyāsī rebellion that took place in the last quarter of the eighteenth century. Following the mother-oriented outlook of the earlier poets. Dwijendralal Ray composed numerous poems glorifying the cultural heritage of India and especially in many of his dramas he pointed out the liberating principles of Śāktism. Even the great poet Rabindranath Tagore, in whom the Śākta religious practices had created a hostile feeling and whose own religious convictions were virtually opposed to the Śākta religion, could not help reflecting the spirt of Śāktism in his nationalistic songs and poems dedicated to the motherland. The tendency of identifying motherland with the Devī or Śakti, although emanated from Bengal, could easily attract the imagination of many a poet in different parts of the country. In Oriya literature this tradition was upheld by Madhusudana Dasa and others and in Hindi literature the intimate relation between the concept of Śakti and the forces of nationalism is remarkably demonstrated in the poems of Balmukunda Gupta and his followers. Restatement of Purāṇic themes, centering round Śakti or Devī is found in the writings of Maithili Saran Gupta, Himmat Simha, Ramananda Tiwari, Jayasankar Prasad, Suryakanta Tripathi 'Nirala', Anupa and others. Mummadi Kṛṣṇarāja had translated in Kannaḍa numerous Śākta works evidently for the purpose of bringing a new orientation in the social and religious life of the country. To Subramania Bhāratī, "the incarnate Agastya" of Tamil literature, Mother India and Mother Tamil were divine realities. In his *Pāñcāli Saptam* he made Draupadī's predicament in the Kaurava court the symbol of enslaved Mother India's plight. In this work Draupadī is identified on the one hand with Mother India and on the other with the Great Mother, the Parāśakti herself.

The main theme of Bankim Chandra's *Ānandamaṭha,* inspired the Bengali youths to sacrifice themselves during the period of freedom movement. The central plot of the novel moves round a band of revolutionaries who called themselves *santānas* or children who dedicated their everything to the cause of the country. They worshipped their motherland as the goddess Kālī, and in their temple they installed three images of the goddess, representing respectively, 'Mother that was', 'Mother that is' and 'Mother that will be'. No other novel so profoundly moved the youths as did this *Ānandamaṭha.* The imagery of the goddess Kālī in the *Ānandamaṭha* leaves no doubt that Bankim Chandra owed his inspiration to the Śākta tradition. His own Vaiṣṇavite convictions did not prove any bar in this respect. Likewise Vivekananda, who inherited from Rāmakṛṣṇa the Śākta-oriented synthetic outlook which helped him to interpret the Vedānta in terms of humanitarian principles, insisted on the cult of Śakti in the programme of national regeneration. He regarded the country as the living image of the Divine Mother and went so far as to state that "for the next fifty years this alone shall be our key-note—this, our great Mother India. Let all other vain gods disappear for that time from our minds."[15] Elsewhere he said,

> O India forget not that the ideal of thy womanhood is Sītā, Sāvitrī, Damayantī; forget not that the God thou worshippest is the great ascetic of ascetics, the all-renouncing Śaṅkara, the Lord of Umā; forget not that thy marriage, thy wealth, thy life are not for sense-pleasure, are not thy individual personal happiness; forget not that thou art born as a sacrifice to the Mother's altar; forget not that thy social order is but the reflex of the infinite *Universal Motherhood,* forget not that the lower classes, the ignorant, the poor, the illiterate, the cobbler, the sweeper are thy flesh and blood, thy brothers. Thou brave one, be bold, take courage, be proud that thou art an Indian and proudly proclaim, 'I am an Indian, every Indian is my brother'. Say, 'The ignorant Indian, the poor and destitute Indian, the, Brāhmaṇa Indian, the Pariah Indian is my brother.' Thou, too, clad with but a rag round thy loins proudly proclaim at the top of thy voice, 'The Indian is my brother, the Indian is my life, India's gods and goddesses are my God. India's society is the cradle of my infancy, the pleasure garden of my youth, the sacred heaven, the Vārāṇasī of my old age'. Say, brother, 'The soil of India is my highest heaven, the

good of India is my good', and repeat and pray day and night, 'O Thou Lord of Gaurī, O Thou Mother of the Universe, vouchsafe manliness unto me. O Thou Mother of Strength, take away my weakness, take away my unmanliness, and make me a Man.'[16]

The conception of the country in the form of Divine Mother was of a general character acceptable to all irrespective of caste and creed, and it had evidently enhanced the patriotic feeling among the Indians. But once it was formed it did not remain simply as a patriotic conception. The demand of action leading to freedom introduced revolutionary movements in different parts of India. Secret societies were started in order to propagate revolutionary ideas, collect arms and rise in rebellion. The chief means of propaganda was the publication of books and periodicals to preach the gospel of revolution.

'The first book, entitled *Bhavānī Mandir*, published in 1905, gives detailed plan of establishing a religious sanctuary as the basis or centre of revolutionary activities—a temple of the goddess Bhavānī in a secluded spot, far from human habitation, in a calm and serene atmosphere. This was to be the centre of a new order of political devotees. They might or might not become Sannyāsīs (ascetics) but were to lead the life of Brahmacārī (novice), and would return to the life of a householder only when the object was achieved. This object was the freedom of India from the foreign yoke. The book is a very remarkable one, and lays main stress on the glorification of Kālī under the names of Śakti or Bhavānī, and preaching of the gospel of force and physical strength as the necessary condition for political freedom. The central theme of the work was the organisation of a band of workers who would prepare the way for revolution in India and should have no other attachment in life. There is no doubt that this central idea was taken from Bankim Chandra's *Ānandamaṭha* to which reference has been made above, and it is a further evidence of the great influence exercised by that book upon the revolutionary activities in Bengal.'[17]

References

1. Yasin, *SHII*, 150.
2. *Camb. HI*, IV.241.
3. Ibid., 242.
4. *Kalyāṇa*, Śakti issue, 417-19.
5. Macauliffe, *SR*, V.83.

6. Singh, *SHS*, I.68.
7. *Dabistan*, II, 154, 164.
8. *Vaiṣṇavatoṣaṇī*, com. on the *Bhāgavata*, X.55.1.
9. *Haribhaktivilāsa*, I.58 ff; II.9 ff; III.4, 220-23; IV.100-102.
10. In Bengali there are many works on Śākta lyrics. A collection of the Śākta lyrics has been published by the Calcutta University. They have been introduced to the English-reading persons by Thomson and Spencer who translated and classified a select number of these songs under the title *Religious Lyrics: Śākta* (1923), J.N. Sinha (1990) has made an English translation of the songs of Rāmaprasād. L. Nathan and C. Seely's translation was published in 1982. Rachel Fell McDermott's excellent and very faithful English renderings of the poems of Kamalakānta awaits publication.
11. Yumjao Singh, *RASM*, I.
12. M. Kirti Singh, 'Śākta Worship in Manipur', Sahitya Akademi Seminar, Guwahati, 12-13 Dec. 1989.
13. Ibid., also see my *RCNEI*, chs. II-III; Chatterji, *KJK*, 77ff.
14. *M*, 13, 30, 32-33.
15. *CWV*, III, 301.
16. Ibid., IV, 477f.
17. Majumdar, *HFMI*, II, 269-70.

9

A Note on Śākta Philosophy

Notwithstanding the antiquity of the Śākta-Tantric cults and rituals and their theoretical aspects, there had been no consistent attempt in the past to give them a complete philosophical shape. This can be attributed to the fact that the Śākta-Tantric teachings were transmitted from teacher to pupil as a secret and mysterious knowledge to be understood and retained only by those considered competent. That is why in the philosophical compendiums—the *Sarvadarśanasaṃgraha, Ṣaḍdarśanasamuccaya, Sarvasiddhāntasaṃgraha, Vivekavilāsa,* etc.—Śākta philosophy as a whole has no place, although some of its aspects have been referred to in connection with other philosophical systems.

The need for reconstructing the Śākta viewpoint on the basis of the available Tantric texts was felt in the last quarter of the 19th century by the advocates of the Neo-Tantric movement who wanted to identify Tantrism with the totality of Hinduism and regard it as the essence of the Vedas. The greatest exponents of this line were Sir John Woodroffe and his associates who composed numerous interpretative works on Tantrism during the first three decades of the 20th century. In 1937 Panchanan Tarkaratna published his Śākta commentaries on *Brahmasūtra* and *Īśopaniṣad* in which he made a laudable attempt to put forward what is known as the Śākta viewpoint in Indian philosophical tradition. This branch of study was further developed by M.M. Gopinath Kaviraj.

It is worth remembering that all these great scholars while interpreting the essentials of Śāktism depended on the sophisticated Tantric tradition which was burdened with Brahmanical superimpositions and Vedāntic elements. We have repeatedly said that the logic and the doctrine of the Tantras were given a very sophisticated tone and colour; a philosophy of extreme idealism was grafted onto them as opposed to the original materialistic outlook which Tantrism basically upheld. Since these accretions have now become an integral part of Tantrism, they should also be properly studied in the light of what has been understood by these great Tantric scholars.

Most of the Tantric works are medieval efficient and inefficient renderings or rewritings or the teachings of the earlier lost texts. It is said that the traditional sixty-four Bhairavāgamas were monistic, ten Śaivāgamas were dualistic and eighteen Raudrāgamas were of diverse views. Most of the original texts are lost. Generally, the Jñanapāda sections of the Āgamas contain some philosophical speculations. Among the Tantric texts of philosophical significance mention may be made of *Svacchanda, Mālinīvijaya, Vijñānabhairava, Triśirobhairava, Kulagahvara, Paramānanda Tantra, Āgamarahasya,* etc. The Śrīvidyā school has an extensive literature of its own. This school claims Agastya, Durvāsā and Dattātreya as its earlier exponents. References to a lost *Dattātreyasaṃhitā* are found. Some of its contents are said to have formed part of the *Tripurārahasya,* the Jñāna section of which throws much light on Śākta philosophy. Gauḍapāda's *Śrīvidyāratnasūtra,* which is said to have been commented upon by Śaṅkarācārya himself, is a useful Śākta text. Philosophically important are *Prapañcasāra,* attributed to Śaṅkara and commented upon by Padmapāda, *Prayogakramadīpikā*, Lakṣmaṇa Deśika's *Śāradātilaka,* and the texts of the Kāśmīra Śaiva school. Abhinavagupta in his numerous works has successfully established the foundation of Śākta philosophy. Among his successors, Gorakṣa or Maheśvarānanda composed an original work called *Mahārghamañjarī* and commentaries like *Parimala, Saṃvidullāsa,* etc. Puṇyānanda's *Kāmakalāvilāsa* is an authoritative work on Śākta philosophy. Its commentary, known as *Cidvallī* was composed by Nathanānanda. Amṛtānanda, a disciple of Puṇyānanda, wrote an important commentary known as *Yoginīhṛdayadīpikā* which was made on the Yoginīhṛdaya section of the *Nityaṣoḍaśikārṇava* of the *Vamakeśvara Tantra.* He was also the writer of *Saubhāgyasubhagodaya* and other texts of great philosophical significance. Svatantrānanda's *Mātṛkācakraviveka* is an exceptional work in five parts in which the aspects of Tantric secret knowledge have been explained. The best exponent of Śākta philosophy is Bhāskararāya who flourished in the 18th century. His most celebrated work is *Setubandha* which is a commentary on *Nityaṣoḍaśikārṇava.* His other works include *Kaula-tripurā, Saubhāgyabhāskara* (commentary on the *Lalitāsahasranāma*), *Guptavatī* (commentary on the Devīmāhātmya), *Śāmbhavānanda-kalpalatā, Varivasyā-rahasya,* etc.

Śākta philosophy, as we have noted, was deeply influenced by the non-dualistic and dualistic interpretations of the Vedānta, though other systems like the Sāṅkhya etc. formed its original basis. The

Śākta philosophical terminologies are not different from those used in the Indian philosophical tradition in general. As in all idealistic systems, the ultimate reality in Śāktism is pure consciousness. It is known as Saṃvit. In the Vedānta, specially according to its non-dualist interpretation, Saṃvit is not limited by time, space and cause. In it the world is reflected just as an object is reflected in a clear mirror. From this analogy of the mirror we have three probabilities: the mirror (Saṃvit) is, but there is nothing (world) reflected in; the mirror it is, and the thing (world) is inside it; and the mirror it is, and the thing (world) reflected in it belongs to the outside. In all the three cases, the mirror (Saṃvit or pure-consciousness) is one and only one without any change. That is why it is called Nirvikalpa which literally means without any transformation. The first probability shows that there is nothing inside nor outside the ultimate reality; the second probability shows that the ultimate reality may be self-expressive inwardly but not outwardly: and the third probability shows that its inwardly self-expression may have outwardly contents. But the problem is in regard to the relation between the pure and unattached Saṃvit and the worldly objects which are reflected in it. According to the Vedānta, specially to its extreme non-dualistic brand, creation does not proceed from Saṃvit or Brahman, the so-called world of existence is false and illusory.

But the Śākta Agamas hold a different view. They recognise the independence of Saṃvit and its power to create motion, although owing to the influence of Vedānta some of the texts hold that the world is an appearance. In Śāktism Saṃvit is conceived of in terms of the functioning of Śakti in *prakāśa* and *vimarśa* aspects, the static and dynamic condition. Saṃvit is both immanent and transcendent, the former condition prevails when Śakti in its static state assumes the form of matter and the latter condition prevails when Śakti in its dynamic state assumes the form of consciousness. The first category is known as *anaham* and the second category as *aham*. In the sophisticated Tantras it is categorically stated that *anaham* is the so called unmanifested material entity and it is caused by the conscious principle expressed by the concept *aham*. In other words, it is stated that matter is produced from consciousness. In modern philosophical terms this standpoint is known as idealism. This approach (in Indian philosophical tradition known as *cetana-kāraṇavāda*) is opposed to the earlier Tantric materialist approach to life and universe. It is obviously due to the Vedāntic influence. But like the Vedānta, the sophisticated Tantras also fail to explain conclusively how matter can be produced from consciousness.

We are not concerned with the fallacies of Tantric or Vedāntic thinking, though it should be noted that there are many. Here we shall see how the Śākta-Tantrics put forward their premises. They say that at the time of the dissolution of the universe pure consciousness or Saṃvit remains absolutely free from material contaminations—it remains as pure *cit-śakti* or *parā-prakṛti*. But when the alternatives or material entities develop (they develop owing to the self-contraction of Saṃvit, but the Tantras do not explain with any amount of reason how the contraction of pure consciousness can yield gross things), then Śakti manifests itself as Avidyā or material Prakṛti. Thus the ultimate reality functions in its two aspects, as subject and also as object. It is stated that pure consciousness is universal in nature, that there is nothing to limit or cover it and that the material world is contained in it. The evolution of the material world from pure consciousness has been conceived of in three stages. The first is the seed stage in which matter does not express its existence and appear as an entity different from consciousness. This stage is regarded is pure. In the second stage there is a marked difference between consciousness and matter, both of which are subject to subtle manifestations. This is regarded as the mixed state. In the third stage the categories of the mixed state have gross manifestations. In this stage we have evolution of Prakṛti, the primordial matter, in the shaping of the material world.

The evolution of the material world has been traced to the following categories: Parameśvara, Śakti, Para-Nāda, Para-Vindu—subdivided into Apara-Vindu and Vīja, and Apara Nāda. Parameśvara is the Supreme Being with whom Śakti or Kalā is in inseparable relation. Just as oil issues from oil-seed so also in the beginning of creation Śakti appears. This appearance of Śakti is like the reappearance of the memory of a person who rises from deep sleep. The appearance of Śakti causes an unmanifested sound called Para-Nāda that fills up the vacuum and eventually concentrates itself on a point or centre which is called Para-Vindu. This Para-Vindu is again subdivided into three parts known respectively as Apara-Vindu, Vīja and Apara-Nāda. In this Apara-Vindu the Śiva element dominates and in the Vīja the Śakti element. In Apara-Nāda, there is Śiva-Śakti equilibrium. The sound caused by the subdivision of Para-Vindu is often called Śabdabrahma. These transformations are due to the inseparable Śakti of the Supreme Being in the form of *icchā* (will) and *kriyā* (functioning).

In the Tantras the whole process is explained with reference to the human body. The space holding the thousand-petalled lotus in the cerebral region is called *brahmarandhra* or Śūnya. It is the breeding spot of Icchā-Śakti and Para-Nāda. It is a part of the *visargamaṇḍala* which is great causal state of Brahman or Saṃvit symbolised by Śabdabrahma or Kulakuṇḍalinī. The three subdivisions of Para-Vindu, namely Vindu (Apara), Vīja and Nāda (Apara), constitute the *kuṇḍalinī* triangle. The subtle elements of matter differs from *kuṇḍalinī* and they reside in different centres of the forehead and nerves. The aforesaid triangle symbolized by Śiva (Apara-Vindu), Śakti (Vīja) and their equilibrium (Apara-Nāda), is called A-Ka-Tha triangle, each of its lines being consisted of sixteen letters. Apart from the Para and Apara-Nādas, there is a third Nāda, known as Mahā-Nāda, caused by the unmanifested sound of the letters which is conveyed by the *kuṇḍalinī*. It serves as a link between the Para and Apara-Nādas, between conscious and non-conscious elements. The upward and downward motions of the Nādas are carried through the main nerves.

To put the whole thing in a more intelligible way, it may be said that Saṃvit or pure consciousness exists. In the Śākta Tantras it is conceived of as the non-dual existence of static Śiva and kinetic Śakti—two positions of the same thing. But, side by side, there is the existence of an unconsciousness, the material world. How can this be explained? According to the non-dualist Tantras it is said that the material world is caused by the self-expression or manifestation of pure consciousness. How can that be possible? The Tantras say that pure consciousness works through its 'Śakti' or inherent power. This Śakti at first appears an Icchā-Śakti or will-power, the desire to be manifested. Subsequently it works in its two aspects—Vidyā-Śakti and Avidyā Śakti or Māyā-Śakti. Both of these are conscious principles with the difference that while the former is illuminating consciousness, the latter is veiled consciousness, i.e. consciousness appearing as unconsciousness. This Māyā-Śakti is composed of these *guṇas*—Sattva, Rajas, Tamas—and known as Triguṇa-Śakti or Kāmakalā symbolised by the triangle. Hence this Māyā-Śakti is not unreal (this is a departure from the Vedāntic line), and it is the cause of the material world.

Śakti, operating as *Cit* and *Māyā*, is real. It is that aspect of the

Supreme Being which is in fact, both the efficient and material cause of the world. Owing to the *vṛtti* of *Māyā*, or Śakti in the form of desire for creation in Parama-Śiva or the Supreme Being, there takes place what is known as *sadṛśapariṇāma* in which the Supreme Vindu appears. This, in its triple aspect is also known as Kāmakalā, the process of the manifestation of Śakti. Śakti as identical with the Supreme Being is immutable and without any transformation, but in its functional aspect it is *pariṇāmī* (subject to transformation). When Śakti passes from a potential state to one of actuality it produces Nāda or cosmic sound from which issues Vindu or Para-Vindu. The *Prapañcasāra* says that Śakti longs to create (*vicikirṣu*) and becomes massive or crystallised (*ghanībhūta*) and appears as Vindu. This Vindu or Para-Vindu divides or differentiates itself in the three-fold aspects of Apara-Vindu, Vīja and Apara-Nāda, as has been most comprehensively dealt with in the *Śāradātilaka* and other texts. The first category is Śivamaya or Śiva-oriented, the second Śaktimaya or Śakti-oriented, and the third Śiva-Śaktimaya in which Śiva and Śakti operate equally. These three categories equated with all the tripartite concepts of Tantra—like Para-Sūkṣma-Sthūla, Icchā-Jñāna-Karma, Tamas-Rajas-Sattva, Moon-Fire-Sun and so on. These are all different phases of Śakti.

Creation is thus the self-expression of the Supreme Being, the subject viewing itself as object. I (*aham*) as it (*idam*). In the dualistic Tantras, however, the whole process has been viewed from a different angle. Here both Śiva and Śakti, the static (*prakāśa*) and kinetic (*vimarśa*) aspect of the same reality, are treated as individual conscious principles. Śiva is unity behind all diversity. Śakti is the same but, since it acts on different things, it is expressed as the inherent nature of the things themselves on and through which it works. Still Śakti is not different from Śiva. Vindu is an eternal material entity outside the realm of Śakti, but it is dependent on the functioning of Śakti. Thus, these three separate entities are the three permanent categories described as three *ratnas*. In the matter of creation Śiva is the efficient cause, Śakti is the instrumental cause, and Vindu is the material cause. Because Śakti is not material in nature; at the time of its activity it undergoes no change, but it may have transformation in Vindu.

In view of what has been stated above we find that in the Śākta scheme *Māyā* is not an unconscious principle but it is consciousness veiling itself as a Śakti of the Supreme Being. Śakti and Śaktimān (possessor of *Śakti*) are one and the same. *Māyā-śakti* is therefore that particular aspect of *cit* or consciousness which it assumes as the material cause (*upādāna-kāraṇa*) in creation. Śiva as Śakti is the cause of the universe and as Śakti in the form of *jīva* (all manifested forms) appears in them. There are two principles or aspects in the Brahman or Saṃvit—Prakāśa (static aspect) and Vimarśa (the kinetic and vibrating aspect), which in creation explicate into the universe. Vimarśa Śakti again has two forms. In the subtle state it is in the form of consciousness (*cidrūpiṇī*) and in the gross state it is in the form of the universe (*viśvarūpiṇī*). The ultimate reality is therefore Śiva in indistinguishable union with Śakti. This Śakti, conceived of as a Female Principle, when in non-dual state with Śiva is unmanifested *cit* or consciousness. The relation between Śiva and Śakti is one of inseparable connection or inherence such as that between I-ness (*ahanta*) and I (*aham*), existence (*bhava*) and existent (*bhavat*), attribute (*dharma*) and attributed (*dharmī*), and so forth.

The evolution of the Supreme Being or Supreme Consciousness into the universe is described in a scheme of thirty-six *tattvas*, divided into three groups named Śiva-*tattva*, Vidyā-*tattva*, Ātma-*tattva* and Śuddha, Śuddhāśuddha and Aśuddha *tattvas*. Without going into the details of these thirty-six *tattvas*, it may be said that they are accepted both by the Śaivas and the Śāktas; they are taken from the northern Kāśmīra Śaiva philosophical school, which itself was based upon the older Āgamas like the *Mālinīvijaya* and others. The point which needs to be discussed is the nature of the evolution of the Supreme Being. It is not a case of complete transformation as we find in the case of milk transforming into curd. The Supreme Being is not exhausted by the transformation. The change is not qualitative. As already stated *aham* (I-ness, the subject) and *idam* (It-ness, the object) exist in an unitary state in Para-Saṃvit, in which Śiva represents the Prakāśa and Śakti the Vimarśa aspect. The latter contains the potentialities of the universe within it. It begins to function leaving the Prakāśa standing alone as an 'I' without a 'This'. The purpose of this functioning is to make the subject experience itself as object. Then stage by stage the *Māyā-śakti* or 'consciousness veiling itself' unfolds itself, and in this process we come across the emergence of multiple selves and objects forming the universe. At every stage of this evolution the Vimarśa Śakti contracts itself into gross and more gross entities until it assumes physical forms and works as the life-principle of all things. At the end of this process, in dissolution, it again returns to its source and remains there in undifferentiated state with her other part, the Prakāśa aspect of the Supreme Being.

The process has also been described using the analogy of a *canaka* or grain by which the cosmic evolution is conceived of as a process polarizing the Supreme Being into static and kinetic aspects. A *canaka* has two seeds which are so close to each other that they seem one; they are surrounded by a single sheath. The seeds are Śiva and Śakti and the sheath is *Māyā*. When the sheath is unpeeled, *Māyā-śakti* operates, and the two seeds come apart. The sheath unrolls when the seeds begin to germinate. It is like reawakening from a dreamless slumber. As the universe in dissolution sinks into a memory which is lost, so it is born again from the germ of recalled memory or Śakti. After the dreamless slumber (*suṣupti*) of the Saṃvit or the world-consciousness the remembrance of the past gives rise in it to create thinking or the will to create (*sṛṣṭi-kalpanā*). It is thus that the indistinguishable unity of Śiva-Śakti or subject and object of the Supreme Being, is broken. It does not, however, take place all at once. There is an intermediate stage of transition, in which there is a subject and an object, but both are part of the Supreme Being which knows its objective form. Their separation becomes a reality when the object manifests itself apart from the subject. The process and the result are the work of Śakti whose special function is to negate, that is to negate its own fullness, so that it becomes the finite centre contracted as a limited subject perceiving a limited object, both being aspects of one ultimate reality. The principle of negation is a feature of *Śakti-tattva* (*niṣedha-vyāpāra-rūpā-śaktiḥ*). Where there is pure experience there is no manifested universe. Śakti negates the pure experience of consciousness because it disengages the unified elements, subject and object, which are latent in the pure Saṃvit in absolute non-dual relation.

The Supreme Being of Śāktism is not a personal God. In its own nature it is more than that. The Śākta standpoint posits the reality of God as the cause of the universe. But it holds that while the effect as effect is the cause modified, the cause as cause remains what it was, what it is, and what it will be. It holds that the Supreme Being is manifested in one of its aspects in an infinity of relations; and though involving at relations within itself, is neither their sum total nor exhausted by them. Śakti, which is its functional aspect, works by negation, contraction, and finitisation. As a Mother power she unfolds herself into the world and again withdraws the world into herself. The purpose of her worship is to attain unity with her forms, and this is the experience of liberation—a state of great bliss (*ānandaghaṇa*). In the natural order of development, Śakti is developed in worldly things but it is controlled by a religious *sādhanā*, which both prevents an excess of worldliness and moulds the mind and disposition (*bhāva*) into a form which develops the knowledge of dispassion and non-attachment. *Sādhanā* is a means whereby bondage becomes liberation.*

*Based upon the interpretations of sophisticated Śākta *mantras* made by Śivacandra Vidyārṇava, M.M. Gopīnāth Kavirāj and Sir John Woodroffe.

Bibliography

Airi, R., *Concept of Sarasvatī*, New Delhi, 1977.

Allan, J., *Catalogue of the Coins of Ancient India*, London, 1936.

Altekar, A.S., *The Rāṣṭrakūṭas and Their Times*, Poona, 1934.

—, *The Coinage of the Gupta Empire*, Varanasi, 1957.

Atre, S., *The Archetypal Mother*, Pune, 1987.

Aurobindo, Sri, *The Life Divine*, Pondicherry, 1939.

Avalon, A., *Garland of Letters*, third ed., Madras, 1952.

—, *Tantrarāja Tantra*, Madras, 1952.

—, *The Great Liberation*, fifth ed., Madras, 1952.

—, *Hymns to Kālī*, sec. ed., Madras, 1953.

—, *Principles of Tantra*, rep., Madras, 1955.

—, *Shàkti and Shakta*, rep., Madras, 1956.

—, *The Serpent Power*, rep., Madras, 1958.

Bachofer, L., *Early Indian Sculptures*, 2 vols., Paris, 1929; rep., New Delhi, 1973.

Bachofen, J.J., *Das Mutterrecht*, Stuttgert, 1861.

Bagchi, P.C., *Pre-Dravidian and Pre-Aryan in India*, Calcutta, 1929.

—, *Studies in the Tantras*, Calcutta, 1939.

—, *Kaulajñānanirṇaya and Minor Texts of the School of Matsyendranātha*, Calcutta Sanskrit Series no. III, Calcutta, 1934.

—, "On some Tantric Texts studied in Ancient Kambuja" in *IHO*, V, 1928, 754-69; VI, 1930, 97-107.

—, *Bauddha Dharma ↄ Sāhitya* (in Bengali).

Bagchi, S.G., *Eminent Śākta Centres in Eastern India*, Calcutta, 1980.

Banerjea, J.N., *Development of Hindu Iconography*, Calcutta, 1956; rep., New Delhi, 1973.

—, *Pauranic and Tantric Religion*, Calcutta, 1966.

Banerjee, S.C., *Tantras in Bengal*, Calcutta, 1978.

—, *A Brief History of Tantric Literature*, Calcutta, 1988.

Banerji, R.D., *Eastern Indian School of Medieval Sculpture*, Delhi, 1933.

Bapat, P.V., *2500 Years of Buddhism*, New Delhi, 1956.

Bardoloi, N.P., *Devī*, Guwahati, 1986 (in Assamese).

Barth, A., *The Religions of India*, Eng. trans. by J. Wood, London, 1881, rep., Delhi, 1969.

Barua, B.M., *Prolegomena to the History of Buddhist Philosophy*, Calcutta,

1918; rep., New Delhi, 1974.
Basumatari, D.R., *Boḍo-Kachāier Saṃskritir Kiñcit Ābhās,* Nalbari, 1950 (in Assamese).
Beal, S., *Buddhist Record of the Western World,* London, 1884; rep., New Delhi, 1983.
Beane, W.C., *Myth, Cult and Symbols in Śākta Hinduism: A Study of the Indian Mother Goddess,* Leiden, 1977.
Belvalkar, S.K. and Ranade, R.D., *History of Indian Philosophy,* vol. II. *The Creative Period,* Poona, 1927; rep., New Delhi, 1974.
Beyer, G., *The Cult of Tārā: Magic and Ritual in Tibet,* London, 1973.
Bhandarkar, D.R., *List of Inscriptions of Northern India: Appendix to Epigraphia Indica,* vols. XIX-XXIII.
Bhandarkar, R.G., *Vaiṣṇavism, Śaivism and Minor Religious Systems,* Strassburg, 1913; Indian ed., Poona, 1926.
Bharati, A., *The Ochre Robe,* London, 1961.
—, *The Tantric Tradition,* London, 1965.
Bhattacharyya, B.C., *Jain Iconography,* Lahore, 1939.
Bhattacharyya, B.T., *Introduction to Buddhist Esoterism,* London, 1932.
—, *Sādhanamālā,* GOS, Baroda, 1925-28.
—, *Guhyasamāja Tantra,* GOS, Baroda, 1937.
—, *Niṣpaṇṇayogāvalī,* GOS, Baroda, 1949.
—, *Śaktisaṅgama Tantra,* GOS, Baroda, 1932, 1941, 1947.
—, *Indian Buddhist Iconography,* Calcutta, 1959.
Bhattacharyya, N.N., *Indian Puberty Rites,* Calcutta, 1968; sec. ed., New Delhi, 1980.
—, *Indian Mother Goddess,* Calcutta, 1971; sec. ed., New Delhi, 1977.
—,*History of Indian Cosmogonical Ideas,* New Delhi, 1971.
—, *Ancient Indian Rituals and Their Social Contents,* New Delhi, 1975.
—, *Jain Philosophy: Historical Outline,* New Delhi, 1976.
—, *History of the Researches on Indian Buddhism,* New Delhi, 1981.
—, *History of the Tantric Religion,* New Delhi, 1982.
—, *Ancient Indian History and Civilization: Trends and Perspectives,* New Delhi, 1988.
—, *A Glossary of Indian Religious Terms and Concepts,* New Delhi, 1990.
—, *Buddhism in the History of Indian Ideas,* New Delhi, 1993.
—, *Religious Culture of North-Eastern India,* Shillong, 1995.
Bhattacharyya, P., *Kāmarūpaśāsanāvalī,* Rangpur, 1931 (in Bengali).
Bhattacharyya, S., *Tantra Paricaya,* Santiniketan, BS 1359 (in Bengali).
Bhattasali, N.K., *Iconography of Buddhist and Brahmanical Sculptures in the Dacca Museum,* Dacca, 1929.

Bloch, J., *Sexual Life of Our Times*, Eng. trans. by Eden Paul, London, 1908.

Bose, M.M., *Post-Caitanya Sahajiyā Cults of Bengal*, Calcutta, 1930.

Breasted, J.H., *History of Egypt*, New York, 1910.

Briffault, R., *The Mothers*, 3 vols., London, 1927; rep., 1952.

Brown, C.M., *God as Mother. A Feminine Theology in India*; An Historical and Theological Study of the *Brahmavaivarta Purāṇa*, Hartfort, 1974.

—, 'Kali the Divine Mother' in *The Book of Goddess Past and Present: An Introduction to Her Religion*, ed. C. Olson, New York, 1983.

Brunton, G. and Caton-Thompson, G., *The Badarian Civilization*, London, 1928.

Butler, S., *The Authoress of the Odyssey*, London, 1897.

Caldwell, Robert, *A Comparative Grammar of Dravidian Language*, third ed., London, 1913; rep., New Delhi, 1974.

Chadwick, H.A., *The Heroic Age*, Cambridge, 1912.

—, *The Origin of the English Nation*, Cambridge, 1916.

Chakravarti, C., *The Tantras: Studies on Their Religion and Literature*, Calcutta, 1963.

Chakravarti, P.C., *Doctrine of Śakti in Indian Literature*, Calcutta, 1940.

Chanda, R.P., *Indo-Aryan Races*, Rajshahi, 1916, ed. by N.N. Bhattacharyya, Calcutta, 1968.

Chatterji, S.K., *Indo-Aryan and Hindi*, Ahmedabad, 1942; sec. ed., Calcutta, 1969.

—, *Kirātajanakṛti*, Calcutta, 1951.

Chattopadhyaya, D.P., *Lokāyata*, Delhi, 1959.

—, *Indian Atheism*, Calcutta, 1969.

—, ed., *Tāranātha's History of Buddhism*, Eng. trans. by Alaka Chattopadhyaya and Lama Chimpa, Simla, 1971.

Childe, V.G., *New Light on the Most Ancient East*, London, 1954.

—, *What Happened in History*, London, 1957.

Coburn, T., *The Devī Māhātmya; The Crystallization of the Goddess Tradition*, Delhi, 1985.

Colebrooke, H.T., *The Sāṅkhya Kārikā*, London and Calcutta, 1887.

Conze, E., *A Short History of Buddhism*, London, 1960.

Coomaraswamy, A.K., *History of Indian and Indonesian Art*, London, 1927, rep., New Delhi, 1972.

—, *Hinduism and Buddhism*, New Delhi, 1986.

Cowell, E.B., *The Jātakas*, Eng. trans in 6 vols., Cambridge, 1895-1913; rep., New Delhi, 1990.

Cunningham, A., *Archaeological Survey of India: Reports.*

Das, H., *Tantrism: Cult of the Yoginīs,* New Delhi, 1980.

Das, S.K., *Śakti or Divine Power,* Calcutta, 1934.

Das, U.N., *Śāstramulak Bhāratīya Śakti Sādhanā,* Shantiniketan, 1966 (in Bengali).

Dasgupta, S.B., *An Introduction to Tantric Buddhism,* Calcutta, 1950.

—, *Obscure Religious Cults,* third ed., Calcutta, 1969.

—, *Bhārater Śakti Sādhana O Śākta Sāhitya,* Calcutta, 1960 (in Bengali).

—, *Śrīrādhār Kramavikās,* Calcutta (in Bengali).

Dasgupta, S.N., *History of Indian Philosophy,* 5 vols., Cambridge, 1922-55.

Desai, D., *Erotic Sculptures of India: A Socio-Cultural Study,* New Delhi, 1975, sec. ed., New Delhi, 1986.

Deussen, P., *Philosophy of the Upaniṣads,* Eng. trans. by A.S. Geden, Edinburgh, 1919; rep., New Delhi, 1979.

Dewan Singh, R., *Folklore of the Garos,* Calcutta, 1960.

Dhal, U.N., *Goddess Lekṣmī: Origin and Development,* New Delhi, 1978.

Dikshit, S.K., *Mother Goddess,* Poona, 1943.

Dikshitar, V.R.R., *The Lalitā Cult,* Madras, 1942.

Edkins, J., *Religions of China,* London, 1878.

Ehrenfels, O.R., *Mother-right in India,* Hyderabad, 1941.

Eliade, M., *Le Yoga: Immortalite et Liberte,* Paris, 1954; Eng. trans., *Yoga: Immortality and Freedom,* by W.R. Trask, New York, 1958.

Eliot, C., *Hinduism and Buddhism,* 3 vols., London, 1921.

Elliot, H.M., *History of India as told by Its Own Historians,* vol. I, London, 1867.

Elmore, W.T., *Dravidian Gods in Modern Hinduism: A Study in the Local and Village Deities of Southern India,* Hamilton, 1915; sec. ed., Madras, 1925.

Erman, A., *Life in Ancient Egypt,* London, 1894.

Farnell, L.R., *Cult of the Greek States,* 7 vols., Edinburgh, 1896-1909.

—, *Greece and Babylon,* Edinburgh, 1911.

Fergusson, J., *History of Indian and Eastern Architecture,* revised by Burgess and Spiers, 2 vols., London, 1910; rep., New Delhi, 1971.

Frazer, J.G., *The Golden Bough* (ab) rep., London, 1959.

—, *Adonis Attis Osiris,* London, 1907 (also 1913 ed., part I).

Freeman, E.A., *History of the Norman Conquest of England,* London, 1870.

Gait, E.A., *History of Assam,* Calcutta, 1903.

Garbe, R., *The Sāṅkhya Pravacana Bhāṣya,* Cambridge, 1892.

—, *Aniruddha's Commentary on the Original Parts on Vedāntin Mahādeva's Commentary on the Sāṅkhyasūtra,* Calcutta, 1892.

Gardner, P., *Catalogue of the Coins of the Greek and Scythian Kings in the British Museum,* London, 1886.

Getty, A., *The Gods of Northern Buddhism,* Oxford, 1914; rep., New Delhi, 1978.

Ghosh, A.B., *Śiva and Śakti,* Rajshahi, 1935.

Ghosh, N., *Concept and Iconography of the Goddess of Abundance,* Burdwan, 1979.

Giles, H.A., *The Travels of Fa-Hsien,* Cambridge, 1923.

Goudrian, T., *Hindu Tantric and Śākta Literature,* vol. II, facs.2 of *A History of Indian Literature,* ed. J. Gonda, Wiesbaden, 1981.

Goyal, S.R., *A History of Indian Buddhism,* Meerut, 1987.

Gupta, Sanjukta, *Lakṣmī Tantra,* Leiden, 1972.

Hargreaves, H., *Handbook to the Sculptures in the Peshawar Museum,* Calcutta, 1930.

Harrison, J.E., *Prolegomena to the Study of Greek Religion,* Cambridge, 1908.

Hartland, E.S., *Primitive Paternity,* London, 1909.

Hawley, J.S. and Wulff, D., ed., *The Divine Consort Rādhā and the Goddesses of India,* Berkeley, 1982.

Hobhouse, L.T. et al., *Material Culture and Social Institution of the Simpler Peoples,* London, 1930.

Hopkins, E.W., *The Religions of India,* Boston, 1885; rep., New Delhi, 1977.

Hutton, J.H., *The Caste in India,* rep., Calcutta, 1951.

Iyer, L.K.A.K., *Cochin Tribes and Castes,* 2 vols., Madras, 1909.

James, E.O., *Prehistoric Religion,* New York, 1957.

—, *Cult of the Mother Goddess,* London, 1959.

Jastrow, M., *Religion of Babylonia and Assyria,* New York, 1898.

Jerret, H., *Ain-i-Akbari,* vol. II, Calcutta, 1881; rep., New Delhi, 1978.

Joshi, L.M., *Studies in the Buddhistic Cultures of India,* Delhi, 1967.

Kakati, B.K., *The Mother Goddess Kāmākhyā,* Gauhati, 1948.

Kane, P.V., *History of Dharmaśāstra,* 5 vols., Poona, 1930-62.

Kaviraj, G., *Tāntrik Vāñmaya men Śākta Devī,* Patna, 1963 (in Hindi).

—, *Tantra O Āgama Sāhityer Digdarśan,* Calcutta, 1963 (in Bengali).

—, *Tāntrik Sādhanā O Siddhānta,* Burdwan, 1969.

Keith, A.B., *Religion and Philosophy of the Veda,* 2 vols., HOS, Cambridge (Mass.), 1925; *The Vedas of the Black Yajus School,* HOS, Cambridge (Mass.), 1914.

King, L.W., *Babylonian Religion and Mythology*, London, 1896.
Kinsley, D., *The Sword and the Flute:* Dark Vision of the Terrible and Sublime in the Hindu Religious Tradition, Berkeley, 1975.
—, 'Blood and Death out of Place: Reflection of the Goddess Kālī' in Hawley and Wulff, eds., *The Divine Consort*, Berkeley, 1982.
—, Freedom from Death in the Worship of Kālī, in *NUMEN*, XXII (3).
—, *Hindu Goddesses: Visions of the Divine Feminine in the Hindu Religious Tradition*, Berkeley, 1986.
Kosambi, D.D., *An Introduction to the Study of Indian History*, Bombay, 1956.
—, *Culture and Civilization of Ancient India in Historical Outline*, London, 1965.
Kramrisch, S., 'The Indian Great Goddess' in *History of Religions*, XIV (4), 1975, 235-65.
—, *Art of India through the Ages*, London, 1954.
Kumar, P., *Śakti Cult in Ancient India*, Varanasi, 1974.
Levy, G.R., *The Gate of Horn*.
Lévy, S., *Le Nepal*, 3 vols., Paris, 1905.
Lorenzen, D.N., *The Kāpālikas and Kālāmukhas*, New Delhi, 1972.
Macauliffe, M.A., *The Sikh Religion*, Oxford, 1909.
Macculloch, J.A., *The Religion of the Ancient Celts*, Edinburgh, 1911.
Macdonell, A.A., *The Vedic Mythology*, Strassburg, 1897.
Mackenzie, D.A., *Crete and Pre-Hellenic Europe*, Gresham, London.
—, *Migration of Symbols*, Gresham, London.
Mackay, E., *Further Excavations at Mohenjodaro*, Delhi, 1938.
Maine, H., *Dissertation on Early Law and Custom*, London, 1883.
Maity, P.K., *Historical Studies in the Cult of the Goddess Manasā*, Calcutta, 1966.
Majumdar, N.G., *Guide to the Sculptures of the Indian Museum*, Delhi, 1937.
Majumdar, R.C., *Inscriptions of Kambuja*, Calcutta, 1953.
—, *Ancient Indian Colonies in the Far East*, 3 vols., Dacca, 1937-38.
—, ed., *History of Bengal*, vol. I, Calcutta, 1943.
—, *Classical Accounts of India*, Calcutta, 1960.
—, *History of the Freedom Movement in India*, 3 vols., Calcutta, 1963.
Marshall, J., *Mohenjodaro and the Indus Civilization*, vol. I, London, 1931.
—, *Guide to Taxila*, Delhi, 1936.
—, *Buddhist Art of Gandhāra*, Cambridge, 1960.

—, *Taxila*, 3 vols., Cambridge, 1953.
Mathan, L. and Seely, C., *Grace and Mercy in Her Wild Hair: Selected Poems to the Mother Goddess by Ramprasad Sen*, Boulder, 1982.
Max Müller, F., *The Science of Religion.*
Mespero, G., *Life in Ancient Egypt and Assyria*, London, 1910.
Mitra, R.C., *Decline of Buddhism in India*, Santiniketan, 1954.
Monier-Williams, M., *Indian Wisdom*, London, 1818.
—, *Brahmanism and Buddhism*, London, 1891.
—, *Religious Thought and Life in India*, London, 1891, rep., New Delhi, 1975.
Mookerjee, A. and Khanna, Madhu, *The Tantric Way: Art, Science and Ritual*, Delhi, 1977.
Morgan, K.W., *The Path of Buddha*, New York, 1956.
Muir, J., *Original Sanskrit Texts*, 5 vols., London, 1858 ff.
Mukherjee, B.N., *Nana on the Lion*, Calcutta, 1969.
Mukherji, P.C., *Report on the Antiquarian Remains in the Lalitpur District*, Roorkee, 1899.
Murray, G., *Rise of the Greek Epic*, Oxford, 1911.
Nagam, Aiya V., *Travancore State Manual*, Trivandrum, 1906.
Nagaswami, R., *Tantric Cult of South India*, Delhi, 1982.
Narzi, B., *Boḍo-Kāchārir Samāj āru Saṃskṛti*, Guwahati, 1971 (in Assamese).
Needham, J., *Science and Civilization in China*, 6 vols., Cambridge, 1954-56.
Neumann, E., *The Great Mother: An Analysis of the Archetype*, Eng. trans. by R. Manheim, New York, 1963.
Nivedita, Sister, *Kālī, the Mother*, Almora, 1950.
Nutt, A., *Studies in the Legends of the Holy Grail*, London, 1888.
O'Flaherty, W.D., *Women, Androgynes and Other Mythical Beasts*, Chicago, 1980.
Oldenberg, H., *Buddha: His Life, His Teachings, His Order*, Calcutta, 1927.
Olson, C., ed., *The Book of the Goddess: Past and Present: An Introduction to Her Religion*, New York, 1983.
Pal, D.N., *Śiva and Śakti*, Calcutta, 1910.
Pande, G.C., *Bauddha Dharma ke Vikās kā Itihās*, Lucknow, 1963 (in Hindi).
Payne, E.A., *The Śāktas: An Introductory and Comparative Study*, Calcutta, 1933.
Petrie, W.M.F., *Social Life in Ancient Egypt*, London, 1923.

Piggott, S., *Prehistoric India*, London, 1950.

Playfair, A., *The Garos*, London, 1909.

Prester, J.J., *Cult of the Goddess: Social and Religious Change in a Hindu Temple*, New Delhi, 1980.

Preston, J., ed., *Mother Worship: Themes and Variations*. Chapel Hill, 1982.

Przyluski, J., 'The Great Goddess of India and Iran' in *IHQ*, X, 405-30.

Radhakrishnan, S., *Indian Philosophy*, 2 vols., London, 1923.

Rajeswari, D.R., *Sakti Iconography*, New Delhi, 1989.

Ray, N.R., *Maurya and Śuṅga Art*, Calcutta, 1965.

—, *The Sikh Gurus and Sikh Society*, New Delhi, 1975.

Raychaudhuri, H.C., *Studies in Indian Antiquities*, Calcutta.

Rhys Davids, T.W., *Buddhism*, London.

Ridgeway, W.G., *The Origin of Tragedy*, Cambridge, 1910.

Rowland, B., *Art and Architecture of India*, London, 1953.

Sachau, E.C., *Alberuni's India*, London, 1888; rep., New Delhi, 1992.

Sahai, B., *Iconography of Minor Hindu and Buddhist Deities*, New Delhi, 1975.

Sahu, N.K., *Buddhism in Orissa*, Bhuvaneshwar, 1958.

Saraswati, S.K., *Survey of Indian Sculpture*, Calcutta, 1957, rep. edn., New Delhi, 1975.

Sarkar, H.B., *Dvīpamaya Bhārater Prācīn Sāhitya*, Calcutta, 1970 (in Bengali).

Sarkar, J.N., *History of Aurangzeb*, 5 vols., Calcutta, 1912-23.

Sastri, H., *Origin and the Cult of Tārā, MASI*, 20.

Sayce, A.H., *Religions of Ancient Egypt and Babylonia*, Edinburgh, 1902.

Schoff, W.H., *Periplus of the Erythraean Sea*, London, 1912, rep., New Delhi, 1995.

Seffert, O., *Dictionary of Classical Antiquities*, London, 1864.

Sen, K.P., *Rājamālā*, Agartala, Tripura year 1336 (in Bengali).

Sharma, R.K., *The Temple of Caunṣaṭh Yoginī at Bherāghāt*, Delhi, 1978.

Sharma, R.P., *Śakti Tattva Darśana*, Birlagram, 1977 (in Hindi).

Shastri, H.K., *South Indian Images of Gods and Goddesses*, Madras, 1916.

Singh, T. and Singh, G., *A Short History of the Sikhs*.

Sinha, J.N., *The Cult of Śakti: Ramaprasad's Devotional Songs*, Calcutta, 1981.

Sircar, D.C., *Select Inscriptions bearing on Indian History and Civilization*, vol. I, Calcutta, 1942.

—, *The Śākta Pīṭhas*, Calcutta, 1948.

—, ed., *Śakti Cult and Tārā*, Calcutta, 1967.

—, *Foreigners in Ancient India and Lakṣmī and Sarasvatī in Art and Literature*, Calcutta, 1970.

Smith, V.A., *Early History of India*, fourth ed., Oxford, 1962.

—, *Jaina Stūpas and other Antiquities in Mathura*, New Delhi.

Smith, W. Robertson, *Kinship and Marriage in Early Arabia*, London, 1903.

—, *Religion of the Semites*, London, 1899.

Srivastava, B., *Iconography or Śakti*, Delhi, 1978.

Srivastava, M.C.P., *Mother Goddess in Indian Art, Religion and Literature*, New Delhi, 1978.

Stein, M.A., *An Archaeological Tour in Waziristan and North Baluchistan*, *MASI*, 37, Calcutta, 1929.

—, *An Archaeological Tour in Gedrosia*, *MASI*, 43, Calcutta, 1931.

—, *Rājataraṅgiṇī*, Eng. trans., 2 vols., Westminster, 1900.

Swami, Nikhilananda, *The Holy Mother: Being the Life of Śrī Śāradā Devī*, New York, 1962.

—, Mahendra Nath Gupta's (*Śrī Ma*) *The Gospel of Śrī Rāmakṛṣṇa*, Eng. trans. of *Rāmakṛṣṇa Kathāmṛta*, New York, 1970.

Thomas, N.W., *Kinship and Group Marriage in Australia*, Cambridge, 1906.

Thompson, E.G., *Bengali Religious Lyrics: Śākta*, Calcutta, 1923.

Thomson, G., *Aeschylus and Athens*, London, 1941.

Tiwari, J.N., *Goddess Cult in Ancient India*, Delhi, 1985.

Tod, J., *Annals and Antiquities of Rajasthan*, ed. William Crooke, London, 1920.

Underhill, M.M., *The Hindu Religious Year*, Calcutta, 1921.

Upadhyaya, K.N., *Early Buddhism and Bhagavadgītā*, Delhi, 1971.

Van Gennep, M., *Les Rites de Passage*, Paris, 1911.

Van Kooij, K.R., *Worship of the Goddess according to the Kālikā Purāṇa*, Leiden, 1972.

Vats, M.S., *Excavations at Harappa*, Delhi, 1950.

Warriar, A.G.K., *The Śākta Uapniṣads*, Madras, 1967.

Watters, T., *On Yuan Chwang's Travels in India*, 2 vols., London, 1904, rep., New Delhi, 1995.

Westcott, G.H., *Kabīr and the Kabīr Panth*, Calcutta, 1953, rep., New Delhi, 1986.

Westermarck, E., *History of Human Marriage*, 3 vols., London, 1921.

Whitehead, Rev. H., *Village Gods of South India*, sec. ed., Calcutta, 1921.

Whitehead, R.B., *Catalogue of the Coins in the Punjab Museum,* Oxford, 1914.
Wilson, H.H., *Essays and Lectures on the Religion of the Hindoos,* London, 1862.
—, *Sketch of the Religious Sects of the Hindoos,* Calcutta, 1846.
Wilson, T., *The Swastikā,* Washington, 1896.
Winternitz, M., *History of Indian Literature,* 2 vols., Calcutta, 1927, 1933, rep., New Delhi, 1973.
Woodroffe, J., (See under A. Avalon).
Yasin, M., *A Social History of Islamic India, 1605-1784,* Lucknow, 1958; rep., New Delhi, 1974.

Index